Chaos and Culture

Chaos and Culture

Renzo Piano Building Workshop and the
Stavros Niarchos Foundation Cultural Center
in Athens

Victoria Newhouse

The Monacelli Press

For Si

All rights reserved. Published in the United States
by The Monacelli Press, LLC

Cover: SNFCC, Faliro Bay, and Acropolis, Athens, aerial view
Photograph by Iwan Baan

Frontispiece: SNFCC and Faliro Bay, aerial view
Pages 6–7: Canal along east side of SNFCC during "Metamorphosis"
celebration, June 23–26, 2016

Library of Congress Cataloging-in-Publication Data
Names: Newhouse, Victoria, author.
Title: Chaos and culture : Renzo Piano Building Workshop and the Stavros
    Niarchos Foundation Cultural Center / Victoria Newhouse.
Description: New York : The Monacelli Press, 2017. | Includes bibliographical
    references.
Identifiers: LCCN 2017002202 | ISBN 9781580934886 (hardback)
Subjects: LCSH: Stavros Niarchos Foundation Cultural Center. | Renzo Piano
    Building Workshop. | Architecture and society–Greece–History–
    21st century. | Athens (Greece)–Buildings, structures, etc. | BISAC:
    ARCHITECTURE / Buildings / Public, Commercial & Industrial. |
    ARCHITECTURE/ Criticism. | ARCHITECTURE / History / Contemporary
    (1945–).
Classification: LCC NA6811.5.G8 N49 2017 | DDC 720.1/03–dc23
LC record available at https://lccn.loc.gov/2017002202

www.monacellipress.com

10 9 8 7 6 5 4 3 2 1
First edition

Printed in China

All dollar amounts were converted from Euros at the rate of $1.114 = €1,
accurate in December 2016.

Timeline

2006

Third year of New Democracy government led by P.M. Kostas Karamanlis

OCTOBER 29
Stavros Niarchos Foundation (SNF) announces Stavros Niarchos Foundation Cultural Center (SNFCC)

NOVEMBER
SNF chooses Cooper Robertson (CR) as master planner

2007

MARCH
SNF signs contract with CR; CR selects Theatre Projects Consultants, Arup (acoustics, structural, mechanical, civil, traffic, and security engineering), and Betaplan, together with other Greek engineers and archaeologists, as part of master planning team

JUNE
SNF confirms commitment to build SNFCC by signing Memorandum of Understanding with Greek government

SEPTEMBER
Andreas Dracopoulos meets Renzo Piano

2008

Onset of European financial crisis

FEBRUARY
SNF interviews architects in Zurich and chooses Renzo Piano Building Workshop (RPBW)

CR hires Faithful+Gould (F+G) for preliminary cost estimate based on master plan

MARCH
Expedition Engineering joins SNFCC team

Schematics begin

APRIL
Master plan is finalized

JUNE–SEPTEMBER
SNFCC hires F+G, with regional director Martin Hirko designated to oversee design and construction program (cost and schedule management, LEED coordination, design and construction contracts administration)

JUNE
RPBW chooses Deborah Nevins & Associates as landscape designer

JULY
RPBW presents design concept to SNF board

SEPTEMBER
RPBW completes conceptual design and feasibility study

OCTOBER
Arup departments begin work

2009

MARCH
SNF signs contract with Greek government

OCTOBER
Greek government forecasts debt of $442 billion, making the country one of the hardest-hit in the global economic crisis

Election of PASOK government led by P.M. George A. Papandreou

DECEMBER
Design development (through July 2010)

2010

MAY
Greek government accepts austerity measures to secure $145 billion loan from the Troika (International Monetary Fund, European Union, European Central Bank)

2011

JUNE 26
Building permit issued

Greek government appoints Myron Michailidis artistic director of Greek National Opera (GNO)

SEPTEMBER
FALIRO 2014, team of Greek architects and engineers, conceptualizes and designs waterfront plan for Faliro in collaboration with RPBW

NOVEMBER
Provisional coalition government led by P.M. Loucas D. Papademos

DECEMBER
Excavation begins

Construction drawings completed

Continuation of violent protests against austerity measures

JANUARY
Election of Syriza-ANEL coalition government led by P.M. Alexis Tsipras

Construction Milestone 3
(projected): Completion of canopy

JUNE
Anti-austerity referendum

AUGUST
Canopy erected to self-supporting position

Appointment of interim government led by caretaker P.M. Vassiliki Thanou-Christophilou

SEPTEMBER
Reelection of Syriza-ANEL government led by P.M. Alexis Tsipras

NOVEMBER
Construction Milestone 4
(projected): Completion of project

MARCH
SNF hires Mecanoo to redesign public library areas (contract expires after six months)

SEPTEMBER
Construction Milestone 1
(projected and actual), as agreed to by Salini Impregilo–Terna: Foundations completed, including seismic isolators for opera house and hill

FEBRUARY 23
Celebration of SNFCC delivery to Greek government

OCTOBER (projected)
GNO and NLG transferred to SNFCC

| 2012 | 2013 | 2014 | 2015 | 2016 | 2017 |

MAY
Caretaker P.M. Panagiotis Pikrammenos appointed to head interim government

JUNE
SNF appoints Ioannis Trohopoulos as SNFCC CEO and managing director

Election of New Democracy government led by P.M. Antonis Samaras

SEPTEMBER
Salini Impregilo–Terna joint venture company wins construction competition

OCTOBER
Construction begins; 15,140 workers eventually employed

FEBRUARY
Greek government appoints Filippos Tsimpoglou director general of National Library of Greece (NLG)

JULY
Construction Milestone 2
(projected and actual): Completion of superstructure (all concrete and steel work)

MARCH
Construction Milestone 3
(actual): Completion of canopy

APRIL
Trohopoulos resigns as SNFCC managing director

Dimitris Protopsaltou appointed CEO of SNFCC

JUNE 23–26
"Metamorphosis: The SNFCC to the World" (celebration of completion of construction)

AUGUST
Construction Milestone 4
(actual): Completion of project

SNF issues temporary occupancy certificate

DECEMBER
Greek government appoints Giorgos Koumendakis artistic director of GNO, replacing Michailidis

DECEMBER 29
Scheduled handover of SNFCC to Greek government

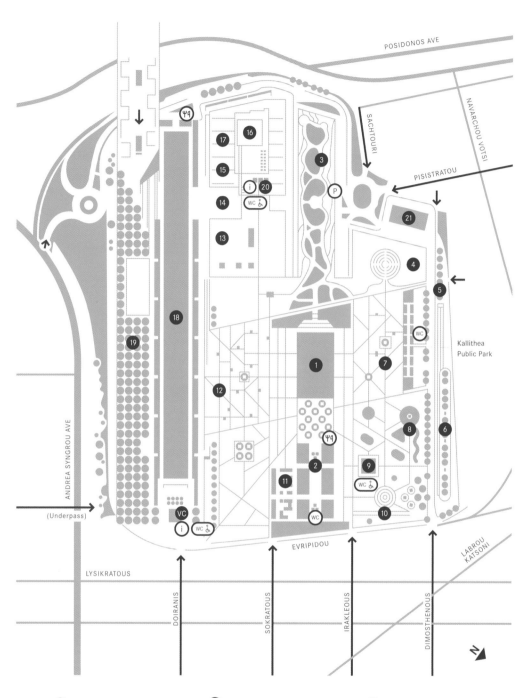

POSIDONOS AVE

SACHTOURI

NAVARCHOU VOTSI

PISISTRATOU

Kallithea
Public Park

ANDREA SYNGROU AVE

(Underpass)

EVRIPIDOU

LYSIKRATOUS

DOIRANIS

SOKRATOUS

IRAKLEOUS

DIMOSTHENOUS

LABROU KATSONI

1	Great Lawn	9	Café	17	Panoramic Steps
2	Pine Grove	10	Splash Pool	18	Canal
3	Southern Walks	11	Sound Garden	19	Esplanade
4	Labyrinth	12	Mediterranean Garden	20	Small Agora
5	Outdoor Gym	13	National Library of Greece	21	Outdoor Parking Lot
6	Running Track	14	Agora	VC	Visitors Center
7	Western Walks	15	Greek National Opera	Ψ٩	Canteens
8	Playground	16	Lighthouse	P	Parking

Introduction

Chaos and Culture: Renzo Piano Building Workshop and the Stavros Niarchos Cultural Center in Athens is the story of a great philanthropist, an extraordinary architect, and a small country that in 2009 began to shake the foundations of the European Union. On October 29, 2006, the Stavros Niarchos Foundation announced its intention to design and build in Athens a cultural center that would include a new national library and a new national opera house in a 40-acre landscaped park, a project that would eventually cost more than $842 million. The decision represented a major escalation of the foundation's activities and coincided with the Greek government's resolution to upgrade the two institutions.

In March 2009, the foundation signed an agreement to proceed, with the provision that the government would assume the cost of running the Stavros Niarchos Foundation Cultural Center once it was built. Little did the directors of the foundation anticipate that by the time the cultural center was completed in 2016, those with whom they had negotiated the deal ten years earlier would long since be gone—replaced by seven successive administrations, none of which were equipped to pick up the tab for maintaining and running the remarkable new facility.

Indeed, in 2008, the year that Renzo Piano Building Workshop was chosen as the architect for the project, Greece had already emerged as the European country hardest hit by the global economic crisis. The passionate conviction of both the client and the architect that their building would be a landmark—even a stimulus—for Greece's survival as a sovereign nation overrode aesthetic, commercial, and any other considerations. The impetus to build a new cultural facility usually originates with an inspiring vision.[1] But the SNFCC is unique as a vision for Greece's reform. The honest, efficient, environmentally sensitive, and transparent process of constructing the center was to be a model for the government to emulate, "a microcosm of the country, if and when the country changes."[2]

Every large building project is complex, and cultural buildings are especially so. Not only do they call for a wide range of specialized technical knowledge, but the very act of designing them—from the making of initial schematic renderings to design development and the execution of final construction drawings—is tremendously demanding. It is difficult to imagine the remarkable technical ingenuity and complex methods of construction needed to realize an apparently straightforward, pared-down building such as the SNFCC. My description of some major aspects of this process is a potent reminder that such an undertaking is not for the faint-hearted.

Experimentation with forms, materials, and means of sustainability has been a constant throughout Renzo Piano's career. In Athens he pushed the envelope of all three, and the result is two large wings of a single structure, constructed in reinforced concrete with some steel elements and separated by a sizable open-air agora—all of this embedded in a man-made hill. A huge but seemingly weightless canopy, tapered like an airplane wing, floats above this construction. Made of ferro-cement (thin-shell reinforced mortar over a layer of metal mesh and closely spaced thin steel rods), it provides support for solar panels, as well as shade, and it conspicuously signals the cultural center's presence. A newly created park covers most of the site, climbing up the hill over the library and the garage. The center is just two miles south of the Acropolis and only a few hundred feet from the beautiful Saronic Gulf, both of which can be seen from the new building.

Investigation and collaboration on the canopy was particularly intense. In an amazing combination of old and new, hundreds of workers, usually on their hands and knees, hand-wove the connecting wire mesh of the structure's components. The form was then filled and covered by a thin layer of sand/cement mortar. It is the most expensive element of the endeavor (it cost more than $57.6 million)—the kind of effort that ends up being called visionary if successful, a folly if not.

The man who set in motion this endeavor is Andreas Dracopoulos, the devoted great-nephew of the shipping magnate Stavros Niarchos, who serves as the SNF's director, co-president, and determining decision-maker. From the moment he met Piano, he was captivated by the man and by the startling originality of his concept of raising the site's flat surface by 105 feet to create a hill as the location for the new home of the Greek National Opera and the National Library of Greece. Inspired by the mountains surrounding the capital (one of whose quarries, Penteli, supplied the marble for the Parthenon), Piano imagined a hill excavated as if for a quarry. The hilltop would provide panoramic views of the sea and the city from the SNFCC. To reconnect the city and the sea, which were separated by a four-lane highway, and to provide backup irrigation for the park, the architect envisioned a canal running parallel to the structure and extending the entire length of the site.

With the country facing such dire financial problems, embarking on an undertaking of this magnitude—the SNFCC is approximately 1.28 million square feet—defied logic. For a foundation to spend a fortune on culture in this heavily indebted country, where labor strikes were frequent even before the crisis accelerated in 2009, presented a paradox—and it was not the only one. The government's call for a new facility for the NLG was convincing, especially because its magnificent collection of books, manuscripts, and documents was divided among three separate temporary venues; but the rationale for a luxurious new opera house was less evident. Granted, the Olympia Theater, where the GNO had performed since 1958, is woefully inadequate for opera, but the company had also occasionally appeared in the Megaron concert hall (completed in 1991), in Athens, with great success. That very success may be what encouraged construction of a new theater built specifically to present operas.[3]

Other incongruities that make the SNFCC unique were the ample resources available for the kind of project that is usually plagued by financing difficulties; construction of the first purpose-built opera house in the capital of the country where theater originated more than twenty-five centuries ago; the architect's partial enclosure of the building, which lessens the visually transparent quality that is typical of his architecture; and, perhaps most surprising of all, the nearly trouble-free realization of this gigantic project in the midst of constant political, social, and economic turbulence. The SNF paralleled its vast expenditures for the cultural center with generous humanitarian aid. But the enthusiastic reception of the SNFCC by the public and politicians is due rather to its having inducted 15,140 workers as of May 31, 2016 (and to the prospect of hundreds of staffing positions for its subsequent operations), stimulating the Greek economy and spurring redevelopment in the surrounding neighborhood.

Construction of the SNFCC encapsulates the multiple and overlapping design responsibilities that have transformed the architectural profession in recent decades. The high degree of specialization in present-day architectural practice echoes that of the medical profession: every issue calls for a different expert.[4] When *Architectural Record* reported the completion of Skidmore, Owings & Merrill's Lever House in Manhattan in 1952, credit was given solely to the architects (Gordon Bunshaft and Natalie de Blois, the building's chief designers), the structural engineers, and the interior designers.[5] For most buildings—apart from the services of engineers and theater acousticians, when called for—there was little need for outside professionals. Currently, however, architects work with teams of specialists. The SNFCC's reliance on a multitude of distinct skills stretches far beyond even today's norms.

Changes in the vocation date approximately from the 1990s, when computers began to replace hand drawing. A few years later, newly developed technologies have led to the creation of materials such as structural glass; and since then, the evolution of sustainable technology, such as high-efficiency photovoltaic panels, has made many aspects of construction more complex, as have higher expectations for thermal comfort and energy efficiency.

Emblematic of changes in the profession was the name of the firm that Piano founded in 1981, Renzo Piano Building Workshop, a name that emphasizes the team rather than the individual—although public tributes to RPBW's projects invariably credit Piano alone. (In the 1950s creative architects generally rejected teamwork as a lowering of standards.[6]) There are eleven partners and twenty-one associates in the firm's Genoa, Paris, and New York City offices; each partner is in charge of one or more projects, and works with at least one associate. Piano describes the process in Athens as "a mix of disciplines that played together like a good orchestra."[7] Many people have likened Piano to an orchestra conductor, for his ability to work harmoniously with all manner of collaborators.[8] With the numerous highly specialized international consultants involved in a project, it might appear impossible to designate a single designer. And yet, strange as it seems, the trend toward more inclusive credits has paralleled the advent of the "starchitect" and the exceptional design fees paid to practitioners of Piano's status—as much as 52 percent more per square foot than the fees of less well-known architects.[9]

Piano is the most successful museum architect in the world (vying in numbers only with Tadao Ando), an understandable accomplishment given the practitioner's undeniable talent as well as a kind of irresistible charm.[10] He explains that he moved from his youthful, rebellious theory of designing "piece by piece" (focusing on individual details) to a more mature attitude. He now prefers to consider the organism as a whole, having concluded that strict adherence to his earlier theory may sometimes produce a "Frankenstein monster." When he describes his design process, Piano stresses "the articulation *between* pieces, the magic of how, for example, a column and beam meet. My favorite part of the process," he says, "is the end, when everything comes together. The rest is a nonstop struggle."[11]

A big part of the struggle can be the lack of input by a project's users and its director, which is an essential component of the design process. For the SNFCC, neither the opera nor the library had a director in place, and therefore no one in charge to work with when the architects began to design the building. A comparable situation arises when an art museum is designed without an existing collection: the creation of one-size-fits-all spaces is often disappointing. At the GNO, however, there was input from the incoming staff of the 1,400-seat multiuse hall and 450-seat Alternative Stage theater, and advice from specialists with experience at similar venues. The library turned out to be a stickier issue.

Greece's first national public library was founded in 1832 on the island of Aegina, 17 miles from Athens, and moved later that year to Nafplio, Greece's new capital; it relocated to Athens two years later, and in 1842, it merged with the library of the University of Athens to form a single library, the National Library of Greece. In addition to the NLG's current collection of more than a million books and thousands of journals and newspapers, it holds in its archives hundreds of priceless ancient Greek and Byzantine manuscripts. In 2008 the library had been without a director for three years; and even more astounding, there was no complete catalogue of its holdings. Consequently, the committee in charge of transferring materials from the old, grand building erected in central Athens in 1903 to the new building did not know exactly what it was dealing with. Perhaps more consequential, no one was able to realistically define the new library's purpose.

Even though seats in the old library's beautiful reading room were largely unoccupied, moving the NLG to a new building provoked the kind of passionate reaction that met the attempts in 2011–2013 to add a circulating book department to the New York Public Library on Forty-second Street and to make room for it by removing the research collection's seven-level book stacks and transferring nearly all those volumes to a storage facility fifty miles away in New Jersey. Scholars, writers, and architecture critics signed petitions protesting not only the programmatic change but also the desecration of the historic stacks, and many opponents of the plan regularly picketed in front of the building until library officials abandoned it in 2014. A similar situation would arise in Athens: adding a public library to the national library provoked more dissent than any other aspect of the SNFCC.

Updating national libraries is never an easy task, as witnessed on a grand scale in the late 1990s by the new Bibliothèque Nationale de France in southeast Paris and the new British Library in London. In London, although the functional results—if not the aesthetic ones—are generally satisfactory, it took thirty-five years, from the time the project was launched in 1962 as an extension of the British Museum, to realize the revised design by Colin St. John Wilson in a new location. Dominique Perrault, the architect of the new Bibliothèque Nationale de France, accomplished the task more rapidly, completing it seven years after its initial design in 1989. But it was achieved only at tremendous expense ($1.5 billion and costly annual maintenance), with questionable results:[12] the entranceway is inhospitable; a below-grade reading room deprives users of city vistas; and the building's four light-inundated glass-and-steel storage towers would have severely endangered the books within if protective wooden shutters had not been added after the fact. At the opening of the library in December 1996, President Jacques Chirac revealed that he had never before encountered a computer mouse. A report of this admission on national television a few months later raised serious doubts about his purported modernity.[13]

Also influencing the design of the NLG were larger shifts in library use and function. Since a person's physical presence is no longer needed to obtain access to a library's holdings, many have adopted a new goal of increasing social inter-action among visitors to the actual building. This is what the Niarchos Foundation wanted, but it took more than two years to achieve, the hiring of more consultants, and innumerable redesigns, even one by an outside architect, all incurring additional expense.

The history of the GNO is briefer than that of the NLG. The opera house's antecedents, however, like the library's, can be traced to antiquity. The first real operas, as they are known today, were composed and performed in Florence and Venice in the late sixteenth and early seventeenth centuries. These were attempts to reinvent Greek drama, which was believed to have been accompanied by chanted or sung choruses and instrumental music; and it was the interest of Renaissance architects in ancient Greek and Roman theaters that inspired theater and opera house design then—Andrea Palladio's Teatro Olimpico in Vicenza (1583) is a prime example—and now. An example from antiquity, the Hellenistic amphitheater at Epidaurus (4th c. B.C.E.), and one of its Greco-Roman descendants, the Odeon of Herodes Atticus (161 C.E.), built on a slope of the Acropolis in Athens, are still in use today and even suggested details for the new opera house. So it is all the more unexpected that Athens has never enjoyed the benefits of a purpose-built opera house.

The GNO was founded in 1939 and operated as part of the National Theater of Greece, giving performances in its historic neoclassical building on central Aghiou Konstantinou Street, designed by the German architect Ernst Ziller (1837–1923). In 1944 the company became a state-run corporation and was officially named Greek National Opera. Its first production in the old Olympia Theater at Academias Street was *Rhea,* an opera by the Greek composer Spyros Samaras. In 1946 the opera ensemble became an independent company, by 1949 giving daily performances at the Athens Metropolitan summer venue and at the Kyveli Institute during the rest of the season. A school of dance was added in 1950, and in 1958, the GNO inaugurated the newly renovated and expanded 740-seat Olympia Theater, where it performed until its move to the SNFCC. Conceivably the greatest challenge for the latter is to render this elitist and costly genre democratic, in conformance with the image desired by the SNF for the overall compound.

The lush Stavros Niarchos Park, which covers most of the site, will play an important role in making the cultural center a popular destination. Myron Michailidis, who in 2011 was finally appointed as the NGO's artistic director, held his first major press conference in the park early in 2015—an indication of the importance he attaches to this part of the cultural center.

Unlike previous models of landscape conservation, which stressed the need to protect natural resources, scenic wilderness, and rural areas from urbanization, recent approaches to landscape design have dissolved the opposition between city and nature, seeking to use parks as a means to introduce natural

ecologies into urban areas. Leaving behind the Romantic idea of a park as a natural idyll that offers an escape from urban activity, most contemporary designers
prefer to integrate nature and urbanism as Piano did in aligning the paths in
the cultural center's park with those of neighborhood streets.

The park and the other two major additions to the city of Athens were made
possible by the foundation established according to the terms of Stavros Niarchos's will. That donation is part of a long tradition in modern Greece of private
support for public institutions. Niarchos began earning a living as an impecu-
nious apprentice in the flour-milling business of his maternal uncles, and then
persuaded them to expand the business by buying ships. After World War II,
he founded his own shipping company and by 1956 had built it into the largest international private fleet in the world.[14] His foundation came into being
in 1996—the year of his death—and has worked actively ever since. However,
because the SNFCC was by far its most ambitious project (and its first important
architecture project), the directors seriously questioned the advisability of their
extravagance in December 2008, when cities throughout Greece were wracked
for more than a month by violent protests. Though triggered by the killing of
a 15-year-old student by the police in Athens, the demonstrations were fueled
by widespread outrage and frustration, especially among young people, over the
country's growing economic difficulties.

So extreme were the problems by late 2009 that the phrase "becoming
another Greece" entered the vernacular as a reference to drastic financial instability. In May 2010 the government agreed to austerity measures in order to secure
a $145 billion loan from the International Monetary Fund, the European Union,
and the European Central Bank (known collectively as "the Troika"). These measures were to prove catastrophic. Coupled with Greece's ineffective rule of law,
weakly enforced property rights, rising incidence of tax evasion, and pervasive
corruption, the so-called Economic Adjustment Program contributed to massive
unemployment (27 percent by mid-2013, with youth unemployment near 60 percent, and more than 850,000 jobs lost), widespread deprivation, and a growing
population of homeless people.[15] Eventually, hundreds of thousands of protesters
again filled city streets throughout Greece, and strikes repeatedly paralyzed the
nation (and, a few times, the Greek National Opera). All of this created a fore-
boding sense of a country on the brink of collapse, in which the Niarchos project
might look at worst like an unnecessary luxury and at best like the right idea at
the wrong time.

The question of whether the government could assume the ownership and
the costs of running the completed cultural center became paramount, haunt-
ing the undertaking throughout its construction. The foundation's ultimate
decision to carry out its plan was based on what Piano hoped would be "art's
transformative potential in the face of adversity."[16] He cited, as an example, the

rebuilding of Milan's La Scala opera house within six months after the end of World War II—an analogy that ignores the fact that La Scala was a beloved, old institution, whereas the SNFCC is a novelty.

Between the foundation's signing of the agreement in March 2009 declaring its intention to proceed with the project and completion of construction in 2016, Greece held four national elections and one referendum. After George Papandreou resigned as prime minister in 2011 in the midst of the economic crisis, the country was ruled by three different short-lived governments until January 2015, when Alexis Tsipras became prime minister. Tsipras had been elected for his strong opposition to the radical austerity measures of more spending cuts and tax increases that Greece's E.U. partners were trying to impose on it. That June, he organized a national anti-austerity referendum and won the people's support for rejecting the new bailout conditions (the third set, which followed the 2010 and 2012 loans), a position that might have led to Greece's exit from the E.U. and destabilized the entire politico-economic alliance. However, a month later, in an about-face, he pulled back from the brink and renegotiated the terms of the bailout, accepting austerity. He thereby staved off the crisis for the moment but did not really resolve the fundamental differences between the two sides.

Unique and severe, the crisis fits a pattern of boom and bust, bankruptcies and foreign bailouts that has plagued Greece's modern history. After nearly four hundred years of Ottoman rule, Greece won its independence in 1830 (recognized internationally in 1832) after the war of 1821–1829, which was brought to world attention by Lord Byron's participation in it. Independence, however, came with a series of additional foreign interventions, beginning with the imposition by Britain, Russia, and France (precursors of the twenty-first-century Troika) of a Bavarian monarch, and the need to borrow from the protecting powers.

Dependence on the goodwill of the Great Powers was not an unusual stance for younger, weaker nations in the early nineteenth century.[17] But in the case of Greece, the large foreign loans of 1824 and 1825 raised in London to finance the war of independence were just the beginning of Greece's borrowing from external creditors, which recurred in the 1880s, the 1920s, and the 2000s. It took the country a hundred years to recover from the first loans, the price being prolonged bouts of foreign political interference and financial oversight.[18]

Geographically and culturally on the frontier of West and East, Greece occupies an ambiguous position between the two. With the remains of cities such as Pergamon and Troy confirming ancient Greek civilization's geographical reach into the East, Greeks today are seen—and see themselves—alternatively as Europeans (from antiquity's Hellenes, or descendants of the ancient Greeks) and as easterners (influenced by the civilization of the Byzantine Empire, also known as the Eastern Roman Empire).

Its Byzantine and Ottoman heritage distanced the nation from its European neighbors for many centuries, isolating it from the progress that western Europe experienced during the Renaissance and the Reformation, and leaving a lasting legacy. Today's resistance to paying taxes, for example, may well stem in part from the Ottoman legal and taxation system, which was marked by discrimination against non-Muslim males, official corruption, and clientelism.[19] Yet the influence of the European Enlightenment and the French Revolution led to the uprising against the Ottomans and independence. Greece broke completely with its Ottoman past in some areas of public life, especially in its sustained efforts to construct a democratic administration and a modern state.

In the absence of a locally based entrepreneurial middle class, Greece's economic development was undertaken mainly by the government, producing an exponential increase of civil servants and public employees. Powerful local elites that had been entrenched in the Ottoman government retained their sway over the newly independent order—their ever-shifting alignments forecasting Greece's political future.[20] Together with excessive military spending, this huge bureaucracy has contributed to the country's financial problems, which stem also from its lack of natural resources and the preponderance of Greek wealth held abroad. Greece's twentieth-century history has gone hand in hand with military strife and political unrest.

The country was engaged in military conflict with the Ottoman Empire and its successor Turkey (over control of areas with a majority Greek ethnic presence, including Cyprus) repeatedly over the course of the twentieth century. During World War II, it was invaded and occupied by Germany and two of that nation's allies, Italy and Bulgaria, until late in 1944, when the Greek government returned to power. But following its liberation, the country experienced several rounds of civil war between the right and left through 1949, when the right prevailed. A period of imperfect democratic rule lasted until 1967; from that time until 1974, the country was ruled by a military dictatorship, during which the rights guaranteed under Greek democracy were suspended. In the 1950s and 1960s, the nation enjoyed economic advances and some middle-class prosperity in the big cities, although there were large-scale exoduses from the war-ravaged and underdeveloped provinces.

Democracy was restored in 1974, and membership in the European Community, beginning in 1981, brought Greece a step closer to the West.[21] However, in the 1990s the government again resorted to taking foreign loans.[22] In 2001, although its claims that it had curtailed inflation and government debts and deficits were inaccurate and overoptimistic, Greece joined the monetary union established by nineteen of the twenty-eight E.U. member states. But membership in the Eurozone did not bring about reform of the old wasteful economic policies. Among its other problems, Greece offers the generous entitlements of a

Scandinavian country without the financial resources to sustain them. In retrospect, uniting with the Eurozone went a step too far—in the words of historian Alexander Kitroeff, "stretching the system which ultimately broke."[23]

Greece's problems with the European Community were only just beginning their dramatic escalation in June 2011 when Piano participated in the SNFCC's inaugural press conference. A brief disruption of the event, orchestrated by environmentalists, subsided when it became apparent that the building would introduce a new level of environmental sensitivity to Greek architecture. The only exception to generally favorable press coverage has been from the far left-wing media, which opposed allowing the SNF to use the land, criticized what it saw as tax exemptions for the foundation, and denounced what it labels private interference with government-run institutions.[24]

Be that as it may, every mainstream newspaper in Athens carried a laudatory front-page story about the June 25, 2014, "Dance of the Cranes" that took place at the construction site in anticipation of the completion of the SNFCC's superstructure (see pp. 46–47). Fifteen hundred people, including myself, watched the sun set in the cloudless Mediterranean sky as ten giant cranes gracefully interacted in a fifteen-minute performance choreographed to the music of Gustav Holst's suite *The Planets,* played by the GNO orchestra. The event replicated a similar "Dance" staged by Piano—ever the consummate showman—in Berlin in 1996, during the erection of his Daimler-Benz complex at Potsdamer Platz.

Dracopoulos, the SNF's director, concluded the performance with a short assertion of his optimism, calling the SNFCC "an inspired project, imparting a sense of magic and a dreamlike quality to each and every one of the citizens of this country." Piano took over the microphone to repeat his belief in the "therapeutic power of beauty."

Dracopoulos and Piano are not the first to entertain such ideas in the face of adversity. The Empire State Building (1931) and Rockefeller Center (1930–1939) in New York City, both remarkable architectural achievements, were constructed during the height of the Great Depression that ravaged the U.S. economy for ten years. More than half a century earlier, in Paris, the Palais Garnier opera house (1875) rose during and immediately after the Franco-Prussian War (1870–1871), in an era of turbulence even more extreme than the Greek crisis. These projects overcame the troubles of their times to become enduring masterpieces. It remains to be seen whether the Athens project will be equally lasting.

Stavros Niarchos Park, installation of an olive tree, symbol of peace and of Athens

Client

In 1956 Stavros Niarchos (1909–1996; fig. 1), Aristotle Onassis (1906–1975; fig. 2), and George Livanos (1927–1997) were described in a *Time* magazine cover story as the "New Argonauts," the most successful shipowners in the world.[1] Although the major players in Greece's merchant marine industry have changed since then, it continues to be one of the biggest shipping industries in the world, valued at $27.3 billion in 2015.[2]

It was this phenomenal wealth that resulted in the creation of the Onassis and the Niarchos foundations in 1975 and 1996, respectively. One reason for Niarchos's dominance in shipping was that he, along with Onassis, took full advantage of their country's lenient tax laws for shipowners and, in the United States, even sidestepped the law.[3] Already in the early 1930s, Onassis adopted the practice initiated by U.S. shipowners in 1922 of registering his ships in Panama, thereby doing away with taxes as well as exchange and currency regulations. A controversial 1953 Greek law protecting foreign capital invested in Greece (LD 2687/53) made the procedure official for vessels registered by Greek owners as a foreign investment. The law gives exceptionally favorable tax conditions—and an equally favorable regulatory regime—to Greek shipowners whose ships sailed under non-Greek flags, such as Niarchos and Onassis. These tax exemptions are still in place, depriving the country of an important source of revenue: receipts from shipping and related businesses in 2015 were some $17 billion a year, almost 7.5 percent of GDP and just behind the $18 billion brought in by tourism. However, a Reuters analysis shows that in 2013 only $700 million had a direct onshore impact, making a mere $500 million contribution to Greece's GDP. With dividends and payments to suppliers and sailors included, the contribution to the economy was still only about $2 billion, which is just slightly more than 10 percent of the amount cited by the industry.[4]

Tax evasion is a given in Greece, but there are many other lacunae in the financial system. One of the most egregious is the flouting by employers of their social security contributions, amounting in 2013 to $10.82 billion owed to IKA

View of Piraeus Port from the sea, c. 1910

2 Stavros Niarchos

2 Aristotle Onassis

3 Andreas Dracopoulos

(Idrima Kinonikon Asfaliseon—literally, "Foundation of Social Security"), the country's biggest fund for private-sector workers. That year, the latter provided health coverage to 5.5 million people and pensions to more than 800,000, but reportedly had to borrow $203 million from the state to pay pensions in October.[5]

The co-president and director of the Stavros Niarchos Foundation, Andreas Dracopoulos (b. 1964; fig. 3), who worked closely with Niarchos during the last eight years of his great-uncle's life, candidly admitted that philanthropy is Niarchos's "way of giving back to society at large and his motherland."[6] The board of directors designated four main categories of philanthropic activity for the foundation: education, health and sports, social welfare, and arts and culture. Between its inception in 1996 and 2016, the charity committed nearly $2 billion to not-for-profit organizations in 120 nations. Making grants that total approximately $93 million a year,[7] the foundation is ranked relatively high in disbursements compared to U.S. foundations—about sixty-third on the Council on Foundations' list of top 100 grant makers.

The cultural center, announced in 2006, arose from the coincidence of the SNF's search for a more ambitious project and the Greek government's offer of state-owned property formerly occupied by the city's racetrack. Its funding is easily the largest single amount the SNF has awarded, and it is one of the largest individual cultural/educational projects worldwide. Dracopoulos has overseen every aspect of the center's development. As a senior foundation executive says, "He is the inspiration, driving force, and guide in everything we do in this organization."[8]

Niarchos was born in Greece to naturalized Greek-Americans soon after they returned to their native country and settled in Piraeus.[9] Spyros Niarchos and his Greek wife, Eugenie Coumandaros, had emigrated to the United States at the end of the nineteenth century, become U.S. citizens, and started what became a thriving candy store in Buffalo. They returned to Greece three months before Stavros was born. When Stavros was twenty, his mother's family provided him an entrée into the local business and social worlds. Members of the Coumandaros family were leading Greek flour millers, with a company in Athens, and when Spyros lost his fortune in the stock market crash of 1929, Stavros abandoned his plans to study law and went to work for his maternal uncles, successfully persuading them to buy ships of their own for transporting wheat. This move proved exceptionally profitable.

Stavros started his own shipping business in 1945 and soon expanded it to other activities. He advanced quickly, aided by a keen business acumen and a lifetime of exceptionally good luck, beginning with the windfall of insurance monies from the destruction in World War II of his first vessel, which had been leased by the Allied Forces. That provided the young entrepreneur with the initial capital he needed to enlarge his fleet. A fast learner, he shrewdly exploited the call for ever bigger oil tankers.

The term supertanker was first used in the 1950s by Aristotle Onassis when he launched the *Tina Onassis*, named after his first wife. Niarchos soon followed suit, building what in 1956 was the world's largest international private fleet (more than eighty tankers and other vessels), and initiating a ferocious, lifelong rivalry that affected every aspect of the two men's lives.

When they first met in 1934, the twenty-six-year-old Niarchos was penniless but was nevertheless an established member of Athens society. Onassis, only three years his senior, was already wealthy, an up-and-coming shipping tycoon. Yet Onassis was snubbed by the Athens-based social elite because of his background—a Greek who had fled the cosmopolitan Ottoman city of Smyrna, his birthplace, as a penniless refugee.[10] Although Onassis enjoyed an opulent lifestyle and impressive social connections, which culminated in his marriage to Jacqueline Kennedy in 1968, he himself acknowledged to his biographer, Peter Evans, that he had style, but "they say I have no class . . . You can't buy class, but you can buy tolerance for its absence."[11]

By contrast, Niarchos never had to worry about his position in society. As he amassed a great fortune, he created an aristocratic persona for himself, becoming prominent internationally as a mover and shaker of café society as well as royalty, a dashing lady's man, a competitive sailor, and the owner of champion racehorses. His sure taste in fine art guided his formation of one of the world's greatest private collections of Impressionist and modern works, which he divided among his luxurious residences in New York City, major European capitals, and Greece. The Niarchos and Onassis homes and other possessions were invariably acquired in competition with one another. At one point they were each married to one of the two Livanos sisters—Onassis to Athina ("Tina") from 1946 until their divorce in 1960, and Niarchos to Eugenia from 1947 until their divorce in 1965. After Eugenia died in 1970, Niarchos married Tina (his fifth wife, her third husband) in 1971.

The rivalry in life is perpetuated by the moguls' respective philanthropies. The Stavros Niarchos Foundation, based in Bermuda, and the Alexander S. Onassis Public Benefit Foundation (named for Aristotle's late son), based in Liechtenstein, continue a rich Greek philanthropic tradition that originated with diaspora Greeks in the nineteenth century.

In contrast with Europe, where private donations have only recently started to supplement publicly financed endeavors, it has been a common practice in the Islamic world for at least a thousand years to set up philanthropic foundations consisting of privately owned property endowed in perpetuity for charitable purposes. By the fifteenth century, and until the early nineteenth century, health, education, and welfare in the Ottoman Empire were entirely financed in this way.[12] In a nod to this precedent, the Greek Orthodox subjects of the Ottoman Empire had a tradition of giving and philanthropy rooted in their religion. This was a feature of their lives in the Byzantine era that they continued long after Byzantium fell to the Ottomans.[13] Wealthy diaspora Greeks continued the tradition of philanthropy after Greece became an independent state, making substantial donations to public institutions and especially to the country's education system.[14]

Before the SNF embarked on the Stavros Niarchos Foundation Cultural Center, the Onassis Public Benefit Foundation had funded two projects in Athens: the Onassis Cardiac Surgery Center (completed 1993) and the Onassis Cultural Center (completed 2011). In 2006, responding to government inquiries about modernizing the National Library of Greece and the Greek National Opera, the SNF announced its intention to underwrite development of a major cultural center in the capital. Certainly, at more than one million square feet, the SNFCC eclipses the 194,000-square-foot Onassis Cultural Center; and, compared with the localized visibility and significance of the Onassis Cardiac Surgery Center, it will have an international presence. By the same token, competition with the huge new SNFCC might underlie the Onassis Foundation's aggressively publicized support in 2012 for a European architectural competition, "Rethinking Athens," for the redesign of the city center.

Wealthy Greeks, especially those who made their fortunes abroad, have repeatedly shown great magnanimity to their country of origin. Evangelos Zappas (1800–1865), a Greek patriot and businessman who was born and spent most of his life in Romania, sponsored the "Zappas Olympics" in Athens, sports events involving Greek athletes, which were the precursor to the modern Olympic Games and were held in 1859, 1870, and 1875. The Zappas donation also financed an initial renovation of the Panathenaic stadium as well as the Zappeion Exhibition Hall near the stadium and schools, libraries, and other institutions there. Another prodigiously successful Greek businessman, George Averoff (1815–1899), was born in Metsovo but moved to Alexandria, Egypt, where he became a prosperous banker and entrepreneur. He made vast donations for educational institutions and other projects in Alexandria, Metsovo, and Athens, including extensive renovations of the Panathenaic stadium, where the first modern Olympic Games were held in 1896, with athletes from more than a dozen countries. One more notable Greek philanthropist was Panayis Athanase Vagliano (1814–1902), born on the island of Cephalonia, who became a prominent shipowner based in London and made significant donations to that island and to Greek education, including the funding of the NLG. He is honored by a statue in front of the national library's first building.

During the global economic crisis, sadly, this charitable tradition lagged just when it was needed more urgently than ever. The Onassis and Niarchos foundations are among the few that have been upholding the custom, and doing so in styles that are as different as their founders.

When I met Dracopoulos in the spring of 2013 at the SNF's pristine, modern midtown Manhattan office, he wore a conservative dark blue suit, white shirt, and tie—a contrast to the casual garb he sports in his appearances on the foundation's websites, YouTube videos, and DVDs. He eagerly described every aspect of the organization's structure and mode of operation, and its involvement in the Athens project, with an openness and charm that belie the Greek shipping industry's reputation for tightly guarded secrecy.

Dracopoulos received a B.S. from the University of Pennsylvania's Wharton School of Business in 1986, four years after coming to the United States, and he compares his role at the foundation to "running a business. But instead of monetary gain, we seek to benefit humanity."[15] His training at Wharton, a stint at Salomon Brothers, and his membership on the boards of the Peterson Institute for International Economics and the Center for Strategic and International Studies all point to his deep involvement in issues of international economic policy. He has also embraced the public aspects of science (he is a trustee of Rockefeller University and John Hopkins University).

From 2003 to 2010, the SNF director served as a trustee of the New York Public Library, where, according to Anthony Marx, director of the NYPL since

July 2011, he remains "one of the people I see most and rely on most for advice. He is informed on everything."[16] (Dracopoulos favored the controversial NYPL plan, ultimately withdrawn, to include a circulating division in the main research library building, which he believes would have modernized the library and increased its value for the public.)[17]

Dracopoulos's strict code of ethics and his family life are very different from those of the high-living, four-times-divorced Niarchos, and he has shaped the foundation in ways that relate more to his American education than to his great-uncle's flamboyant business practices. It is more oriented to serving the public interest than many other European philanthropic organizations.

The director's determination to improve education is matched by his equally strong conviction that in Greece the wealthy are morally obligated to help their country overcome its current problems. In 2013 he called the nation "a dying animal" and blamed politicians for "a big part of the problem."[18] And in 2015, he criticized, not for the first time, "all these people who have money but who don't do any of the three things they should do: they don't do philanthropy, they don't pay taxes, and they don't start businesses."[19]

Transparency International, a corruption watchdog group in Berlin, ranks Greece as Europe's most corrupt country,[20] placing it fifty-eighth among 168 countries worldwide.[21] It is also one of the most bureaucratic countries in Europe: the average ministry has about 440 departments, 20 percent of which have no staff other than a department head.

Dracopoulos points out that even the country's philanthropies receiving donations must be monitored as to how they handle the grants they accept from the SNF. To do this, as well as manage its other activities, the SNF has three offices: one in Athens, which attends to 80 percent of the donations, including those for the SNFCC; one in Monaco, which oversees mainly causes in Europe and Africa; and one in New York City, which manages projects in the rest of the world. The foundation's staff—fifteen people in New York, ten in Monaco, and fifty in Athens— is modest compared to what a U.S. institution of comparable size would have, suggesting that the family plays a prominent role in running it. "The foundation is still young," says Dracopoulos. "It is like a teenager—active and experimenting."

Indeed, like the trials of adolescence, the SNF's June 2007 commitment to the originally estimated $796 million cultural center project played out against a rocky context. Within less than a year of the foundation's formal 2009 memorandum of understanding with the state, the latter agreed to the first of a series of loans from the European lenders known as the Troika; these political and financial institutions were accused of trapping Greece in a vicious circle consisting of austerity-generating recession followed by more austerity, new taxes, and deeper recession—which was strangling economic growth, inhibiting job creation, and straining social cohesion.[22]

Pervasive mistrust in Greece—of the government, of the media, and of every business transaction—prompted the SNF to take certain precautions even before the magnitude of the nation's debt was revealed. The memorandum with the government concludes with what the SNF lawyers call a potential "bombshell": should the state fail at any time to meet its part of the bargain in terms of maintaining and running the center, all monies spent on creating the facility must be returned to the foundation within three months, to be used for public benefit programs within Greece. The foundation would have the right to withdraw Niarchos's name from the center, which would presumably cease to function.[23] As the center was nearing completion in mid-2016, it seemed likely that the state would not be able to keep its commitment due to its financial instability, but that very instability clearly would make the SNF's punitive proviso difficult if not impossible to enforce.

Because of the uneven results of public/private business partnerships in the United States, most foundations in Greece have concluded that their philanthropic contributions can only supplement, not replace, government funding.[24] Dracopoulos has fully endorsed this attitude, repeatedly citing the foundation's promise to turn over ownership of the cultural center to the state.

The terms of the agreement with the state include the creation of a legal entity (the SNFCC Ltd.) to administer construction of the SNFCC and its delivery to the government; and the assurance that, upon delivery, the foundation's board of directors would resign, and the state would appoint new board members. As additional insurance for the center's future, the contract guarantees that the state would honor, for a period of at least five years, all agreements with the suppliers, the parking/restaurant operators, and the bookstore concessions that were signed before the center's handover.[25] The SNFCC Ltd. met with a government advisory committee approximately once every six weeks starting in June 2007 to develop programming and to help negotiate the various agreements.

Some leftist politicians and fringe media organizations immediately attacked and have continued to snipe at this five-year contingency plan, denouncing it as private interference with a public institution. The government's return to the SNF of the value-added tax (VAT) levied on it to pay for maintenance of the center—which would come into play at the moment the SNF handed the complex over to Greece—is among the issues objected to by the marginal Communist press.[26]

What for the Greek government is a "gift from heaven" was also condemned by some abroad.[27] Gerard Mortier, then director of Madrid's Teatro Real, who brought that company's production of Bertolt Brecht and Kurt Weill's *The Rise and Fall of the City of Mahagonny* to Athens in March 2012, expressed indignation that the government endorsed the new opera house while at the same time failing to pay his artists fees agreed upon by contract.[28] Mortier was not the only one to find fault with nonpayment by the GNO: in November 2015 the opera's technicians' union called a series of strikes to protest repeated delays in payment of their salaries.[29]

In addition to its support for the cultural center, the foundation continued to issue grants to relieve the humanitarian crisis in Greece, while implementing three additional major initiatives of approximately $125 million each, in 2012 and 2015. In 2013, a long-term grant of $138 million for a "Recharge Youth" program to help unemployed young people was announced. The SNF also hosts an annual international conference in Greece on philanthropic, economic, and social programs in Europe.

As soon as the foundation received a conceptual design from RPBW in mid-2008, it began to try to raise public awareness of the project, using the local press. And once construction began in October 2012, the SNF added to its website a 24-hour webcam showing the work in process. At the same time, the foundation encouraged live viewing of the construction site, going so far as to erect a 330-foot-long temporary pedestrian metal bridge over part of the work area.

In 2013 the SNF held an architectural competition, limited to Greek architecture students, for the design of a temporary visitors center at the end of the bridge. The winners, chosen by Renzo Piano from 93 entries, were Agis-Panagiotis Mourelatos and Spyridon Giotakis. The duo received an award of $24,000; five runners-up also received cash awards. Reminiscent of the platform built to overlook the construction site of Potsdamer Platz in Berlin (for which RPBW designed the master plan and eight of the eighteen buildings), the 2,150-square-foot glass box, which featured interactive displays, was inspired by Piano's signature transparency and lightness. It opened to the press on October 4, 2013; but with the Greek public preoccupied with securing the basic necessities of life during the continuing economic crisis, attendance got off to a slow start. Supplemented by a weekly Sunday-morning bus tour of the site that began in April 2014, the number of spectators increased considerably; overall, 75,474 people visited between October 2013 and June 2016.[30] The $1.1 million cost of operating the center until January 2016 was covered by the foundation.

The SNFCC was a pale bright spot amid the city's troubles in 2013. In June, demonstrations denounced the government's sudden suspension of the state-owned radio and television broadcast company ERT (the Hellenic Broadcasting Corporation), and a general strike protested the Greek parliament's approval of an omnibus bill to overhaul the civil service, enact a new tax code, and make other budget cuts. Greeks were not appeased by Prime Minister Antonis Samaras's optimistic announcement in August that by the end of the year the country would host a record-breaking 19 million tourists, or by the deal he announced for the Trans Adriatic Pipeline, which would carry Azerbaijani gas from the Caspian

Sea to European markets through Greece and Albania and which represented a $40 billion investment in the region as well as the potential for job growth.[31]

On September 23, to protest salary cuts for 25,000 civil servants and the specter of their transfer or dismissal, Greece's public transportation, all public services and hospitals, and to a certain extent all public media ground to a halt nationwide.[32] Government employees (whose salaries and pensions had already been cut by 30 percent between 2010 and 2013) were joined in the strikes by public schoolteachers, hospital staff, and lawyers, staging protests that resulted in clashes, at times violent, between the strikers and security forces.[33] There was fear that the country could be brought to the point of collapse by such demonstrations.

In a supreme twist of irony, Samaras arrived in Washington, D.C., to meet with United States and IMF officials just three days before the American government was shut down by its own congress on October 1, 2013. But even with this reminder of ubiquitous political uncertainty, by November Samaras's attempt in August to portray Greece as "a bastion of stability" was subject to ridicule when the country was once more brought to a standstill by a general strike.

A crackdown on corruption, which the Greek government began in 2014, unearthed one Greek official, Antonis Kantas, who testified that he had accepted so many bribes he couldn't recall all of them. Even though he was only a lowly military officer, Kantas was able to amass nearly $19 million in payoffs in five years. Notwithstanding a country hardened to wrongdoing, Kantas's testimony revealed a system of illegal activity much more widespread and infinitely more costly than suspected.[34] By the end of 2014, as the British newspaper the *Guardian* noted:

> *Since the financial meltdown, only one senior politician, the former defense minister, Akis Tsochatzopoulos, has been imprisoned partly because the scale of his avarice made his ill-gotten gains difficult to hide. Last month, the erstwhile finance minister Yiannos Papantoniou was given a suspended four-year jail term for producing a false declaration of assets and revenues. But with the exception of Thessaloniki's ex-mayor, who was found guilty of embezzlement and imprisoned for life, they are the only high-ranking officials to have paid the price of breach of duty.*[35]

Dracopoulos himself had stated early in 2014, "Things are improving, but not widely enough and not fast enough."[36] Regrettably, this prognosis would eventually apply to the government's attitude toward the SNFCC.

Preceding pages: SNFCC, Renzo Piano's presentation to public at agora site, June 29, 2011

Site with beginning of hill

Stage pit excavation and demarcation of main and rear agoras

Overleaf: Completed hill without topsoil, foundations being poured: parking garage (left), level of seismic isolators for opera and library wings (right)

Site, canopy fabrication shed (left), Kallithea Public Park (far right)

Stavros Niarchos Park with first olive trees

Opera house auditorium

Concrete superstructure

Opera house under construction, monumental staircase

South elevation of opera house beside south-facing wall at car park ("cliff")
(left)

Opera house auditorium

Overleaf: "Dance of the Cranes," June 25, 2014

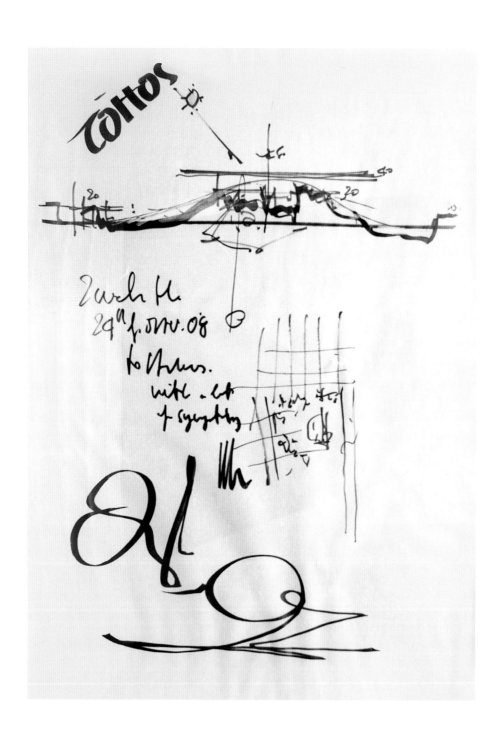

Beginnings

Even before officially announcing the Niarchos Foundation's project for Athens, Andreas Dracopoulos commissioned a master plan from the New York architecture and planning firm Cooper Robertson (fig. 1). Master plans, devised either by the architect for a project or by an outside firm, are the keystone of every major architectural venture. Here, the one developed by Cooper Robertson established the physical requirements for what was to be built—functionality, ability to fit the program to the site, layout of vehicular circulation—and the list of consultants. The master plan helps to calculate a general estimate of costs both for construction and for running the facility, and it plays an important role in a project's aesthetic success or failure. "In order for a project to proceed," said Scott Newman, the CR partner-in-charge of the Athens undertaking, "the program, the master plan, and the budget must all work."[1] Richard Meier's Getty Center in Los Angeles is one example of a master plan that fell short, because more was crammed onto the site than it could gracefully accommodate (fig. 2).

Development of the master plan was one of the many phases of the SNFCC that suffered from the lack of a defined client. Without a director for either the national opera or the national library providing consistent leadership, Newman and his three teams—one for the opera house, one for the library, and one for the 42-acre park—took their directives from a committee consisting of government ministers, representatives of the SNF, the administrations of the opera and library, several consultants, and local experts. As with all state-run institutions in Greece, the hiring of directors and staffs for both institutions was subject to a constantly changing political scene. Of the four ministers who signed the memorandum of understanding with the foundation, only Antonis Samaras, at the time Greece's minister of culture, remained in office, eventually becoming prime minister, a position he held from June 2012 to January 2015.

A master plan typically consists of a model, which conveys the physical qualities proposed by the planners, and a document, which puts forth the

Renzo Piano, conceptual sketch of SNFCC, February 29, 2008

49

2   Richard Meier, Getty Center, Los Angeles

ı   Cooper Robertson, SNFCC, master plan, model

background of the project, what the users hope to achieve, and how the planners intend to satisfy those hopes. The comprehensive text for the SNFCC master plan, completed in April 2008, contained three components:

- A *survey of existing conditions* made use of the floor plans of the old library and opera house buildings, along with site visits and meetings with department heads, to study how spaces were being used. These findings established a baseline against which to measure future growth and change.
- A *needs analysis* compiled information gleaned from the department heads, in workshops, and by touring comparable facilities in other countries to define operational, technical, and space requirements that would be valid for at least twenty years. The analysis proposed sizes and shapes for the various spaces as well as ideas for public circulation, both pedestrian and vehicular, inside and outside the buildings. Local experts advised on topography (including sub-surface conditions), environmental impact, transportation, and political factors in the surrounding neighborhood. In addition to its usefulness for the architects, this information was essential to obtaining the necessary building permits.

4 Snøhetta, Oslo Opera House

3 Snøhetta, Alexandrina Library

5 Oslo Opera House

- A *roster of requirements* included such considerations as bulk and height, massing, and location for buildings on the site, as well as the park, all of which were described in physical terms and contributed to the cultural center's program.

To help determine the crucial choice of an architect, the planners drew up a long list of candidates; experience with complex undertakings was the single qualification. Thirty names were proposed by Cooper Robertson, including the winners of the Pritzker Prize. There were three finalists: Snøhetta in Oslo, Ateliers Jean Nouvel in Paris, and Renzo Piano Building Workshop in Genoa. Each had major auditoriums to their names; two of them, Snøhetta and RPBW, had designed libraries.

Snøhetta was propelled to international attention by its design for the new Alexandrina Library in Alexandria, Egypt (2002), especially its enormous tilting roof and multidisciplinary facilities (fig. 3). In its design for the Oslo Opera House six years later, it was again the roof, dramatically sloped for pedestrian use, that was the building's defining image (figs. 4, 5). That sloping roof instantly became the city's favorite promenade and may have influenced some

6 Ateliers Jean Nouvel, Dansk Radio Byen Concert Hall, Danish Broadcasting Company, Copenhagen

7 Dansk Radio Byen Concert Hall

8 Renzo Piano and Richard Rogers, Centre Georges Pompidou, Paris

9 RPBW, Menil Collection, Houston

of the ideas for the Athens project's design. The acoustics of the traditional, horseshoe-shaped theater within the opera house were also much praised.

Nouvel's Dansk Radio Byen Concert Hall for the Danish Broadcasting Company (2009), part of that company's four-building media center in Copenhagen, was under construction at the time of the search; the auditorium's spectacular multilevel seating resembling a vineyard's terraces, which surrounds the stage—similar to a theater-in-the-round—is at the top level of an enormous boxlike structure (figs. 6, 7). The building weathered public outrage about its cost overruns and opened to mixed reviews of its acoustics.[2]

With fifty people in the Genoa office, seventy in Paris, and a small satellite office in New York, Renzo Piano has produced a wide-ranging body of work that includes outstanding buildings worldwide, from the huge Kansai International Airport Building in Osaka (1994) and the Shard skyscraper in London (2013) to the jewellike Pathé Foundation headquarters in Paris (2014). Two of the firm's recent projects are the Paris Courthouse (begun 2010) and the École Normale Supérieure Cachan (begun 2014), prestigious commissions that bookend the French capital to the north and south.

ıı   Parco della Musica, Sala Santa Cecilia

ıo   RPBW, Parco della Musica, Rome

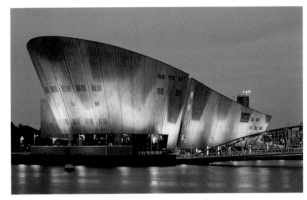

ı2   RPBW, National Center for Science and Technology NEMO, Amsterdam

Many of the cultural buildings Piano has completed worldwide have become benchmarks for their respective type of institution. Among these are the Centre National d'Art et de Culture Georges Pompidou (with Richard Rogers, Paris, 1977; fig. 8) and the Menil Collection (Houston, 1986; fig. 9).

However, although several of the performance spaces designed by Piano have been outstanding—including the fully reconfigurable "Prometeo" (Venice, 1983–1984) and the Niccolò Paganini Auditorium (Parma, 2001)—RPBW's most ambitious venue for music, the Parco della Musica complex in Rome (2002), is the least engaging architecturally of the three contenders' recent performance venues. Grouped around an open-air space that holds up to 3,000 people, its three separate structures range in size from 700 to 2,700 seats (figs. 10, 11). The interiors are handsome, but the curved lead-panel exteriors look like shiny scarabs or beetles (in fact, locals have nicknamed them "beetles"), and the acoustical quality of the largest hall varies depending on where the listener sits. As with RPBW's other buildings that feature opaque, curvilinear forms (for example, the National Center for Science and Technology NEMO in Amsterdam, 1997; fig. 12), the Parco della Musica, though a popular success, is less satisfying aesthetically than the transparent, Euclidean architecture for which the firm is best known.

Visits to some of the competitors' buildings by a team from the foundation were an important part of the selection process, but Dracopoulos obviously preferred to choose according to personality. As a part of this process, he arranged for the board to meet the three finalists, first in New York City late in 2007 and then in Zurich early in 2008. For these interviews, the candidates were asked to present whatever they wanted.

The SNF director remembers the board meeting Kjetil T. Thorsen, a founding partner of Snøhetta, for breakfast in Zurich. Thorsen had interesting new ideas, but for Dracopoulos the "deal breaker" was the fact that he had not visited the area in Athens.[3]

In contrast to the Snøhetta team, Jean Nouvel had visited the site by helicopter as well as on foot. But at a dinner meeting in Zurich, the directors, despite being impressed by Nouvel's architecture, balked at what they felt was his self-serving description of the cultural center as "a new Acropolis," which overlooked the fact that the old Acropolis has a revered place in the Greek mind.

Dracopoulos clearly favored Genoa-born and -based Piano, with whom he had "hit it off" when the two men met over lunch in New York in 2007. That encounter took place at the Morgan Library and Museum, for which Piano completed the redesign in 2006. "Within the first three minutes," Dracopoulos says, "I knew this was the guy. He said all the right things; he was calm, ethical in his approach, and intelligent."

One could say that Piano was destined for the job. The project resonates with his affinity for the classical tradition and his love of the sea, which he calls the "other face of the earth."[4] The tall, wiry Italian (b. 1937) fiercely defends the summer month he spends on the Mediterranean, cruising on the *Kirribilli*, a sleek, 60-foot-long sailboat he designed in 1999–2001. The architect says he loves Greece because "the Mediterranean is part of my DNA. I'm Italian, so I'm vaccinated against trouble; the troubles of Greece are familiar to me. We have to be grateful to Greece for the beginning of democracy. Now it is like a beautiful but fragile child that Europe must help."[5]

Piano also described a prophetic Mediterranean trip that took place in 2006. He was aboard the private yacht of the friend of a client, Jean-Louis Dumas-Hermès, who at the time was chief executive of the French fashion and luxury goods company. When the vessel docked at the port of Faliro, just south of Athens, Piano, his wife, and young son disembarked and took a cab into the capital.[6] In an uncanny coincidence, the taxi was stopped by the police for speeding at exactly the spot where the SNFCC would begin to rise six years later. Standing there, waiting for the car to proceed, Piano noticed that he couldn't see the sea, although it was only a few hundred feet away.

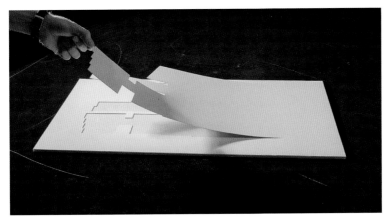

13   SNFCC, conceptual model

Choosing an architect on the basis of personality is not necessarily a guaran-tee of the best outcome; nevertheless, early in 2008, Piano's imaginative idea of creating a 100-foot-high hill and inserting the building within it reinforced the board's preference. His presentation of the extraordinary concept was greeted with enthusiasm at a meeting in Zurich in which he exhibited only a tiny wood model (now lost) and a small, informal sketch. Inscribed "To Andreas, with a lot of sympathy," the sketch explains why a single, two-wing structure (rather than the two separate buildings proposed by CR) was needed to provide space for the central, open-air agora (see p. 48).

At the very beginning, Piano had oriented the complex to the north, so that in his words, it would "talk to the city, and face the Acropolis." But the scheme felt too monumental; it brought the agora between the library and opera house too close to the adjacent road system; and there were few interesting views on the flat terrain.

Early in the design process, Piano visited the roof terrace of the Onassis Cardiac Surgery Center (the highest point near the site, just two blocks to the north) and spent hours studying the outlook: a panoramic vista that includes views of the Aegean Islands at the southeast, Piraeus and Salamis Island at the northwest, and the Acropolis due north. The architect realized that to offer views of the scenic bay, a building would have to rise 80 to 100 feet above the existing ground level. When I discussed the hill concept with Piano several years after he had started work on the project, he still marveled at the fact that such a relatively small increase in height would be enough to provide expansive views

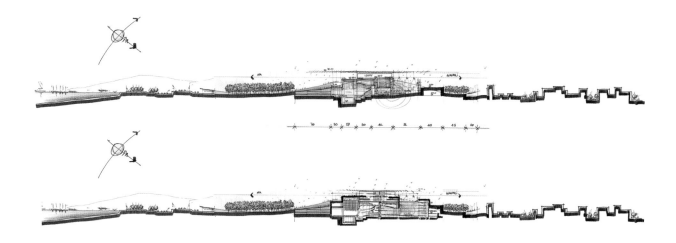

14   SNFCC, hill peaking at north end of site, sectional sketches

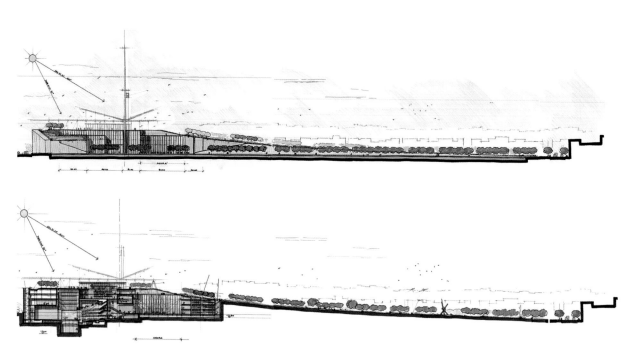

15   Hill peaking at south end of site, sectional sketches

16   RPBW, Il Vulcano Buono, Nola, Italy

of the city and, in particular, of two of its determining features—the Acropolis and the sea: "It was an almost childish idea: I simply lifted the ground's surface to make way for the architecture" (fig. 13). It is a modest statement considering that the hill quickly became the project's defining feature and saved a considerable amount of energy.[7] Having decided on construction of a hill that would rise from north to south, the building was reoriented to face southeast, with both volumes situated at its southeast end (figs. 14, 15).

Manipulation of the ground plane and an accessible roof were not new concepts for Piano. RPBW had just completed Il Vulcano Buono, in Nola, Italy, in 2007, a mixed-use shopping and leisure center with a grass-covered cone-shaped volume that visually echoes nearby Mount Vesuvius (fig. 16); and NEMO in Amsterdam offers an inclined rooftop for pedestrian use. I asked Piano whether he had any of these earlier buildings in mind when designing the current one, and he responded, "You can't think too much about the past—oblivion helps. Architecture is about mixing things up; it's what [Jorge Luis] Borges described in his fiction as between memory and forgetting."[8]

In addition to the precedents in Piano's recent and in-progress works, the mountains surrounding Athens offered their own inspiration. One characteristic of the Attican hills is the quarries that have, for millennia, provided marble for Greek architecture, including the Parthenon. The architect adapted the characteristics of a natural quarry to his scheme, not only burying the building in a hill but also, in an early phase of the design, cladding exterior and interior vertical surfaces in marble. Only the first part of this concept—insertion into a hill—was retained in the building's final design.

Piano and his office began their design with the master plan and these initial concepts. Among the early team members were Giorgio Bianchi (b. 1958), a RPBW partner who was in charge of the project; Vassily Laffineur (b. 1976), an associate; and two others. They were subsequently joined by as many as twenty-three colleagues. Bianchi is one of seven architects who entered the firm in the

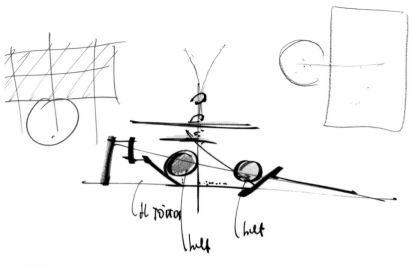

17 SNFCC, development sketch

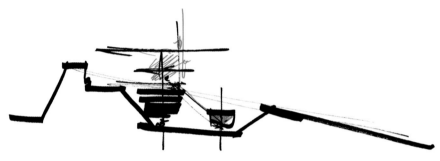

18 Development sketch

1980s and subsequently became a partner. (There are now eleven partners.) When he arrived there straight out of school in 1985, he was twenty-seven years old. A fiercely passionate man, he is devoted to his boss: "Renzo Piano was my master—I learned everything from him—design, drawing, people, how to be modest. It's my life."

Using Piano's schematics, Bianchi worked with Laffineur to produce hundreds of elegant sketches (figs. 17–20); Bianchi's are typically more general, Laffineur's more detailed. Together with the models that were made, these played a large role in the early stages (fig. 21). Computer drawings then fine-tuned the initial ideas so that they could be built. Bianchi explains, "If an idea doesn't work, you have to come up with a new concept: sometimes we made as many as ten different models in one day."[9]

The cultural center was created with the help of a technology widely used in architecture today, Building Information Modeling (BIM), which links the design, schedule, construction, and management activities and costs of different disciplines by means of a virtual information model; a change in one discipline is automatically updated in the others. The contractors and the owner/operator

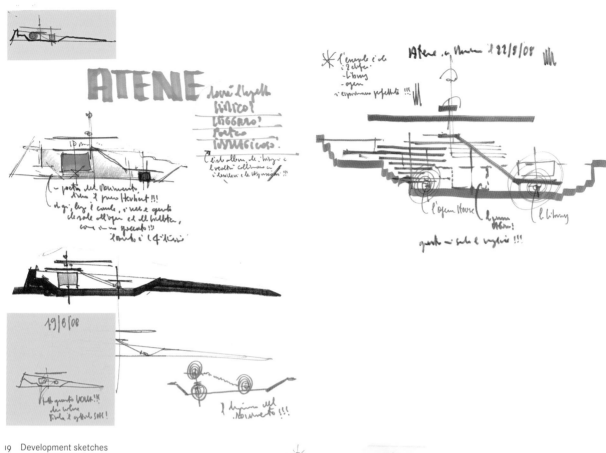

19 Development sketches

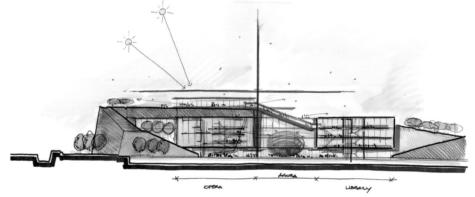

20 Development drawing, section

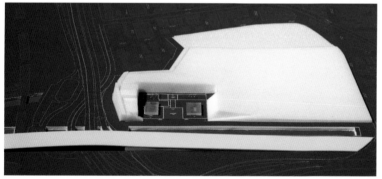

21 Conceptual development, cutaway model

use the model to ensure better coordination and more accurate cost estimates during construction. In addition, such models can be adjusted to provide guidance for operating and maintaining completed buildings.[10] The SNFCC is the second project for which RPBW has employed the software program Revit for BIM. (The first was Columbia University's Manhattanville Campus plan in 2002, for which the client required the use of this program.) It is now their preferred software. All official communication for the project took place via Aconex, a cloud- and web-based collaboration tool for construction management, which stores everything related to a project—down to the most inconsequential e-mail—in an easily accessible database.

Piano has certain principles that guide him in making the sketches with which he begins a project: they are not meant to be beautiful objects, he emphasizes, but rather to document a vision and an emotion. "If they were beautiful," he says,

> you would fall in love with them. The bottom line isn't the drawing, but the building. The drawing is to explore, to say only one (maybe two) simple things. I learned this from my friend Italo Calvino, who came often to the Pompidou construction site with a piece of paper folded in eight, on each side of which he took notes. He even used ongoing work there for a description in his book Invisible Cities: "a forest of pipes that end in taps, showers, spouts, overflows." At the end of the day I disperse the sketches to my colleagues: I don't want to mystify. What I do want is to feel the ping pong of collaboration, how you can build from a sketch.[11]

The architect has similar feelings about models, which he uses as a design tool, not a means of influencing the client. He cautions against

> [falling] in love with the model, because the building ends up looking like a big scale model. These are the traps of architecture—instead of a finished building with a relationship to the city, you end up with an isolated object. Many things go into the process of architecture. We are like musicians, obsessed with the final thing—not with something in between.

The critic Peter Schjeldahl has expressed, in an interview, a similar idea about ways in which art can fail: "One of them is for the maker to enjoy it too much. That's treason. I compare it to a chef eating his own cooking and then proudly handing you an empty plate. The proper chef barely tastes the food, and gives it all to you."[12]

Somewhere between a drawing and a model are "bas-relief drawings" or "three-dimensional drawings" (fig. 22). These are particular to Piano and are used, in part, to explain architectural concepts to clients. The team starts with a sketch on paper, drawn to scale. The sketch is cut out and mounted on a sheet

22   SNFCC, east elevation, schematic bas-relief drawing

of polystyrene foam core, which is then stacked atop additional sheets to make a solid form. To liven things up, Piano resorts to storytelling references to bodily fluids (blood) and sex appeal (for the sensuous smoothness of certain surfaces), along with anything else that will vividly bring to life what he is trying to accomplish.

The SNFCC is one of the rare instances for RPBW in which the firm was responsible not only for the design but also for the construction drawings. In many cases these are prepared by architects who specialize in such documentation. Construction drawings have been a requisite part of making architecture since the Renaissance. Until that time, the head mason in charge of erecting a structure was answerable for the execution of a design; the shift to a reliance on drawings, initiated by Leon Battista Alberti (1404–1472), a humanist who epitomized the "Renaissance man," switched responsibility to the architect. This new paradigm, now a basic procedure in architecture, would eventually lead to three-dimensional computer modeling software and other innovations.[13] In his discussion of this major change, the historian and theoretician Mario Carpo gives a glimpse into the profession's imponderables: no such drawing, he says, "no matter how rich, can ever hope to encapsulate *all* aspects of a physical object yet to be built."[14]

The procedures used by Piano, the son of a Genoa builder, recall pre-Renaissance practice in their emphasis on a craftsman-like approach. He bestows especially careful attention on full-scale mock-ups for every aspect of a project. Painstaking examination of the mock-ups—how they look in different light conditions, their appearance when painted in subtle variations of the chosen colors, and their feel—produces a constant series of alterations.

Like Genoa, always a touchstone for Piano, Athens is closely connected to its port. For Athens, it is Piraeus, and long before a port was constructed in that harbor in the fifth century B.C.E., it was Faliro. In the mid-twentieth century, superhighways were inserted along the water's edge in both Genoa and Athens,

23 Seaside highway, Tae Kwon Do stadium (left of
center), volleyball stadium (upper center), Athens

24 RPBW, Columbus International Exhibition, Genoa

25 Reimagining of Phidias's *Athena Promachos*

severing the connection to the shoreline; RPBW has found a way to reestab-
lish each city's relationship to the water despite the barriers created by seaside
avenues (fig. 23). In Genoa, the firm's design for the Columbus International
Exhibition (1992; fig. 24) provided the opportunity to create attractions at the
waterfront that link it with the historic city; and in Athens, a prominent canal
within the SNFCC park returned the presence of water to the site (see pp. 6–7).
There are also similarities between RPBW's UNESCO Laboratory-Workshop,
established in 1989–1991 at Vesima on the outskirts of Genoa (see p. 130, fig. 23),
and the cultural center: each sits on a hillside where land and sea meet, captur-
ing what for Piano is water's "magic."

In the Athens project, Piano discarded almost all of CR's suggestions related
to design; nevertheless traces of those ideas survive in what was built. The master planners had also sought to provide views of the sea and the city, but by far
more conventional means—elevating the two separate buildings for the opera
house and the library on a podium, with parking underneath. They also considered how the complex would look from the sea, conjecturing that it could evoke
the sculptor Phidias's *Athena Promachos*, a giant marble masterpiece from 456
B.C.E., now lost, which stood just inside the Acropolis (fig. 25). Its gilded helmet
and sword tip reflected the sun, serving as a beacon for sailors.[15]

Bearing in mind the relationship between site and neighborhood, CR proposed constructing a connection to the long north–south esplanade built in
2000 for the 2004 Olympics, which extends to the sea at the east side of the cultural center, passing over the broad thoroughfare. At the west, they envisioned

26   Esplanade steps

a second green space, Kallithea Public Park, intended for the neighborhood's use—a contrast to the national status of the cultural center's park (fig. 26; see also pp. 36–37). The planners also launched the idea of performance spaces in the Stavros Niarchos Park. All of these ideas were carried out.

Also during design development, the park was reconfigured and aligned north–south instead of east–west (fig. 27). The final complex has the seven-level opera house at the southeast and the five-level library just north of it; the two are separated by the 17,220-square-foot open-air agora. The 1,300-foot-long, 100-foot-wide, and 5-foot-deep canal runs the whole length of the site along the building's east facade.

Other changes arising as the design progressed include the position of the opera house auditorium, which was rotated from its first angled location within the building. Originally aligned with a historic path to the Parthenon, it was transposed to a north–south and then to an east–west axis, which provided better access to the back of the house (figs. 28, 29). The smaller, Alternative Stage theater, planned primarily for children's programs and experimental material, was also moved. The architects placed it initially at the building's top level, with access to the roof; this access was sacrificed when the theater was relocated next to the west side of the main auditorium to facilitate sharing of the backstage (with the loading dock at the building's southwest corner) and lobby.[16]

The team also reduced by half the dramatic canopy crowning the complex (figs. 30, 31). They moved the restaurant from the ground floor to the fifth floor and placed the ballet school above the restaurant, partially visible to diners (fig. 32). They also undertook major redesigns of the library's interior (see "Library" chapter). The agora was trimmed in size, colored cladding planned for its concrete surfaces was removed, and surrounding elevated walkways for the staff were eliminated. Also dispensed with was the bridge that had traversed the agora's top level (fig. 33), connecting the library to the lighthouse above the opera

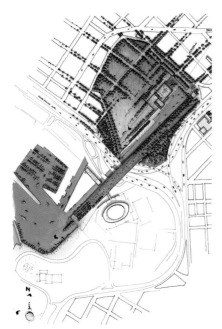

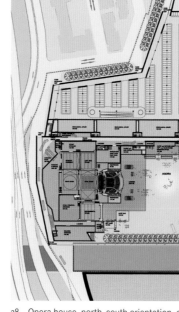

27 SNFCC, east-west alignment of park, early sketch   28 Opera house, north-south orientation, early plan

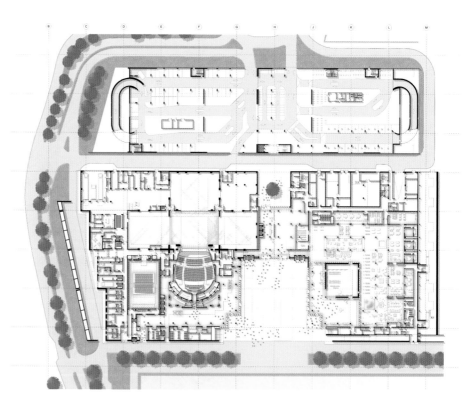

29 Opera house, east-west orientation, plan

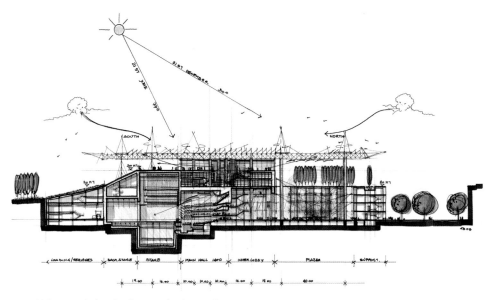

30   Initial canopy design, development drawing, section

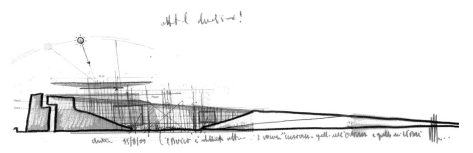

31   Canopy, development drawing, section

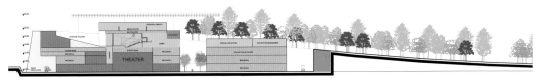

32   Restaurant (in red) and planting on library roof, section

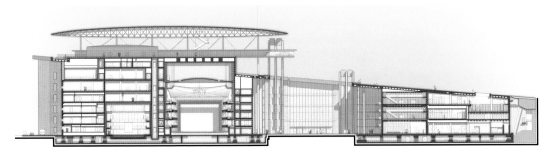

33   Section

34   RPBW, Giovanni and Marella Agnelli Art Gallery, Lingotto Conference
     Center, Turin

house (now accessed by elevators from the agora), first intended as a reading and meeting room for the public library. Its position recalls the rooftop Giovanni and Marella Agnelli Art Gallery at Piano's Lingotto Conference Center (2003; fig. 34).

Piano even made a minor adjustment to the garden elements near the canal promenade—eliminating the planters along the foot of the east-facing park walls. He felt that their replacement by a simple joint gap between the promenade and the walls intensified his wish to convey the effort of the earth being lifted up.[17]

One of the sketches that emerged during this phase became a symbol for the entire undertaking (fig. 35). Used for all the foundation's promotion, it also represents the core of the idea: a black line indicating the hill's surface traces its diagonal incline from north to south, starting from the bottom of the slope (at the right) upward and over the roofs of the library and opera house (at the left). Planting indications on this incline represent the park's unification of the site. Two concrete walls, drawn in white pencil on the blue-gray background, rise in opposite directions at either side of the agora between the hill and the horizontal ground plane. Both walls support stairways: for the opera, the generously proportioned outdoor stair balances the library stair's oblique and replaces the traditional monumental one within. The steps lead to the rooftop restaurant and may prove more successful for outdoor seating than as a means of ascent to the fifth level. Also sketched in white is the lighthouse, the fly tower in its podium. And hovering above the lighthouse is the huge canopy (see "Structure" chapter). The lighthouse, restaurant, and park's hilltop are the major viewpoints.

The architectural historian Vincent Scully has eloquently described the sensitivity with which the ancient Greeks positioned their sacred temples. The structures were sited in relation to nearby hills and mountains to harmonize in an architectural whole, establishing the landscape's religious as well as aesthetic significance.[18] No temple better embodies this idea than the Parthenon, the key structure of the Athenian Acropolis, which was the most important complex

35   Renzo Piano, iconic development drawing of SNFCC, showing
     slope of hill, concrete walls, and canopy, 2009

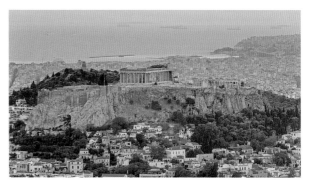

36   Acropolis, Athens

constructed during classical antiquity (fig. 36). It was commissioned by Pericles while he led Athens (461–429 B.C.E.) in recognition of the goddess Athena's
protection of the city and, then as now with the cultural center, to provide work
for its citizens.

The relationship of the SNFCC to the hills around Athens is equally sensitive,
and also recalls other historic precedents. The tilted plane of the artificial hill
conjures up the long, sloping promenades favored by André Le Nôtre, landscape
architect to Louis XIV, as found at the Château de Chantilly (fig. 37); and the canal
is reminiscent of those the Frenchman designed to expand the vistas of his parks.

The SNFCC also bears a striking similarity to the 62-acre Parc des Buttes-
Chaumont (1864–1867), designed by the horticulturist Jean-Pierre Barillet-
Deschamps (1824–1873) and the engineer Jean-Charles Adolphe Alphand to
reclaim a landscape in the north of Paris scarred by, among other things, a gal-
lows, a sanitary sewage dump, and a mass grave (fig. 38). At Buttes-Chaumont,
as in Athens, a painstakingly constructed high artificial promontory was a daring experiment to offer panoramas of the city beyond the industrial vicinity. The
promontory also includes a natural limestone quarry.[19]

Barillet-Deschamps was the chief gardener of Paris, responsible for designing and building the Bois de Boulogne and the Bois de Vincennes and renovating the Jardin du Luxembourg, initiatives of Napoleon III as part of his radical renovation of Paris under the guidance of Baron Georges-Eugène Haussmann (1809–1891). Today, French architect and theoretician Antoine Grumbach asserts that mid-nineteenth-century Parisians felt that the grandeur and otherworldliness of the artificial landscape of Buttes-Chaumont was more natural than nature itself.[20] This may also prove true of parts of the SNFCC park, with its native vegetation and the dialogue between its hill and the two promontories behind it (the Acropolis and, further inland, the Lycabetus).

Implemented during the heady period of design, yet independent from it, was a series of practical decisions essential to the realization of the complex. Construction management was carried out by Faithful+Gould, which was hired initially to review cost estimates. Even though early valuations provided by a local Greek consultant were twice as high as the SNF directors had expected, F+G demonstrated that they were too low.[21] Piano trimmed the size of the building to reduce construction costs; Martin Hirko (b. 1952), a regional director of F+G, together with a local firm engaged by the SNF, established a €550 million ($776 million) lump sum price tag for construction, which eventually rose—because of an increase in the value-added tax and change orders by the SNF—to slightly over €617 million ($854 million), including two grants of €5 million ($6 million) each to the NLG and the GNO for their transition to the SNFCC.

A few months after RPBW was chosen to design the center, Hirko and F+G were engaged by the SNF to oversee construction, for which he put together what he calls a "lean and mean team."[22] He had also witnessed the hiring of what he

When Renzo Piano visits the SNFCC site—here he examines a mock-up of the canopy—he resembles a pop star surrounded by a crowd of adoring teenagers. But these "teenagers" are the various architects, consultants, contractors' representatives, and construction managers accompanying Piano, many aiming cell-phone cameras at the great designer. The multitude produces a present-day Tower of Babel, mixing Greek, Italian, and English (the project's official language). About a third of the architects, engineers, and administrative personnel associated with the foundation and the contractors are women.

37 André Le Nôtre, Château de Chantilly, etching by Adam Perrelle, seventeenth century

38 Jean-Pierre Barillet-Deschamps and Jean-Charles Adolphe Alphand, Parc des Buttes-Chaumont, Paris, engraving, 1873

considered to be a prodigious number of consultants—some even before RPBW and primarily by Cooper Robertson—for room and building acoustics, theater design, and civil, structural, and mechanical engineering, to name just a few. "It was the first time in my career," he says, "that there were so many consultants of different backgrounds involved. It is like working for the United Nations."[23]

The construction supervisor, who looks considerably younger than his years, was born and grew up in Astoria, New York, where he attended public technical and vocational schools. After graduating in 1972, he worked as an office clerk for a firm of consulting engineers, and over time was employed by some of the best-known construction companies in the United States. He says that the SNFCC is "the most interesting, challenging, and rewarding assignment of my 40-year career."[24]

Unlike the routine selection of a builder from two or three candidates, F+G managed the process of choosing a contractor more like an upscale architectural competition. Eight companies participated in the ten-month process, and to help the Greek economy, the foundation made an effort to include some that were based in Greece. However, foreign firms are better placed for bank loans, and so the local company that was chosen, the Greek firm Terna, was asked to collaborate with an international outfit, the Italian firm Salini Impregilo, with the latter controlling 51 percent. The cooperation between firms of different nationalities had a bumpy beginning, but once the principals got used to working with each other, most issues were resolved amicably.

Hirko represented the client—the SNF—on site, ensuring that its intentions and those of the architects were realized. Among other things, this entailed making sure the contractors did not stint on the quality of materials in order to maximize profits. Hirko tried to avoid lengthy and counterproductive searches for the cheapest materials, kept the contractors to a strict schedule, monitored environmental regulations, and maintained the security of a site where there were at times more than 1,200 workers.

39   OMA, Central Library, Seattle

40   Frank Gehry, RPBW, and others, Millennium Park, Chicago

The manager explained that during the first year, the contractors submitted monthly invoices from the subcontractors (including material, labor, and equipment) of approximately $6.5 million, a sum that nearly doubled the second year, when the building began to rise. Greek unions enjoy strong representation, but the average salary for construction workers in Athens (as well as for engineers and other professionals) is less than half of what the equivalent would be in New York City. An unusual aspect of the contractors' agreement was that they assumed complete financial responsibility for satisfactory and on-time completion of the project, even in the face of errors and omissions by the design team. This clause first came into play in respect to the concrete, some of which had to be demolished and recast because its quality did not meet the architects' standards.

More drastic was the $56,000-a-day penalty (which could have amounted to $1.7 million a month) that the SNF had the right to impose if the canopy was not completed by January 28, 2015. That deadline, considered a major construction milestone, was in fact missed, but a four-month extension eliminated the penalties.[25] The original completion date of November 2015 for the building was also extended (to May 2016), with the same elimination of penalties.

Bianchi visited the site every other week, and Piano several times a year. On all of these visits, the two men were accompanied by architects from Betaplan, the Greek architecture firm hired by RPBW as their local partner. Betaplan, with senior architect Eleni Tzanou in charge, provided most of the on-site supervision of the contractors and also helped coordinate the various designers and specialists. Tzanou was one of about ten women and seven men from the firm who were involved from the beginning.

With contracts signed and preparations well under way, a feasibility study put forward in 2010 appeared almost as an afterthought. It was prepared by the Athens office of the Boston Consulting Group, whose more than seven thousand consultants worldwide specialize in business strategy.[26] BCG equated the SNFCC with landmarks like the Parthenon and the Acropolis Museum and compared its potential impact with that of several recent additions to major United States cities, among them the Seattle Central Library (Rem Koolhaas and Joshua Prince-Ramus of OMA, 2004; fig. 39) and Millennium Park in Chicago (Frank Gehry and Renzo Piano, among others, 2004; fig. 40). The library in Seattle became an asset for the city's economy, a catalyst for downtown revitalization, and a new icon for the metropolis, with 166 percent higher attendance at the new building in its first year of operation than at the old building the previous year. In Chicago, Millennium Park each year attracts nearly 5 million visitors, who spend $1.4 billion.[27]

BCG's study predicted that the new cultural center would encourage a similar increase in visitors (1.5 million annually) and in visitor spending, and would bring greater economic benefits to the Athens region than Seattle or Chicago had experienced: spending of nearly $300 million in the local community and annual fiscal revenue of $19.5 million.[28] While the results of such a feasibility study would make or break any other undertaking of this magnitude, Dracopoulos dismissed it as a mere formality. Regardless of its conclusions, he said, "We would have gone ahead."[29]

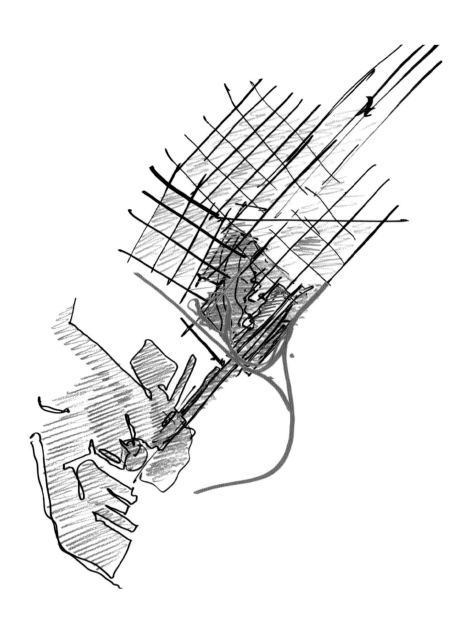

Athens

The 42-acre site for the SNFCC is in a district known as Kallithea (Greek for "beautiful view"), a mere 600 feet from Faliro Bay, one of the many bays along the Saronic Gulf. It is less than two miles south of central Athens, a distance comparable to the stretch between Washington Square and Central Park in New York, or between the Hôtel de Ville and Place de l'Étoile in Paris. Four times the size of Bryant Park in Manhattan, the area is surrounded on three sides by the low-rise, middle-class *polykatoikias* (apartment buildings, literally "multi-residences") typical of Athens. The last row of these residential buildings on the site's northeast side together with the high-speed roads at its southwest and southeast sides create well-defined borders for the project (fig. 1).

The nearby harbor of Faliro is believed to be the oldest port of Athens, dating to the era of Pericles. Shipping activity switched to Piraeus only when the populist Athenian politician and general Themistocles (c. 524–459 B.C.E.) ordered a new harbor as part of his plan to achieve naval dominance in the Mediterranean.

In the early part of the twentieth century, Faliro Beach was among the most beautiful in the Mediterranean, a cosmopolitan destination graced by a pair of luxury hotels, two piers running into the sea, and a summer theater (fig. 2). The activity generated by these lively seaside attractions was lost in the 1970s when Poseidonos Avenue was built, isolating the beach from the interior. The decline of the waterfront occurred more or less concurrently with that of the municipality's nearby racetrack. Inaugurated in 1925, the once-elegant racing facility was finally dismantled in 2003–2004. In 2006, when Piano first saw the area, it was an unsightly, neglected tract used for parking in daytime and car racing at night, frequented by drug dealers and other unsavory characters.

Over a period of almost two hundred years, the site of the cultural center and the city in which it is located have been subject to the kind of political and economic disruptions characteristic of the nation as a whole. The modern urban history of Athens is replete with confusion, controversy, and failed renewal plans. For starters, during the fourteen years after Greece was recognized as a

SNFCC, site plan, showing water theme and Athens street grid, sketch

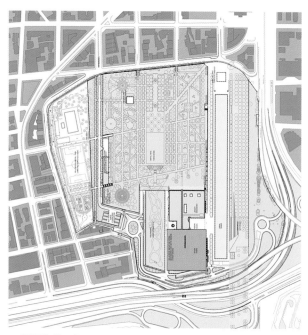

1 SNFCC, Site plan

2 Faliro Beach, Athens, early twentieth century, postcard

3 Carl Ferdinand von Kügelgen, *Athens and the Acropolis from the Northeast,* c. 1820, oil on canvas

fully independent state in 1832, eight consecutive uncoordinated urban plans, only snippets of which were implemented, vied with one another.[1]

These plans could be divided loosely between those that juxtaposed the new capital with its ancient remains and those that separated the two. The plans were introduced by two groups who had little affinity with the city's population: Bavarian and German architects and engineers, and powerful representatives of the educated Greek diaspora.[2]

The first effort at urban renewal came at a time of civil strife shortly after Greece had won its independence and Athens, at that time still just a village, was selected as its capital (fig. 3). Awaiting the arrival from Bavaria of young King Otto (1815–1867), a provisional Greek government established a scantily detailed program and commissioned a design from Stamatios Kleanthes (Greek) and Gustav Eduard Schaubert (Prussian), two young architects who had studied with Karl Friedrich Schinkel, the great German neoclassicist. The plan was revised in 1834, at the behest of King Otto, by Leo von Klenze, court architect to Otto's father, Bavarian King Ludwig I (fig. 4). The new city was to symbolize the nation's reconstruction and westernization.[3]

Athenians welcomed, theoretically, the idea of a rectangular city grid, considered more European than the city's old, narrow streets, which recalled the detested Turkish repression. But in practice, local residents opposed widening the streets because it entailed relinquishing property rights, for which there was often no compensation.

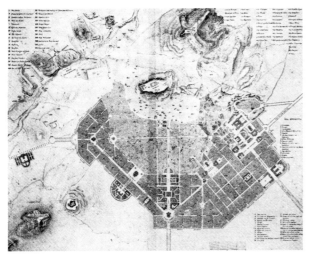

4   Leo von Klenze, Plan of Athens, 1834

5   Neoclassical Athens, 1915, postcard

Kleanthes and Schaubert proposed several monumental buildings for the new capital, which went unrealized for lack of funds. However, a royal palace for King Otto designed by Friedrich von Gärtner was completed in 1843 and became a forerunner of a reliance on prominent institutions as an organizing principle for the city—a trend that continued into the 1960s and is still occurring today, as with the SNFCC.[4]

By mid-nineteenth century, there were still parts of Athens that lacked a definitive plan; moreover, changes to the existing plans were made arbitrarily, and buildings were erected beyond the city limits with only piecemeal approvals.[5] Such problems persisted into the twentieth century, when in 1918, a Greek architect, Vassilios Tsagris, joked that the only way those city plans would ever be seen was if a new museum were built to exhibit them, since there was no hope of ever implementing them.[6]

The urban development of Athens differed from that of other European cities. Following independence, evidence of the thousand-plus years between antiquity and the modern city was wiped out. Ottoman buildings were destroyed because they represented Turkish control; less understandably, Byzantine and medieval monuments met the same fate. All were replaced by neoclassical architecture, perceived as a modern symbol of the country's prodigious ancient past (fig. 5). Additionally, for a large part of its long history, Athens has been relatively small: in 1800 it had a population of 4,000, compared to more than 500,000 in Paris, London, and Constantinople. The lack of centralized planning in Athens might be attributed to a discomfort with the idea of a large city, an idea that dates to antiquity.[7]

Another difference between Athens and other rapidly urbanizing cities in Europe and the Far East was the Greek capital's lack of a heavy-industry base; development in such fields was a low priority for both the private and public sectors because there was sufficient income from shipping, supplemented by remittances from Greeks abroad and United States aid. The lack may also be due to the Greek preference for small-scale, family-owned industrial enterprises.

One of Greece's several Nobel Prize–winning poets, George Seferis, captured the paradox of his country's rich legacy in his poem "Mythistorema":

Remember the baths where you were murdered
I woke with this marble head in my hands;
It exhausts my elbow and I don't know where to put it down.
It was falling into the dream as I was coming out of the dream
So our life became one and it will be very difficult for it to separate again.

I look at the eyes: neither open nor closed
I speak to the mouth which keeps trying to speak
I hold the cheeks which have broken through the skin.
That's all I'm able to do.

My hands disappear and come towards me
Mutilated.[8]

Two mass migrations to the capital in the twentieth century resulted in a populace that looks much as it does now. The first occurred after World War I and the Greco-Turkish War of 1919–1922; one especially notable event toward the end of the latter war was the great fire of Smyrna (September 13–22, 1922), after which as many as 400,000 Greeks and Armenians fled that city. Both of the wars produced a tremendous influx of ethnic Greeks previously living in the Ottoman Empire.[9] Refugees and civilian exchanges with Turkey nearly doubled the population of greater metropolitan Athens (from 435,000 to 802,000). The second mass migration, from 1950 to 1970, consisted of about 1.4 million people who moved from the provinces hoping to find work in Athens and contributed to the city's population exceeding 2,540,000 by 1971 (and 3,016,000 by 1981), more than double its population in 1940[10] (fig. 6). In 1970 roughly one in three Greeks lived in the greater Athens area. Small businessmen profited from the newcomers' housing needs, bypassing professional architects and flouting planning laws.

One historian described the capital's growth after 1922 as resulting in "such a terrible layout that it will probably never be possible for Athens to undertake enough infrastructural works to support all this expansion."[11] In 1933, the Congrès internationaux d'architecture moderne, led by Le Corbusier, held a

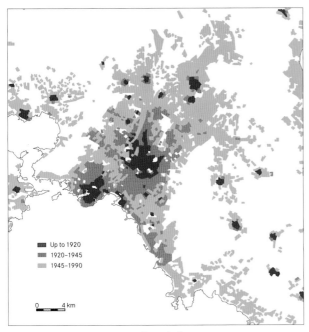

6 Growth of Athens 1920–1990, schematic diagram

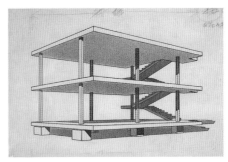

7 Le Corbusier, Maison Dom-ino

8 *Polykatoikias*, Kallithea

conference on a ship that sailed from Marseilles to Athens.[12] In their prepara-tions for the congress, the participants studied a number of cities, Athens among them. They, too, criticized the city's narrow streets, which provided inadequate circulation, and the lack of centralized administrative services and recreation areas. Ironically, the CIAM meeting's eventual statement, the Charter of Athens (1933), had absolutely no effect on the Greek capital; indeed, its advocacy of general fragmentation of cities into separate functional areas has been largely repudiated.[13]

The mid-twentieth century saw the neoclassical city replaced by the *polyka-toikias*—white, modernist, flat-roofed buildings usually no higher than six stories and constructed of concrete slabs and walls of brick, with structural sup-ports similar to Le Corbusier's Dom-ino slab-and-column frame system (1914–1915; fig. 7). Each apartment has a balcony, and there are plentiful retail and commercial activities at ground level (fig. 8). Built by contractors operating on a quid pro quo system of obtaining the right to build on a plot of land by compen-sating the owner with apartments in lieu of payment (known in Greece as the *antiparochi* system), the residences were eventually adapted for office and com-mercial use. Between 1950 and 1980, Athens's thousand multistory apartment buildings multiplied thirty-five times over.[14] The more or less uniform volumes of *polykatoikias* are now ubiquitous in cities throughout Greece.

The relatively low height of these units, which have been developed by mul-tiple small owners, discourages large developments and thus helps keep the scale of Greek cities moderate. Yannis Aesopos, principal of Aesopos Architec-ture and author of *The Contemporary Greek City*, considers the *polykatoikias* "the basis for a new vernacular architecture of modernity"; he is among several architects who are currently reinterpreting the model[15] (fig. 9).

Despite popular resistance to perpetuating the existing grid, a common street pattern that goes back at least to the fifth century B.C.E., *polykatoikias* were laid out in that configuration. However, unlike the planned cities of antiquity, modern Athens relates instead to the formless, smaller-size towns of the Byzantine era, which evolved over time without a master plan. The city's dense mass of white structures in fact recalls the architecture of typical island villages, which in small agglomerations are extremely picturesque. However, on a practical level, conflicting policies by planning agencies created during the years of intense growth are still in place today, leaving zoning regulations so arcane that RPBW architects often turned for guidance to comparable, up-to-date rules in other cities.

Athens and its adjacent coastal areas, now numbering more than 3 million inhabitants, continue to grow, with no real center, little public space, weak definition of plazas and street facades, inefficient zoning, and poor-quality urban infrastructure. Dust from Africa still blows a ghostly cover over the city every few years, but in general pollution has greatly improved since its all-time high in the late 1970s.[16] All of these problems notwithstanding, the charm of Athens's narrow thoroughfares lined with bitter orange, carob, plane, and Judas trees is irresistible. A multitude of shops and numerous inviting cafés whose generous outdoor seating is occupied the better part of the year contribute to the animated street life (figs. 10, 11), while the mountains that surround the city provide a breathtakingly beautiful setting for it.

With so much in the city's favor, it is unfortunate that a succession of governments has embraced short-term plans, based on their ability to achieve quick, politically useful results. Ineffective state agencies regularly waive building regulations in favor of real-estate speculation: 70 percent of the people own their own residences, and the political system is tied to real-estate investments. Thus, the ambitious Athens Regulatory Master Plan of 1985 and subsequent versions remain unrealized, and preparations for the 2004 Olympic Games were limited to sports and transportation initiatives instead of a larger strategic improvement of the city that could have had a lasting usefulness.[17]

Furthermore, there was the daunting precedent of Barcelona, which was transformed by the 1992 Olympics from an industrial backwater to a thriving metropolis, the fifth most popular tourist destination in Europe. But where the Catalan city spent $8 billion for lasting infrastructural improvements—a 15 percent increase in roads compared with 1986, 17 percent expansion of the sewage system, and 78 percent enlargement of new green areas and beaches—Greece spent nearly the same amount (more than $7 billion) with far less to show for it.[18] Additionally, efforts to improve Greece's standing were handicapped by the dearth of international businesses there and throughout the Balkans.

10 Typical street, Athens

9 Yannis Aesopos, office building, Athens

11 *Polykatoikias*, Athens

Granted, the 2004 Olympics—held between August 13 and 30 of that year—brought Athens its much needed and overdue first subway system, a new airport, a tram and light railway network, and the pedestrian esplanade stretching next to the SNFCC over the coastal highway to the bay, together with a bypass highway. But improving traffic flow away from the center encouraged the city's messy profusion in all directions and the flight of many of its more affluent residents to the city's periphery. The resulting vacuum in the city center was filled by thousands of undocumented immigrants from Asia and Africa, with no improvement of public space there. However, endless shopping malls (financed by irresponsible bank loans) were allowed to spring up along the highway and train axes.

Greece had hoped that the prestige of hosting the games would raise the country up from its second-rate status and boost its image internationally, branding it as both the heir to ancient triumphs and a modern, developed, European country.[19] It was, after all, where the games had originated—in 776 B.C.E.—and remained for nearly twelve hundred years. The international media called the Athens Olympics a great success in terms of hosting and organization; unfortunately, Greece was unable to capitalize on its achievement, because there had been no planning for the day after.

In large part responsible for the disappointing results was the government's usual inept commandeering of organizational responsibilities, especially those related to construction, compounded by the perennial game of musical chairs among top ministers. Shortly after the conclusion of the Olympics, most of the thirty-odd sites built or renovated for the games went unused, and some were demolished.[20] A rare exception is the Tae Kwon Do stadium (Sports Pavilion) just east of the cultural center, which occasionally hosts exhibitions and late in 2015 housed refugees from the Middle East (see p. 62, fig. 23).

The prospect of a spectacular new national library, opera house, and park designed by a world-renowned architect appeared to many like a phoenix rising from failed efforts to improve Athens's competitiveness. Not only is the tremendous financial commitment of the SNF a gesture of confidence, but distinguished modern architecture has been uncommon in Greece in recent years. For Athens, the dominance of the Parthenon may have discouraged modernism except for a short period in the 1960s. At that time, Greek architects Takis Zenetos and Nicos Valsamakis added some noteworthy architecture to that of Walter Gropius (United States Embassy, 1961) and Eero Saarinen (East Terminal building of the Hellinikon International Airport, 1969). In a city with few contemporary landmarks, the most significant public building since then is the new Acropolis Museum (2009) by Bernard Tschumi Architects.[21]

Piano, however, insists that the Parthenon inspired him to create a facility whose cultural impact will equal that of the Centre Pompidou. With his usual self-assurance, he talks of "Athens as the future center of the world."[22] Dracopoulos is equally optimistic: he sees the convergence of the government's decision to upgrade two national institutions on state-owned land with the foundation's decision to escalate its operations as a sign that "the stars were aligned for this to happen."[23]

Before any construction or even site preparation could begin, the site hosted a comprehensive archaeological exploration. Archaeological finds that complicate foundation preparation are an everyday occurrence in historically rich countries such as Greece and Italy. (This was recently the case for Tschumi's Acropolis Museum.) Greek laws controlling such finds date to 1834, shortly after the country became independent. Between 1911 and 1915, excavations in the northeast portion of the SNFCC site uncovered vases that are now in the British Museum. Because further discoveries were anticipated, a full year was added to the foundation's original estimated completion date for front-running archaeological excavations while bids for a contractor were in process, well before construction was scheduled to begin.

The archaeologists worked under the stringent guidance of Dr. Stella Chryssoulaki, director of the Department of Prehistoric and Classical Antiquities for Piraeus and the islands. Buried beneath the earlier find spots located in the northeast portion of the site were the remains of two cemeteries, one apparently dating to the seventh–sixth centuries B.C.E. (the Archaic period) and a smaller one to the fifth–early fourth centuries B.C.E. (the classical period). What makes these discoveries noteworthy is their remarkable variety: among the tombs, some appear to have been for the wealthy, yet seventeen of them seem to have contained indi-

12   Archaeological excavations on SNFCC site

viduals buried in prisoners' irons. The finds are hardly surprising in one of the oldest cities in the world, with a recorded history that dates back 3,400 years.

Most of the 1,500 recovered remains were interred in simple pit graves with a third (infants and children) in amphorae; five percent are cremations and a few stone-lined cist graves.[24] Because about a hundred shackled skeletons show evidence of a violent demise, possibly by a method resembling crucifixion, early conjecture identifies one cemetery as a burial ground for people who were punished, enslaved, or condemned to death.

Chryssoulaki claims that this was the most difficult dig of her thirty-five years as an archaeologist because so few people could work in the relatively small area for fear of stepping on, and damaging, bones and other artifacts (fig. 12). Nevertheless, participating at different times, seventy archaeologists, manual laborers, and architects from her department discovered more than a thousand items, some of which will be distributed to existing museums.[25]

In October 2013, I first visited the huge site with architect Theodore Maravelias (b. 1950), the SNF's chief technical officer. Like many professionals in Greece, where graduate education was until recently hard to come by, Maravelias studied outside the country, receiving his Ph.D. at Edinburgh University. By this time, the remains of the crumbling racetrack bleachers had been removed, and construction was in full swing. The Greek architect considers the SNFCC a paradigm of green development—as sustainable architecture and landscaping and as a green space—and notes that this quality helped overcome local resistance.

Maravelias and I began at the north and drove at a snail's pace up the nearly completed hill (see pp. 36–37). Walls of cast-in-situ concrete at the east and west—62.5 centimeters (24⅝ inches) thick—retain the mount's 884 tons of fill, which is laced with reinforced stabilization. Another wall, at the highest, southern end of the hill, is only 30 centimeters (11¹³⁄₁₆ inches) thick, because there the earthwork is held in place by a system that combines compaction with stabilization fabric.

The concrete part of the library's facade, which faces east, is part of the load-bearing structure, whereas the concrete of the opera house facade is detached and curves along the south side to the car park. Referred to as the "cliff," this seaward wall is intended to protect the center from the waterfront highway's roar of traffic.

On the balmy October day of my visit, eleven huge cranes punctuated a cloudless sky. They were coordinated electronically for uninterrupted simultaneous operation (a first in Greece). The installation of the permanent storm water and drainage system was in progress, with black plastic tubes leading to underground tanks to be used in case of extreme rainfall (not for irrigation). Standing at the summit of the mount and looking south, Maravelias and I saw the building's foundations progressing. The ground slabs were being poured at a level that would provide protection against future rises in sea level as well as against local flooding. The agora's vertical elements were also beginning to rise. Most easily identifiable was the deep excavation (113 by 95 feet) for the opera house's stage and orchestra pit, the heart of the building (see p. 35). The notion that control of the auditorium would eventually come from what was then a hole in the ground was a thought-provoking evocation of the future.

Maravelias proudly pointed out the temporary pedestrian bridge that the SNF had built from the esplanade and the temporary visitors center, both constructed to encourage viewing of the site (fig. 13). He was equally pleased with the project's "social and environmental responsibility during construction"; in fact, discussion of sustainability practices and resources occupied a good part of our conversation.[26] Because SNFCC construction management firm Faithful+Gould applied on behalf of the foundation for LEED Platinum certification —the highest rating possible in green design and construction standards (the

Some of the human remains unearthed in excavations at the SNFCC site bear evidence of apotympanismos, or criminal execution. The skeletons' broken bones correspond to descriptions of the practice by Aristophanes (in his play *Thesmophoriazusae*) and Plutarch (in his *Life of Pericles*). Also discovered were burial pots, some possibly for infants, that may be from as early as the eighth century B.C.E.; cooking pots and typically Athenian commercial amphorae that were exported throughout the Mediterranean; and a die made of an unidentified material with faience inlays for the numerical symbols, which might be from as early as the ninth century B.C.E.

13   Agis-Panagiotis Mourelatos and Spyridon Giotakis, temporary visitors center (now demolished)

prestigious status was awarded in November 2016)—exceptional care was taken with site management and construction activities.

Whereas several buildings in Athens had received LEED certification by 2016, the SNFCC is the first Platinum-level LEED public building complex in the whole of Greece and the first of its size and complexity in Europe. Registering for LEED certification comes with numerous strict requirements, among them keeping the site clean and filtering storm water that enters nearby public networks. These rules were meticulously adhered to: a local construction inspector, after examining the SNFCC site, remarked that, compared to sites elsewhere in the city, "it was like walking into another world."[27]

Measures that helped the complex reach Platinum status include more than 87,000 square feet of photovoltaics (expected to satisfy 15 percent of its electricity needs); partially submerging the architecture in the earth and using high-albedo materials for roof and hard-landscaping finishes, thereby significantly reducing cooling loads; and a water conservation strategy that avoids dependence on the city's scarce water supply[28] (see "Park" chapter).

In the same way that technologies are constantly changing, so too is the green-building standard. Just a month after my 2013 visit, it underwent its fourth major overhaul.[29] The SNFCC project, registered on October 9, 2008, is enrolled in LEED 2.2 (an older version of the standard). In March 2014, I asked Eirini Matsouki (b. 1976), the Greek-born sustainability advisor at Atkins in London, F+G's parent company, whether the enrollment would have to be upgraded. Matsouki explained that changes made to accommodate new, stricter requirements in the latest version of LEED could compromise other aspects of the project—such as the completion date and development costs—and that F+G had obtained permission to retain the original application (with an extension of the certification submission deadline from 2015 to 2016).[30] The architects were under constant pressure to stay abreast of advances in technology and related issues by updating components of the building. The canopy panels, for example, now offer 2.0 gigawatt hours in annual energy yield; earlier ones could generate a peak of only 1.85 gigawatt hours.

Instead of obtaining credit for rapidly renewable materials (such as natural rubber, cork, and bamboo), which were hard to find in Greece, RPBW focused on locally produced materials with high levels of recycled content to reduce the demands and impacts associated with virgin materials. Recognition of additional green-building practices, such as remediation of the neglected site, are also part of the sustainability program.

Another question we discussed at some length was how the public would reach the new venue, which isn't within walking distance of the city center. The nearest subway station is nearly two miles away, and a planned extension of the privately owned subway line had been jettisoned. Consequently, two bus lines and a tramline (two of which are slow and indirect) are the sole means of public transportation to the cultural center.

Direct vehicular access to the SNFCC—although dependence on automobiles is at odds with the cultural center's environmental safeguards—is via Andrea Syngrou Avenue. This boulevard, built by Greek banker and philanthropist Andreas Syggrou (1830–1899), is yet another example of public benevolence in Athens. The four-lane highway links the city center to Poseidonos Avenue along the waterfront, thus providing an easy route there from the new Acropolis

Capitalizing on Piano's involvement in the Kallithea district, in October 2010 the Ministries of Environment, Energy and Climate Change; Infrastructure, Transport and Networks; and Tourism asked RPBW to design a master plan for the beachfront. Efforts to improve the area had been attempted as far back as 1965 and continued up to the construction of a pedestrian esplanade that stretches from the mainland over the highway to the beach.

Underwritten by the SNF, the waterfront plan, by RPBW partner Susanna Scarabicchi (in collaboration with FALIRO 2014, a team of Greek architects and engineers, together with landscape designer Helli Pangalou), was completed in 2011 and almost immediately put on hold. In 2016, responsibility for the plan was transferred to the Attica Regional Authority, which, in December, awarded the first phase to Aktor, a contractor that reduced the €150 million ($167.1 million) estimate to €80.3 million ($89.5 million).

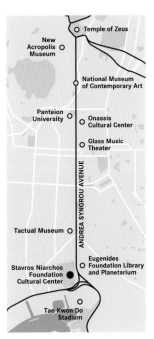

14 Cultural institutions along
Andrea Syngrou Avenue, Athens

Museum and the National Museum of Contemporary Art (in the space of the former FIX brewery, unoccupied for lack of funds). The presence along Andrea Syngrou Avenue of other educational institutions, including the Onassis Cultural Center, the Panteion University of Social and Political Sciences, and a state-of-the-art planetarium established by the Eugenides Foundation, has prompted plans to landscape this roadway so that it becomes less a commercial thoroughfare and more a cultural axis (fig. 14).

In 2013 the SNFCC was just about the only regenerative project for Athens that had not succumbed to Greece's beleaguered economic situation. But early in 2014, the Hellenic Republic Asset Development Fund accepted a bid by the Greek company Lamda (backed by Abu Dhabi and Chinese investors) to develop the abandoned Hellinikon International Airport. The $7 billion, 500-acre luxury housing project, with a master plan designed by Foster + Partners, includes a park, athletic fields, an upgraded public coastal front, and massive tourist infrastructure. It should generate seventy thousand jobs and substantial returns for the government.[31] The boosting of real-estate values in the neighborhood surrounding the SNFCC may well have been an inducement for the huge Hellinikon investment.

However, with the election early in 2015 of the Syriza-ANEL coalition government, headed by Alexis Tsipras, the project was frozen by a hold placed on all private initiatives for publicly owned property in Athens.[32] In 2016, Tsipras's lifting of this intervention showed a less confrontational attitude toward the private sector, which would include funding for the SNFCC.[33]

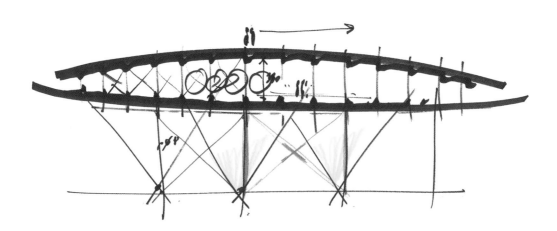

Structure

A recalcitrant government and a challenging design were not the only tests faced in the creation of the SNFCC. Renzo Piano's ability "to make buildable what at first appears impossible to build"[1] depends on the ingenuity of his engineers, just as engineering inventions depend on the vision of an architect. Both combine artistry and science, developing what are often wildly experimental asymmetrical and non-linear forms that must be made sturdy and safe. The engineers, like the other specialists who participated in this project, played a vital part in the design.

At the beginning of the twentieth century, engineers' design abilities became evident in glass-and-steel structures that introduced column-free, air- and light-filled factories to the new industrial culture. A succession of novel construction techniques ensued, including tensile and inflatable structures and different types of concrete, which encouraged a succession of engineering innovations.[2] In the present-day electronic world, engineers have upped the ante: besides advances in making new kinds of spaces and providing natural air and light, they delve into cultural, social, political, and environmental considerations, and their masterful designs are acknowledged more prominently than ever before.

Bruce Martin (b. 1971) is one of the new generation of highly innovative design engineers who share credit and responsibility with the architects and artists they advise. An associate director of the London firm Expedition Engineering, with specialists in civil, structural, environmental, and infrastructure design, he led a team of the firm's structural designers on the SNFCC project in collaboration with the Greek design and supervision group OMETE as consulting engineers.

Giorgio Bianchi calls Martin "the guy."[3] Martin and Chris Wise (b. 1956)—who founded Expedition with Sean Walsh in 1999—are among the most inventive members of the profession. "Chris is the 'big boss,'" says Bianchi. "He was

SNFCC, canopy, conceptual development diagram, sections

87

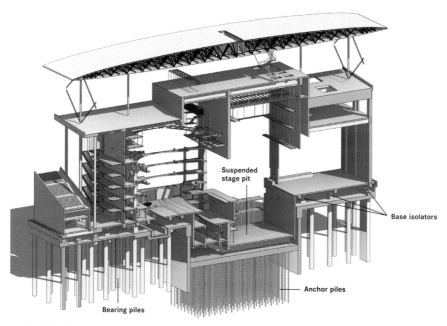

Suspended
stage pit

Base isolators

Anchor piles

Bearing piles

ɪ Expedition Engineering, SNFCC, working drawing, cutaway section

very present at the beginning." But the firm worked more with the low-key Bruce, who is "our kind of person."[4] Martin clearly relishes describing the terrain: underneath man-made deposits are more than four feet of coastal clay; a layer of silty sand sometimes as deep as twenty-nine feet; and alipedon, a sandy, silty clay extending as much as forty feet deep, supported by marl (a loose sedimentary deposit of lime-rich rocks and clay). Because Greece is the most earthquake-prone country in Europe, with tremors often measuring more than 6 on the Richter scale, the site required elaborate preparation before construction could start.[5] "Earthquakes do not kill people, buildings do," say the seismic experts,[6] and anything built in Athens needs to be protected should a quake cause the stratified earth to liquefy—in which case the building would collapse.

For the Piano-designed hill, the construction team excavated and retained for reuse 654,000 cubic feet of earth, together with salvaged demolition materials. To stabilize the huge earthwork and to facilitate drainage, Martin had 3,500 gravel piles—steel tubes filled with stones—driven into the sand every 10 feet. Once the tubes were removed, the stones remained to secure the terrain. Beneath the building, reinforced concrete piles were used to transfer the loads to the rock layer deep below the site (fig. 1).

Like others at Expedition, Martin is passionately committed to pioneering work. Born in Malawi, where his parents have lived since 1966, he is known to be a devotee of exotic travel. In 2013, due in part to the recession, he disappeared on an eight-month leave of absence, some of which were spent kite surfing in Greenland and inventing a new kind of capsize-resistant kite boat.

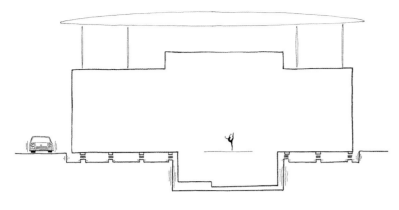

2 Expedition Engineering, base-isolation system, diagram

3 Columns in base-isolation system

"The building in Athens," he says, is "mostly standard construction, with areas of special architectural interest, such as the canopy, the auditorium, the atrium, and the conference room [lighthouse] on top of the opera house."[7]

Piano had met Wise while the latter was a director at Arup, one of the world's foremost engineering companies, but only began to work with him and the other Expedition engineers on a bank headquarters tower in Turin from 2006 to 2013 and the Athens project starting in 2009. The firm, though relatively small (employing 60 people in 2016), has numerous specialists within its own discipline. I would eventually talk with five of them, including Wise.

Jared Keen (b. 1979), an associate director at Expedition and project engineer for the opera house, was assigned the job of making the structure earthquake-resistant. Keen asserts, "Earthquakes are in my blood."[8] Indeed, his hometown, Christchurch, New Zealand, is located in an active seismic region, and it is not surprising that the University of Canterbury, also in Christchurch, where he trained, is known for its Earthquake Engineering research program. He moved to London to join Expedition in 2006.

Traditionally, seismic design focused on making buildings stiffer, which often produced chunky structures and led to higher construction costs. A more advanced approach favored flexibility over stiffness, but it could leave buildings damaged after a quake. The latter method was ruled out in Athens in order to ensure the longevity of the building and the safety of any precious objects on display in the library. The Expedition team, with Piano participating in the most critical decisions, chose to stabilize the hill and the building within it.

Keen demonstrated for me how the building is made resistant to the damage caused by seismic activity using a rectangular Plexiglas box about two feet long and one foot wide that contains two small massing models. When he shook the box, one of the two models immediately fell over, while the other, which he described as being "on roller skates" as part of a seismic protection system called base isolation, swayed with the box's movement (figs. 2, 3). Keen explained that when an earthquake shakes the ground, the building tends to shake at the same speed, often more than doubling the earthquake's force.

The phenomenon, known as resonance, is similar to pushing a child on a swing at the peak of the backswing, causing the swing to go higher and higher—that is, adding energy where the potential energy is already at its highest level. It's the same effect seen when a soprano sings a very high note and shatters a wine glass. Base isolation, the standard procedure to counter the effects of resonance, places a building's supporting columns on sliding bearings similar to those used to support bridges—three pieces of steel, two of which slide past each other on a Teflon-like surface. The bearings slow the building's movement (at the SNFCC, to about one-tenth of the seismic ground movements) so that it remains mostly stationary while the ground whizzes away underneath.

Those who worked with Piano in Athens say he is a tireless problem-solver who walks the building site for hours, eager to see everything and cognizant of the smallest detail.[9] One of the issues that consumed some of this time was how to give the SNFCC "visibility and a symbolic presence." The architect first thought that a mist or cloud above the building could collect energy from natural resources, like the sun and wind; he soon rejected this concept as not visually noticeable enough.

The next idea was to develop a lightweight, three-dimensional steel tensegrity roof (a structure based on a few simple design patterns described by Buckminster Fuller as "islands of compression in a sea of tension")[10] that would hover over both the opera house and the library. With a design in mind, the question arose as to its material.

It would have been difficult to protect metal from environmental problems associated with the seaside, such as rust and birds; and on a metal surface, the photovoltaic cells that were required to reduce the building's energy usage would make the whole appear massive, dark, and too umbrella-like. The design team then considered a ceramic-covered canopy, but this kind of cladding is heavy and doesn't always age well. Further complicating the issue was Piano's insistence that the bottom surface have no visible joints. He wanted the underside of the canopy—the side seen by the public—to appear glossy and perfectly smooth. (Hiding joints became a leitmotif of the project.)

Finally, after more than two years of frustrating deliberation, a solution emerged on October 21, 2010, at what proved to be a crucial meeting of the architects, engineers, SNF directors, and members of the Niarchos family. Wise recalled,

> *We were sitting in the garden of Renzo's beautiful Punta Nave studio (outside Genoa) overlooking the Mediterranean, where models and building parts are scattered like sculpture indoors and out, when we suddenly focused*

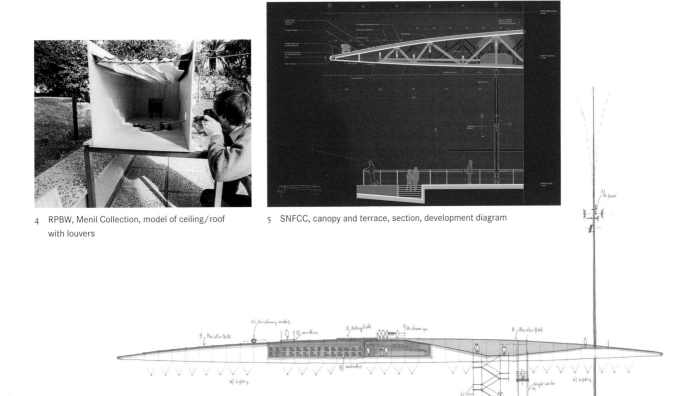

4   RPBW, Menil Collection, model of ceiling/roof
    with louvers

5   SNFCC, canopy and terrace, section, development diagram

6   Canopy, section, diagram

*on part of a louver from the roof of the Menil Collection in Houston. The
ferro-cement [a type of thin-shell reinforced mortar] louver had been outside since the museum's completion in 1987, yet it was still in perfect condition. The material is clean, it can be sculpted, it is light and energy efficient.
Because ferro-cement is insensitive to thermal expansion, even though built
without joints, it lasts a very long time, like masonry.*[11]

The ferro-cement that was used to make the louver was exactly what Piano had
in mind: "an artificial stone, something highly dignified and generous, that is
forever"[12] (fig. 4; see p. 128, fig. 19). Once ferro-cement was designated for the
canopy, Piano and his team monitored construction of the skin's surface with all
the intensity that might be accorded the care of a newborn child.

Wise says the canopy was seminal to the undertaking: "The whole project
came from it; it is the counterpart to the Parthenon" (figs. 5, 6). There is in fact
a parallel between the canopy floating above the artificial hill, with its flexible,
130-foot-high mast gesturing to the heavens, and the Parthenon crowning the
Acropolis, appearing to reach out to infinity.[13] The idea that the canopy might

cover both the opera house and the library was considered early on, but it was ruled out once it became clear that seismic engineering required the two parts of the building to move separately. Piano envisioned a canopy supported by a single column, or at most four, but the final design ended up with thirty slender supports.

The canopy is a daring twenty-first-century version of the heavy, curved parasols designed by Le Corbusier for parts of two buildings at Chandigarh in northern India: the roof of the Governor's Palace (unbuilt, 1951–1955) and the entryway to the Palace of the Assembly (1962; fig. 7). In Chandigarh and in Athens, these protective devices address the problems of extreme sun and rain. The canopy provides shade, harnesses solar power by means of photovoltaic cells, and collects rainwater (the supports are hollow-section steel tubes that contain the drain pipes). Its 107,600-square-foot expanse consists of 717 1½-inch-thick ferro-cement panels, each approximately 23 by 10 feet (with an almost 2-inch splice zone between them); it is less than 1 foot thick at the outer edges but swells to almost 13 feet deep (the height of a single story in a typical high-rise) at the center. The canopy floats 40 feet above the top of the lighthouse; its upper surface is 142 feet from grade. The solar panels are capable of generating—in theory—enough electric energy to light the entire complex, with the exception of theatrical lighting for performances. What is remarkable about this huge, hollow mass weighing 4,700 tons is that it appears paper-thin.

Piano has built forms similar to the Athens canopy—what he calls "flying carpets"—for various other cultural institutions, notably the Giovanni and Marella Agnelli Art Gallery in Turin (2003), part of the former Lingotto Fiat Factory that he transformed into a multipurpose conference center (see p. 66, fig. 34), and his addition to the Art Institute of Chicago (2009; fig. 8). At both the Turin and Chicago buildings, the extended roof structure consists simply of steel-and-glass louvers that control the amount of daylight in the galleries below. The SNFCC canopy is more innovative and far more complex, bringing together for the first time in the RPBW oeuvre a canopy and ferro-cement.

This material is different from reinforced concrete, which is concrete reinforced with steel rods to resist tensile stresses. Although ferro-cement is, in fact, reinforced with steel, the difference is that ferro-cement has a much larger surface of reinforcement due to its thin section and the fineness of its raw materials (sand/cement mortar instead of concrete, small-pattern wire mesh instead of rebar).[14] Indeed, it is different from most other construction materials in that its unique properties require highly sophisticated analysis within a millimeter of tolerance. Patrick Jennings, a British civil and structural engineering consultant who, alone of those working on the project, had used the material successfully for several large projects in the Middle East, advised on the material's fabrication:

8   RPBW, addition to Art Institute of Chicago

7   Le Corbusier, Palace of the Assembly, Chandigarh

9   Pier Luigi Nervi, Palazzetto dello Sport, Rome

The reinforcement usually consists of several closely spaced layers of continuous and relatively small-diameter wire mesh, placed within the sand/cement mortar mix throughout each thin section, relatively close to the surface. Only every four panels of the canopy's upper and lower skin have the same shape; otherwise, each panel has a unique geometry, although each panel has an individual thickness profile. The panels are cast on an adjustable steel form by pumping a high flow sand/cement mortar into the mesh and then compacting it by vibration to produce a dense, smooth surface. Thousands of mesh links protrude from the edges of each panel and must be woven together with the links in adjacent panels; the assembly resembles the mail shirt in a medieval suit of armor. The unmortared splice zones where the projecting mesh wires overlap between the panels were filled by hand casting the mortar.[15]

Ferro-cement is strong and durable, but since the 1950s its dependence on intensive construction labor has largely limited its use to developing countries. Among the paradoxes of the SNFCC, one of the most surprising is the old-fashioned, handmade methods used to fabricate the canopy, which in turn supports the technologically advanced solar panels. Although Piano dismisses the suggestion that considerations of cost influenced his choice of ferro-cement, it is hard to imagine that the cheaper labor in Greece didn't affect the decision.

Ferro-cement has an interesting history. The material was first used for building two rowboats in 1848 and 1849 by a Frenchman, Joseph-Louis Lambot.[16] Italian architect Pier Luigi Nervi's masterpiece, the Palazzetto dello Sport (with Annibale Vitellozzi, 1956–1957; fig. 9), one of three stadiums he designed for the 1960 Olympics in Rome, uses for its dome, 60 meters (197 feet) in diameter, a new kind of prefabricated thin-shell ferro-cement that has a smooth exterior and a ribbed interior side.[17] Almost simultaneously, the Spanish-born architect Félix Candela, working in Mexico, demonstrated that very thin concrete shells, though expensive to build, were endowed with the ability to withstand seismic activity.[18] Because the earthquake force on a structure is proportional to building weight times ground acceleration, the extreme thinness ($\frac{5}{8}$ of an inch to $1\frac{1}{2}$ inches) and concomitant lightness of these forms protects them. The double curvature of the Cosmic Ray Laboratory on the campus of the National Autonomous University of Mexico (1951), which Candela designed in collaboration with Jorge González Reyna, initiated his experiments with undulating forms. These culminated in dramatic hyperbolic paraboloid structures, including Los Manantiales Restaurant (1958; fig. 10), in Mexico City.

Wise attended lectures by Candela at the Royal Institute of British Architects in the late 1980s; profoundly impressed by the Spaniard's explanation of how he used simple techniques and relatively simple mathematics to produce beautiful forms, Wise attributes to these ideas an influence in shaping his philosophy of design. As for Piano, he first deployed ferro-cement in architecture at the Menil Collection, which he designed with Peter Rice and Tom Barker, both of Arup; the louver model in Piano's garden was one of the leaf-shaped light diffusers installed in the ceiling of the museum. It is also worth noting that his yacht was constructed of this material, possibly in a gesture to its previous use in boats and by Nervi in the twentieth century (fig. 11).

One of the Expedition engineers described the directors of the SNF as having been "terrified" at the unusual material's choice at the time, because ferro-cement had rarely been used in Europe and indeed was untried anywhere on such a large scale.[19] Development of a concept and software calculations—required to gain the necessary approvals from the Greek authorities—

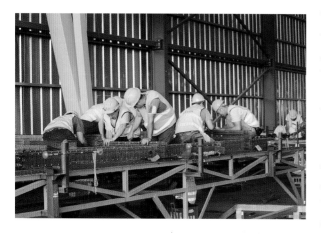

The ferro-cement panels for the SNFCC canopy were fabricated entirely on-site under the supervision of Patrick Jennings, a civil and structural engineer who was hired to advise on their fabrication. The 717 panels were cast in reusable molds—an efficient construction method given the complex forms—and joined by hand. As many as three hundred fabricators, working in a 350-by-130-foot cathedral-like temporary shed, wove the edges together using links of the canopy's metal mesh. Christos Athanassopoulos, an architect and project manager who was in charge of this process, expressed the general feeling on site: "It's a first, a once-in-a-lifetime experience."

10   Félix Candela, Los Manantiales Restaurant,
     Mexico City

11   *Kirribilli II*

involved at least one hundred people, including outside consultants as well as the Expedition team.

Despite the precedents of Piano and others,[20] no design codes existed for the use of ferro-cement, although the American Concrete Institute has published guidelines and studies since 1979. To determine how to proceed and how to choose the optimal method of fabrication for the material, as well as to garner arguments promoting its use, the team visited Paul Nedwell, the teaching and research support manager in the School of Mechanical, Aerospace and Civil Engineering at the University of Manchester. At a series of workshops run by Nedwell, the architects, engineers, and joint-venture contractors all dirtied their hands making ferro-cement.[21]

From Manchester, the engineers traveled to Nantes in western France to test their ferro-cement model in a wind tunnel at the Scientific and Technical Center for Building, a research, testing, certification, and training center that deals primarily with the built environment and construction. Trials on a small-scale model of the canopy (about 1½ square feet) of 70 pounds/square foot in winds up to almost 100 feet per second demonstrated the need for steel bracing ribs to stiffen the structure and prevent it from buckling.

While still working on the experimental stage of the canopy, the engineers were plagued by anomalies between the various software packages that are combined to predict the performance of particularly complex structures. It took them two full months to figure out that their structural model for the canopy was incorrect. The date of this frustrating problem's solution—Good Friday, April 6, 2012—is fixed in the mind of Neil Clemson, project manager and commercial director at Faithful+Gould. Load tests, which used an 18-foot-6-inch by 50-foot-3-inch mock-up piled with bags of gravel and a specially built rig that underwent stress/deflection measurements, finally revealed, as he points out, that "what can be built in a workshop is different from what it is possible to achieve ten stories in the air on a wet and windy day on site"[22] (fig. 12).

The Expedition professionals also looked into environmental conditions at the site. Despite ferro-cement's relative lack of response to temperature-related expansion and contraction, the engineers realized that a problem could arise on a torrid day, when the top of the canopy would be far hotter than the bottom: the top would expand more, making it larger than the bottom, arching it skyward, possibly separating it from the opera house roof and causing it to crack. The contractor came up with a solution to the problem with the insertion of a spring on top of each of the supporting columns. These high-tech hydraulic springs (which also help the canopy withstand wind loads and seismic activity) were used for the first time to install a roof structure when they lifted the canopy into place from its temporary scaffolding (fig. 13).

Pete Winslow (b. 1994) is Expedition's expert in roof structures and unusual geometries. "He is so smart," says Wise, "that no one understands him." Even so, Winslow describes the canopy's fundamental integration of structure and skin in simple terms:

> For the solar canopy (and a number of other aspects of the project) the boundaries between engineering and architecture are increasingly blurred. I remember Renzo saying in one of our design team meetings: it is somewhere between a space ship, a boat hull, and a living-breathing field for generating solar energy. The canopy is unique in that it is not a skin with structure hidden beneath (i.e., it doesn't separate engineering and architectural systems). Instead the ferro-cement skin carries all the structural forces as well as providing the weatherproof barrier, creating the architectural form, and providing the final visual effect. Rather than separate studies by the different design team members, the design process has very much been an integrated exploration of material use and form.[23]

Interaction of this sort between architects and engineers was a lifelong concern of Ove N. Arup, later Sir Ove (1895–1988), the Danish philosopher turned engineer who in 1946 founded the company that still bears his name. Arup remembered that, at the outset of his career in the early 1920s, "As an engineer, I never met any architects"[24]—a situation that ran counter to his conviction that "the architect should be part engineer and the engineer should be part architect in order to achieve a fruitful collaboration."[25]

Peter Rice, who started working at Arup in 1956, shared Ove's attitude. An engineering great and a frequent collaborator of Piano and other internationally renowned architects until his untimely death in 1992, Rice deplored the common view of the engineer's role in modern design as that of a "Iago to the architect's Othello, always trying to undermine the role of the architect."[26]

An egregious example of what can happen in the absence of collaboration between the two disciplines is the Sydney Opera House. When Danish architect

12   SNFCC, canopy mock-up for load test

13   Canopy, hydraulic springs

Jørn Utzon resigned from the project in 1966, in the midst of its construction, the quality of the building's performance spaces was permanently compromised. The ability of the Arup office, with young Peter Rice in charge, to successfully complete this early example of destination architecture established the firm's reputation.

Arup alumni hold an outsize position in the engineering profession, with many of them, including Wise, having founded their own firms. The willingness of some design and structural engineers to take unusual risks is impressive, considering the profession's unforgiving pitfalls.[27] David Billington, an eminent engineer who has lectured at Princeton University since 1960, once made the amazing statement that no built form can be considered structurally sound until it is put to the test. The Citicorp Center in New York City (1978) is a good example of structural failure waiting to happen.[28]

The 59-story Citicorp tower (fig. 14), at the time among the tallest in the world, was designed by Hugh Stubbins Jr. in collaboration with William J. LeMessurier, an engineer expert in high-rise structures. The building's unusual geometry, with nine-story-high columns at the center of each side rather than at the corners, was designed to resist both diagonal and perpendicular winds. But after the building was completed, a student of Billington's pointed out to LeMessurier that diagonal winds would exert more pressure on the bracing system than he had originally calculated and that the bolted joints he had approved as a cost-saving measure would be more vulnerable than welded joints. LeMessurier corrected the problem by having 2-inch-thick steel plates welded over each of more than two hundred bolted joints.[29]

14   Hugh Stubbins Jr. and William J. LeMessurier, Citicorp Center, New York

15   Foster + Partners, Sir Anthony Caro, and Arup, Millennium Bridge, London

Rice himself encountered a setback when the first *gerberette* at the Centre Georges Pompidou—the short cast-steel cantilevers that, among other functions, connect the primary truss system to vertical supports—failed its proving test because of a mistake in translating the German installation instructions into French.[30] Even Wise experienced a problem with unpredictability in one of his last projects at Arup. Right after opening in 2000, London's Millennium Bridge, designed by Norman Foster with the sculptor Sir Anthony Caro, was dubbed the "Wobbly Bridge"[31] (fig. 15). In its first weekend, two hundred thousand visitors (five times the number expected) crossed the bridge, which connected St. Paul's Cathedral with Tate Modern across the Thames. The design had major flaws, including the fact that the syncopated footsteps of a critical mass of pedestrians matched the bridge's horizontal frequencies and created a self-generating swaying motion. Once the Millennium Bridge was closed for repairs, the engineers discovered that several recent pedestrian bridges—in Japan, Canada, and France among others—had experienced the same phenomenon. Of the discovery and resolution of the circumstances, Wise said, "We found ourselves outside normal experience, which was a good thing. It proved that the bridge was a piece of engineering."

On a crisp spring morning in May 2013, I met with Keen, Wise, and George Oates (an associate director at Expedition and the project engineer for the library) in Expedition's London office. All three were casually dressed, relaxed, and seated in comfortable lounge chairs. Wise, who is also a professor of design at University College London, immediately launched into a mini-lecture on a favorite topic, that of waste: "We are mindlessly chucking materials into the built environment," he said. It is an issue that he keeps in mind on every project.

In Athens, one example of the engineers' efforts to avoid wastefulness is the library roof. The meeting between the concrete supporting columns and the roof slab is indicated with a nicely detailed reveal, or shadow gap. Because the slab supports heavy landscaping, a certain minimum thickness, in addition to the

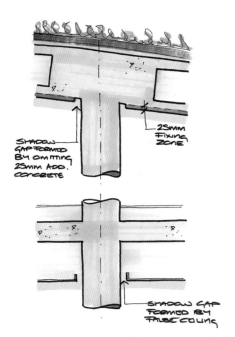

17   Library, intersection between column and roof slab

16   Expedition Engineering, SNFCC, library, intersection between column and roof slab, diagram

depth of the reveal, was needed over the columns. What initially appeared to be a wasteful increase in the roof's volume of concrete was rectified as the design developed by means of an efficient cutaway in the roof slab, which retained the reveal but reduced the amount of concrete used (figs. 16, 17). Wise also finds fault with a more systematic way in which waste is produced: the fees that are considered "normal" for engineering are based on a percentage of construction costs and thereby in their very nature encourage the use of excess material.[32]

Wise's engaging smile makes his arguments all the more persuasive. He idolizes the genius of the Renaissance architect Filippo Brunelleschi as well as the brilliance of the nineteenth-century English engineer Isambard Brunel, known for his ingenious designs and his acceptance of non-standard ideas. By the 1920s, says Wise, the burden of proof shifted engineering to an emphasis on mathematics that stifled its practitioners' creativity. Now, in the early twenty-first century, however, he believes that the computer and its ability to perform straightforward tasks will enable engineers to become more creative once again.

Of the SNFCC, Wise says, "We embraced the Athens project as an opportunity to make something with a life of one thousand years—forever. We figured that everything in the city would change, but this would stay the same." Wise's prediction for the city seems to have been prophetic. Whether his claims for the building are equally prescient remains to be seen.

SNFCC, Renzo Piano inspecting glass facade mock-up

Agora before installation of glass facades

Overleaf: Opera house and canopy under construction, "cliff" at south of opera house (left)

Opera house auditorium

Alternative Stage theater

Opera house lobby balconies

Overleaf: NLG, installation of book shelves

Canopy, internal steel construction

Solar panels on top of canopy

Stavros Niarchos Park, planting

"Cups" sheathing joints between columns and canopy for a seamless surface

Installation of mast

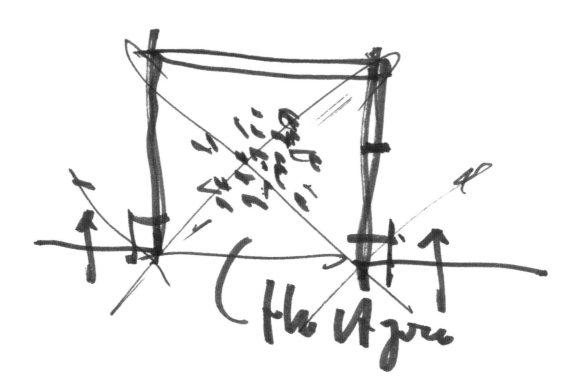

Agora

"Everything starts at the agora," says Piano of the critical ground-level area on the east side of the SNFCC between the library and the opera house (fig. 1). "It is the focus of the cultural center, the place where fear disappears and people can share. It unifies everything."[1] Even before construction was completed, the synergy among the complex's different components was palpable in the agora. Visitors can walk easily from the park, the esplanade, and the canal to this outdoor space, from which the library, the opera house, and their various attractions are accessible. The steps of the grand stairway beside the opera house provide an ideal viewing spot for the day and night events planned for the agora.

In a nod to the illustrious history of Athens, the architect looked to what was the nexus of the city in classical Greece for a term to designate what he usually calls a piazza—an open-air gathering place. The most familiar of Piano's piazzas is the popular square in front of the Centre Pompidou in Paris. Piano hopes that the one in Athens will have the same success, fostering calmer gatherings than the violent clashes between police and the public that have frequently taken place in centrally located Syntagma (Constitution) Square (fig. 2).

The rash of news articles on the Arab Spring and the Occupy movements, both of which sprang up in 2011, often referred to Greece's agora as the first public place used for democratic practices (from about 600 to 350 B.C.E.).[2] Among the present-day spaces that continue to be appropriated by the public for civic action are Syntagma Square, Tahrir Square in Cairo, Puerta del Sol in Madrid, and the National Mall in Washington, D.C. It is possible that the SNFCC agora could become a site like Zucotti Park, the privately owned vest-pocket park in Lower Manhattan that was successfully occupied by protesters in fall 2011.[3]

Most visitors to the SNFCC arrive by car and enter at the back of the building (its west side), traversing the so-called small agora (fig. 3). They then pass through an indoor area that can be used for temporary exhibitions, which features the specially designed permanent display of the Spyros Louis Cup by Michael Breal created for the inaugural modern Olympic Games in Athens in

2 Demonstration in Syntagma Square, July 3, 2015

1 SNFCC, view of agora across canal, scenic elevators at southwest and northwest corners

1896. It also contains a café, bookshop, and information desk; offices occupy the floors above the ground level. Corridors lead indoors from this introductory area into the opera house and the library and also venture outside, into the main agora, in which there are exterior entrances to the two venues (the library at the northeast and the opera house at the southeast). Piano placed these main entrances at the buildings' corners to provide vantage points with comprehensive views of each lobby. Even though the agora (17,220 square feet, accommodating between eight hundred and a thousand visitors) is considerably larger than either of the two lobbies (the opera house's is more than 9,600 square feet; the library's, more than 7,000), it preserves a sense of intimacy. Both the small and large agoras are paved in marble from the nearby Dionysos quarry (two miles northeast of Athens's city center, fig. 4), as are the lobby floors of the opera house and the library and the floors of the public restrooms. The faint yellow tint of the Pentelikon white marble takes on a golden hue in the sunlight.

For those arriving at the cultural center on foot—whether from the park, from the adjacent esplanade, or from public transportation on Andrea Syngrou Avenue—the agora offers a welcoming open expanse between the imposing

118

4   Dionysos quarry

3   Small agora

external concrete stairway that rises along the east facade of the opera house and a narrower one along the east facade of the library. The opaque stone wall behind part of each stairway, punctuated by a few small, vertical windows, contrasts with the transparent glazing of the two volumes.

In ancient Greece, the agora was enclosed by public buildings and some covered areas; at the SNFCC, this gathering place is defined at the north and south sides by the glass facades of the opera house (nearly 80 feet high) and the library (60 feet high). With the canopy, the north and south facades are the most technically innovative part of the complex. "They are unprecedented," says Marc Simmons (b. 1970), a professor at the Georgia Institute of Technology and the founder in 2002 of Front, the facade engineering firm that collaborated on the design. The crystal-clear glass walls provide views into the interior of both institutions, showing elements of the design that immediately identify each building: to the south, the balconies that overhang the soaring opera house lobby; to the north, the multiple levels of book stacks. One of the many challenges faced by the Arup lighting specialists was how to admit daylight but inhibit solar gain.[4] A lower glass facade delimits the west side of the agora; one of Front's own struggles with glare prompted the firm's protection of all three facades with long, off-white automated blinds on the exteriors, similar to those on the south facade of Piano's Morgan Library and Museum expansion in New York (2006).[5]

In addition to the Morgan Library, RPBW and Simmons had worked together on facades for a residence in Colorado for Margot and Thomas Pritzker (son and daughter-in-law of Jay and Cindy Pritzker, founders of the famous

5 Giant radar antenna (early inspiration for glass facade)

architectural prize, 2010) and the Isabella Stewart Gardner Museum addition in Boston (2012). When the RPBW architects first approached Simmons for the Athens project, they had in mind a bubblelike facade with multiple cable nets—perhaps something like a giant radar antenna (fig. 5).

But Piano notes that the idea never even got to the drawing board: "A bubble would be insane because every piece of glass is different." The comment reveals the architect's adherence to orthodox modernism in dealing with the problems he undertakes or rejects for the SNFCC. He and Bianchi eventually switched to what they called "an ephemeral, Cartesian solution—quieter, without the in-your-face technology of cross-bracing." (The entire orthogonal design is in fact based on a repetitive symmetrical grid.) Piano refers to one of his favorite leisure pastimes—sailing—to explain the structural facades. "A sail," he points out, "when hit by a 45-knot [about 52 m.p.h.] wind simply inflates; but a glass wall needs mullions so that it can remain upright, withstanding the pressure or suction that could occur."

In the course of a series of discussions, RPBW and the Front team developed the idea of wide glass fins instead of mullions (fig. 6). The use of such fins as part of a glass facade proliferated after they appeared in the Maison de la Radio by Henri Bernard (Paris, 1963; fig. 7) and the Willis Faber & Dumas Headquarters by Foster Associates (Ipswich, 1975; fig. 8). But the fins in Athens are far taller than those at either of these early, innovative examples, which, because of their relatively low height, do not carry much load.

The Front system relies on the structural interplay between steel mullions running along the edges of the fins and the load-bearing capacity of the glass itself. Placed approximately every 4 feet along the facade and hung from the roof slab, the fins, which extend on both sides of the facade, work like cross-braces to help support the tempered glass curtain wall. It is a completely orthogonal solution," says Simmons, "abstract, elegant, and restrained." Hanging the glass facade from the roof, rather than supporting it at the base, avoids buckling.

6 SNFCC, NLG facade, glass fins

7 Henri Bernard, Maison de la Radio, Paris

8 Foster Associates, Willis Faber
& Dumas Headquarters, Ipswich,
United Kingdom

Neil Clemson of Faithful+Gould recalls what was, for him, a freak incident involving construction of the facade. Construction supervisors were aware of an almost imperceptible misalignment of the opera house. When they came to inspect the building a day after a mild earthquake, they found, to their astonishment, that the tremor had nudged the wall into place.[6]

Once the RPBW architects and the facade engineering firm had agreed on a form, the search began for a subcontractor capable of building it. Three German fabricators were asked to submit bid proposals. The first challenge faced by the one that was selected was to fill the gap between the glass fins and their steel casings in a way that would allow the assemblage to work as a single structural unit. Front had high hopes for a special high-strength epoxy adhesive called Hilti HIT. Though well-known in the industry, here the product would be used in a new and untested way.

The facade consultants envisioned that the structural action of each fin would simulate that of a truss. A small bead of adhesive placed every couple of feet between the glass and the steel frame would transfer the load diagonally across the fin to the steel on the other side. This system moved the load over the entire fin, stressing both glass and mullions in a measurable and seismically resistant manner.

However, concerned that the adhesive might not withstand changes in temperature, the fabricators proposed an alternative solution: inserting a tensioned rod inside the U-shaped mullion. This novel solution would undoubtedly have resulted in a strong facade, but it presented potentially dangerous conditions in case of breakage, and it called for making the middle layer of the fins' three layers of laminated glass a bit thicker (.98 of an inch instead of .75 of an inch) and therefore more expensive. The unacceptably high cost killed the deal.[7]

At this point, Salini Impregilo, the Italian firm collaborating with Terna in the contractor joint venture, recommended Tossoni, a facade manufacturer in Verona, who proposed yet another alternative: securing the fins by means of a complex system of butterfly clips and diagonal screws. However, F+G preferred to continue investigating Front's proposed Hilti HIT system by testing it on a 1:1 scale panel. Spurred on by Tossoni's commercial director, Rinaldo Rinaldi—who was hell-bent on winning the commission—the fabricators agreed, and were persuaded that the adhesive binder worked as intended.

Subsequent tests included one to see how the facade would perform in wind-driven rain. When a mock-up was pummeled with water propelled by winds of 100 knots (115 m.p.h.), the assemblage proved not to be watertight.

In response to the SNF's request for nighttime visibility, Brian Stacy (Arup lighting specialist) and his team created what they call an "enhanced artistic exterior lighting experience." In Athens, generally a city of white light, brightly colored night lighting is mostly used for discothèques and outdoor recreation areas. In response, Stacy proposed, for grand openings, a "symphony": colored light on the buildings and white searchlights beaming into the sky.

After Piano deemed the searchlights "too 'film noir,'" the consultants came up with a scheme that wraps the buildings in the blues of the foundation and the Greek flag. An elaborate lighting system geared to the agora's round-the-clock programming is supplemented with infrastructure that can project work by local artists and texts by Greek poets (for the library). Similar projections of music-related images enhance the facades of Copenhagen's Dansk Radio Byen Concert Hall for the Danish Broadcasting Company by Ateliers Jean Nouvel.

9   Glass fin mock-up, Verona

Just one month later, a trial on the main mock-up, with adjustments in work-manship, saved the day, achieving a rating twice as high as the contractual target (fig. 9). The cost was approximately $500 per square foot, which falls within current industry norms.[8]

Piano says, "You need prototypes to avoid mistakes." Simmons reports that Piano and his partners' examination of mock-ups is more detailed than that of many architects: "They set the standard."

The facade components were manufactured in Verona by Tossoni, with the fins and the glass enclosing the building made in Italy by the French company Saint Gobain. The enclosing glass is double-laminated for structural support, security, and environmental control; low-e (low-emissivity) coating protects against ultraviolet light and excessive solar gain. The exterior portion of the fins is consistent across the facade, while the interior portion varies in relation to structural necessity—the higher the span, the wider the interior segment—making the facade appear even thinner from the inside.

Among Front's numerous tasks at the SNFCC were the concrete facades, of which Simmons says, "The thick concrete walls insulate the building like a ther-mos."[9] Early on, the architects had envisioned cladding the exterior and interior vertical surfaces in marble. The more they thought about marble for the walls, however, the more it brought to mind the image of the pompous monument to King Vittorio Emmanuele II in Rome (1935), widely ridiculed for its vulgarity.[10] RPBW eventually abandoned marble in favor of concrete first for the exterior walls and then for the interior walls, too.

The faultlessly executed concrete—whether in the dove-gray walls of the opera house lobby, hidden walls, or ground slabs—was poured using a routine but substantially refined process. Two different companies and three subcontractors supplied the center's more than 240,000 cubic yards of reinforced concrete (including foundations and external areas): one company was responsible for the fair-faced visible concrete for the opera house, library, and car park; the other for the visible concrete at the hill and "cliff," the south-facing wall at the car park. The ingredients of the concrete and the steel reinforcing vary depending on needs.

Along with two kinds of Portland cement (black-gray and white), the concrete mix included sand and gravel, which were carefully selected from a single lot in order to achieve a uniform color for the surface finish. The use of metal frames and smooth wood for the formwork ensured blemish-free surfaces and made it possible to achieve different effects. For example, wood-plank formwork produced a wood-grain finish on the exposed-concrete ceilings of the opera house and library lobbies.

Poured in layers to minimize porosity, the concrete was watered several times a day for a week after each pour to maximize the curing process and make it 50 percent stronger. Water-cured concrete retains moisture in the slab so that the concrete continues to gain strength; and it delays shrinkage during the drying until the concrete is strong enough to resist shrinkage cracking.[11] Although cement pouring is sensitive to heat, in Athens the workers were able to pour from 7 a.m. until midnight.

In addition to a refined aesthetic quality, the complicated construction procedure provides horizontal stability for the building while allowing an outside layer of concrete to move independently in case of an earthquake. Within each wall, two layers of insulation are separated by a ⅜-inch gap that serves for both water drainage and seismic isolation.

Within the library and the opera house, extremely slender steel-and-concrete columns stand along the glass facades at intervals of 25½ feet, contributing to the sparse, elegant look of the entryways. Surprisingly thin columns—in the architect's words, "fingers holding up the roof"—appear at street level in other large RPBW buildings, such as the addition to the Chicago Art Institute and the new Whitney Museum of American Art, in Manhattan (fig. 10; see also p. 93, fig. 8).

When I expressed curiosity about how such delicate elements could support huge loads, Piano described something he saw in India as a young architect. Women walked through the towns and markets carrying enormous loads on their heads. They were able to do this, he discovered, by avoiding horizontal forces. As long as the women remained strictly upright, centering the weight on their spine, they could transport loads that were sometimes heavier than their own bodies. Piano's subsequent adaptation of the principle in Athens evokes

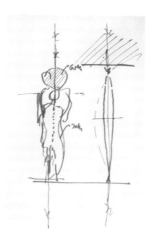

II   Standing woman and steel-and-
     concrete column, sketch

10   RPBW, Whitney Museum of American Art, New York

12   Erechtheion, Acropolis, Athens

the six draped caryatids that serve as supporting columns in the south porch of the Erechtheion on the Acropolis (5th c. B.C.E.; figs. 11, 12). (In fact, the SNFCC building will be subject to lateral loads caused by wind and seismic forces.)

The transparent layers of lobby space, columns, and facade are typical of RPBW projects. In Bianchi's words, "It is part of the firm's DNA that achieved an apotheosis at the Menil Collection, with its connection of rooms, glass, courtyards, and the exterior. At the SNFCC, you see past the columns and facades to the exterior. We use layers instead of windows: there is a joke that we are not able to draw windows."[12]

Hand in hand with the firm's characteristic creation of transparency is the theme of lightness, in the sense of both luminosity and weightlessness. A number of RPBW buildings have a soaring, lightweight quality, among them the Whitney Museum, with its masses, outdoor terraces, and metal stairways projecting over the street. American sculptor Mark di Suvero, who has several sculptures in the museum's permanent collection, remarks that there is "a moment in the Whitney building where you see the Hudson and you feel like you're flying over the water."[13]

13   RPBW, Harvard Art Museums, renovation, Cambridge, Massachusetts

14   Ludwig Mies van der Rohe, glass tower, competition drawing, 1921

Bianchi cites other recurring traits of the firm's practice, such as the use of wood cladding and metal handrails. "We've invented something that works: why change it?" he asks. Even so, it is apparent that RPBW railings can become relentlessly repetitive, as they do at the Harvard Art Museums in Cambridge, Massachusetts (2014), where, in response to the client's request for some additional protection around the atrium for visitors, the metal railings doggedly repeat those on the stairways (fig. 13).

Piano's success in creating transparency and lightness places him within a century-old architectural tradition. In the early 1900s, against a background of intense political and economic unrest, Expressionist architects in Germany regarded crystal edifices as the harbinger of a new civilization.[14] Later, Le Corbusier facilitated the spread of non-load-bearing glass curtain walls by separating wall and structure in his design of the Maison Dom-ino prototype (1914–1915). Willis Polk's Hallidie Building in San Francisco (1918) was among the first curtain wall buildings, and Ludwig Mies van der Rohe conceptualized the idea of a building glazed on all sides on an immense scale in 1921.

Mies's competition entry that year for a glass office building in Berlin—a glass prism with a triangular plan—consisted of a 260-foot-high curtain wall with no base or cornice (fig. 14). Its transparent facade and the stacks of offices it made visible dematerialized the building. The competition project was the German modernist's radical response to Daniel Burnham's Flatiron Building in Manhattan,[15] known in Europe from its June 1917 publication on page 1 of *Neue Jugend*, a proto-Dada journal in newspaper format, where it was stamped

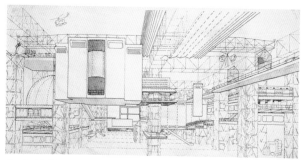

16   Cedric Price, Fun Palace, interior perspective, c. 1964

15   *Neue Jugend*, June 1917

with the word *REKLAMEBERATUNG* ("advertising advice") across its upper portion[16] (fig. 15).

The scheme remained unbuilt, and with a few exceptions, it was only in the years after World War II that what architecture critic Ada Louise Huxtable called the "glass box" appeared throughout the world in a wide range of building types, styles, scales, and glazings.[17] Transparency and reflectivity governed the discourse early on; in the new millennium, concerns about the environmental impact of this technology were added. As if fired by Expressionist ideals, a new generation of practitioners around the turn of the twenty-first century eschewed the ubiquitous boxlike tower in favor of skewed facades, shaped roofs, and technological innovation.

At the forefront of experimentation, RPBW has used two distinct approaches to the design of facades. The first is technological expression, or facades that emphasize either structural or ecological building performance. The second is transparency, or facades that embody the quality of translucence—the approach that was adopted for the SNFCC. Thanks to several factors, including the mild climate of Athens, a nearly invisible structural system, and a design that strove for invisibility, the facades of the cultural center reprise the vision demonstrated by Mies in his glass skyscraper project.

The strategy of highlighting a building's structure is exemplified by Piano and Rogers's Centre Pompidou, an outgrowth of English architect Cedric Price's Fun Palace project (1959–1961; fig. 16). Price, like several of his contemporaries, created conceptual schemes in which the construction framework was

17 RPBW, B&B Italia offices, Novedrate, Italy

18 RPBW, IBM traveling pavilion

19 RPBW, Menil Collection, Houston, ferro-cement ceiling louvers

completely independent of the disposition of interior spaces; these, in turn, were infinitely reconfigurable and adaptable to any number of uses. The Paris cultural center brazenly exposed frame, circulation, and mechanical systems in a revolutionary statement about facade and curtain wall design. That approach has been echoed in many RPBW works, among them the B&B Italia offices in Novedrate, Italy (1971–1973; fig. 17) and the IBM traveling pavilion (1983–1986; fig. 18). In reiterating the transparent curtain wall in his design for the SNFCC, however, Piano made the building's lobbies and the "book castle" visible through the glass while keeping most of its internal structure hidden.

Ecological performance is represented by the complex sunscreen and air-circulation devices that have been built into the walls and roofs of numerous buildings throughout the firm's history. In the Menil Collection building, a system of electronic louvers extends out from the glazed roof into a portico, signaling the importance of light regulation in the scheme (see p. 52, fig. 9); and ferro-cement louvers (whose material inspired the SNFCC's ferro-cement canopy) suspended below the roof inside the galleries moderate the intensity of the light that enters the interiors (fig. 19). At the Jean-Marie Tjibaou Cultural

20　RPBW, Jean-Marie Tjibaou Cultural Center, Noumea, New Caledonia

22　RPBW, Debis Building, Berlin

21　RPBW, New York Times Building, New York

Center in New Caledonia, spaces between the curved, vertical wooden ribs create convection chimneys that contribute to natural ventilation (fig. 20).

The facades of the 52-story New York Times Building in New York City (2007) combine transparency and sustainability in a novel way (fig. 21). For its first high-rise in the United States—its second anywhere, after Aurora Place/ ABN Amro Tower in Sydney, Australia (2000)—the firm teamed up with local architects FXFowle. The design drew in part on RPBW's 21-story Debis Building on the Alte Potsdamer Strasse in Berlin (1997; fig. 22). Terra-cotta is one of the RPBW architects' favorite materials, and the Berlin tower is clad in square, terra-cotta rods, referred to as "baguettes," which shade the windows. The baguettes were adapted, for the Times project, into horizontal, off-white

23   RPBW, UNESCO Laboratory-Workshop, Vesima, Italy

ceramic rods. Three inches in diameter, the rods are placed 8 inches away from the glass facades and extend well above the roofline.[18] Their thinness and slightly irregular spacing allow ample views outward, and despite the partial obstruction of the exteriors, the building is more transparent than high-rises that use low-emission glass tinted or coated with ceramic frit.[19] Bruce Fowle, founding principal of his firm, admits that dealing with Piano's fiery Italian temperament was a small price to pay for a great learning experience: "I got better both in terms of diplomacy and in the details."[20]

The most direct precedent for the SNFCC's glazed facades may be the firm's UNESCO Laboratory-Workshop (1989–1991) at Vesima, just outside Genoa (fig. 23). At the time of its construction the pavilion was shared by the RPBW studio and a UNESCO research station for studying potential architectural uses of plant fibers. Like earlier pioneering glass architecture, such as Joseph Paxton's Crystal Palace for the Great Exhibition in London (1851), it was built as a greenhouse. The workshop's translucent roof, made from a glasslike material that filters out infrared rays, is somewhat different from its nineteenth-century predecessor: the glass facades are not required to bear any weight, thanks to a wood-frame system in which the roof is supported by laminated timber beams joined to crossbeams by steel posts. The posts are secured to the retaining wall that forms the edge of each level. Glass fins not unlike those at the SNFCC are used to accommodate this system. Both the earlier Vesima design and the later Athens project share three important characteristics: translucency (there is no

24   RPBW, Shard skyscraper, London

25   RPBW, Potsdamer Platz B1 Tower, Berlin

solid frame to bar daylight), visual transparency (each fin connects two separate window panels, obscuring the joint between them), and convenience (the
assemblages in both buildings incorporate solar-cell-controlled louvers and
blinds). The primary difference between the Vesima office and the SNFCC is
that the fins at the workshop simply hide the joints, while at the cultural center
they serve a structural function.

Together with Piano's tallest (ninety-five stories) and most dramatically
translucent high-rise, the Shard (2013) in London, Potsdamer Platz B1 Tower
(1999), at the opposite end of the Alte Potsdamer Strasse from the Debis headquarters, has one of RPBW's most transparent facades. Vertical mullions are
entirely absent, a structural refinement that is especially apparent at the corners of the building (figs. 24, 25). As in Athens, the contrast between glass and
opaque masonry emphasizes the structure's ephemeral qualities.

The cultural center's agora facades began to go up in April 2015, an indication that, miraculously, the initial timetable for completion would be met
despite Greece's escalating instability. Already that January, the victory of the
left-wing Syriza coalition party headed by Alexis Tsipras had opened up new
problems.

The young and charismatic prime minister injected a breath of fresh air
as the leader of a party that had not previously held power, and his promise
to relieve nearly five years of austerity policies was irresistible to the Greek
electorate.[21] However, Tsipras's vow to renegotiate the bailout terms that had

been agreed to by the previous Greek government posed a serious threat to the nation's standing in the European Union, and by extension to the rules governing that union.[22]

Less than three weeks after the election, the newly appointed finance minister, Yanis Varoufakis, initiated a series of meetings with Eurozone economic ministers that proved to be disastrous. Repeatedly described in the press as a "combative" and "pugnacious" "firebrand," Varoufakis started his negotiations in Brussels with a confrontational attitude that was exacerbated by his casual untucked shirts and rejection of neckties. In fact, the press focused on the Greek finance minister's unconventional behavior at least as much as his arguments, and one reporter continued in that vein when he seized on the black leather jacket worn by I.M.F. director Christine Lagarde as a signal of her tough approach.[23] Varoufakis's flamboyance turned a serious situation into a media circus.

At issue were the terms of extending the bailout of €273 billion ($300 billion), which was scheduled to expire on February 28. Refusing the lenders' demand to keep the existing terms in place, Varoufakis sought a bridge loan while trying to negotiate less punishing conditions.[24] A deal proposed on February 22, which modified the shape of Greece's obligations without reducing them, outraged many members of the Greek government, and at least one Syriza lawmaker threatened to resign, adding to the uncertainty of the nation's future.[25]

By March, the discussions had deteriorated into an ugly confrontation between Greece and Germany, with Greece calling for reparations for the crimes and unpaid debts of the Nazis. The economic crisis triggered a political standoff when the Greeks accused Wolfgang Schäuble, Germany's finance minister, who was chief spokesman for the creditors, of destroying their country; the Germans, in their turn, depicted Varoufakis as the embodiment of an

Graffiti can be a gauge of popular opinion. Here the phrase "Let's now pretend we are all ducks" expresses the artist's conviction that the Greek people are expected to mindlessly follow whatever the government decides.

In June 2014, numerous buildings in Athens were covered in politically related graffiti. Some were supported by government sponsorship, and many were copyrighted by their artists. It is to be hoped that the expansive walls of the SNFCC will not meet the same fate.

unrepentant Greece, shirking its obligations. The Greek finance minister's antics reinforced a word in the political vocabulary: Grexit.[26] The implication that the nation might withdraw from the Eurozone and return to its former currency, the drachma, piled even more unpredictability onto the uncertainty of the European Union's survival.

Surprisingly, the political upheaval did not affect the progress of the SNFCC, nor was any member of the government critical of the project, with its promise of badly needed jobs. What it did affect, and strongly intensify, were misgivings about the government's ability to fund the maintenance and programming of the cultural center in the foreseeable future.

Prior to Syriza's election, the party had been openly hostile to private-sector (including charitable) involvement with culture, questioning, for example, public funding of the privately run, financially troubled Megaron concert hall complex.[27] However, since coming to power, the party has softened its stance, and in May 2015 the new minister of culture, Aristides Baltas, stated publicly that he was looking forward to the completion of the Niarchos project.[28] For the next year, during which Greece faced a whole new set of problems triggered by the massive influx of refugees that inundated Europe, this kind of support alternated with the government's complaints about the financial burden of the SNFCC.[29]

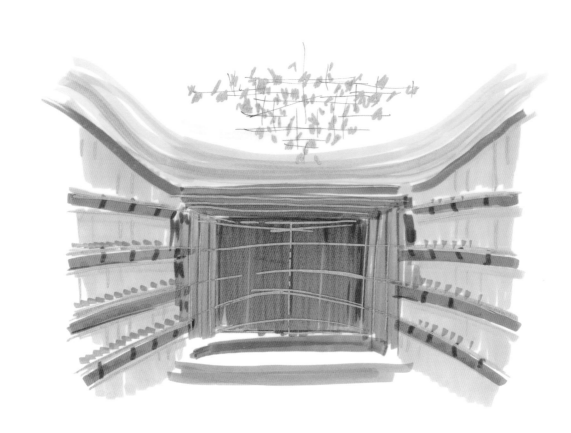

Opera

No drama on stage could possibly measure up to the real-life tragedy of Greece at the time when the opera house, together with the rest of the SNFCC, approached its final phase of construction early in 2016. Anticipation of the elegant building shedding its scaffolding and the attendant promise of diverting performances within paled in comparison to forebodings over what appeared to be the nation's unraveling.

For his early 2015 brokering with Greece's creditors on the loan agreement that had been extended but was about to expire, Yanis Varoufakis appeared to be trying to show the Europeans how to save Europe itself instead of sticking to negotiating Greece's future.[1] He and Prime Minister Tsipras were faulted for being too idealistic and too confident in their ability to persuade their creditors to abandon ideas dear to the Europeans for years.[2] One after another, the finance minister's suggestions, together with his flirtation with the Russians, fell by the wayside.[3] In June 2015, after five months of discussion, the Eurogroup negotiators presented a package of continued fiscal austerity, fiscal reforms, and a funding formula that Tsipras publicly condemned. The prime minister characterized the proposal as "an ultimatum to Greek democracy and the Greek people." He called on Greece to vote on the proposal in a referendum on July 5[4] (fig. 1).

In that referendum, Greek voters soundly rejected the proposal; but, almost immediately, Tsipras bowed to economic realities in an astonishing about-face, accepting the Eurogroup's plan for an €85 billion ($96 billion) bailout, the third since 2010. As a result, Syriza's parliamentary deputies were riven by dissent, and, in order to regain his credibility, Tsipras resigned in August and called for yet another election in September. He was reelected—albeit with a smaller majority than before and the loss of many members of the Syriza party.

Varoufakis's strategy of postponing the Greek loan agreement until the last minute so that a new arrangement could be negotiated turned out to be a monumental miscalculation that, on the morning after the referendum, forced him also to tender his resignation. No matter how seriously he regarded his

SNFCC, opera house, conceptual sketch

Celebration by anti-austerity voters

own intentions, the way in which he pursued them called to mind a trajectory comparable to the legendary Hippoclides: the inebriated young suitor stood on his head at a dinner party, revealing his posterior to his potential father-in-law, Cleisthenes, the tyrant of Sicyon, thereby losing the bid for the hand of his daughter.[5]

What Tsipras's reelection in September showed was that the conservative and socialist parties were discredited in the eyes of the electorate, which was left with Syriza as its only hope for a more socially equitable implementation of the most painful economic measures. Enforcement of these measures, including budget cuts and tax increases, despite the prime minister's promises, put Tsipras on shaky ground.[6]

In addition to the country's financial and political quandary, by September 2015 it was burdened by half a million refugees from the fighting in Syria, Iran, and Afghanistan, a mass migration unequaled since World War II. That fall, several thousand refugees were temporarily sheltered in the Tae Kwon Do stadium, almost at the doorstep of the SNFCC, and in other locations in Athens. In December, the Greek minister for immigration policy announced that three to four thousand migrants and refugees were entering Greece each day.[7]

Far from deterring Andreas Dracopoulos, this upheaval strengthened his resolution to see the SNFCC project through to completion. Although at the outset of the undertaking he had accorded precedence to the library, by this time he had become equally passionate about the opera house. While acknowledging that Greece was "at the front line of Europe's financially weakened condition," he was convinced that the cultural center would symbolize "a new beginning" for his country.[8]

Dracopoulos's optimism, though shared by few of his fellow countrymen, derived in part from video conferences with ministers and other officials in which he participates every six weeks. The SNF's director was sure that the government had started to understand that the cultural center had a role in changes

2   RPBW, Music Theater and Casino, Berlin

that would take place in Greece. "After all," he said, "the library and the opera house are two pillars of civilization. If the state can't maintain them, you might as well close down the country." For him, the project had already succeeded, because "it is the first time things have been done with no corruption, no bribes, or other misdeeds, from the bottom up. It is not about money, but about doing it right. It is tough love."

Planning and design for the GNO's 355,209-square-foot multiuse hall, Alternative Stage theater, and school of dance were well on their way before politics intruded, even prior to the designation of an architect. A full ten months before RPBW was engaged in 2008, Cooper Robertson recommended that the SNF hire international theater and acoustics consultants.

Consequently, in March 2007, the foundation commissioned Theatre Projects Consultants to determine the shape of the auditorium as well as the required backstage facilities, and Arup to advise on acoustics and lighting.[9] These consultants, together with the SNF and RPBW, developed the building program using historic and contemporary precedents, advanced technology, observation of current audience behavior, aesthetic considerations, and even—briefly—a magazine illustration. In the absence of an artistic director for the GNO, who was finally appointed in 2011, the specialists acted heroically as substitutes for the user-client.

Arup and TPC had worked on several projects together, including Henning Larsen's opera house in Copenhagen (2004) and Snøhetta's in Oslo (2008). Before the Athens project, by contrast, RPBW's only theater-related auditorium (as opposed to a concert hall) was the Music Theater and Casino in Marlene Dietrich Platz, Berlin, which was designed by Bianchi (with Christoph Kohlbecher, 1998; fig. 2). But that venue was intended primarily for amplified performances. An auditorium for classical opera poses a whole different set of acoustical issues.

French-born Alban Bassuet (b. 1974), an acoustic consultant at Arup from 2000 until 2015, served as the room acoustician for the GNO—that is,

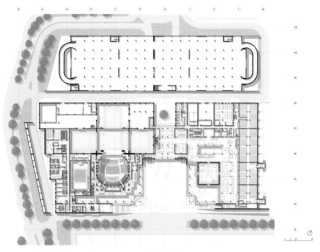

3   SNFCC, opera house, second level plan

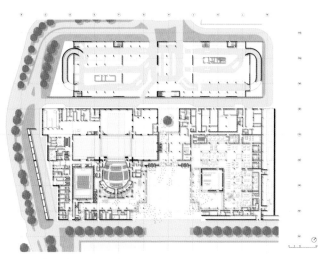

4   Opera house, agora level plan

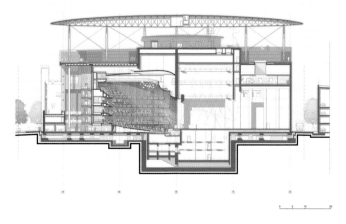

5   Opera house, section

the specialist who advises on how the architecture will affect acoustics. After practicing at Paris's Institute for Research and Coordination Acoustic/Music (IRCAM) and other acoustic laboratories, he came to Arup. Working with Bassuet as project director was Raj Patel (b. 1972), a principal at Arup who specializes in the design and acoustics of performing arts venues, museums, and galleries. Theatre Projects Consultants was established in 1968 by the English lighting designer and theater design consultant Richard Pilbrow (b. 1933); Benton Delinger (b. 1962), a principal consultant at the firm, led the Athens project with fellow consultant John Coyne (b. 1964).

Together with CR and RPBW, the consultants decided on a medium-size auditorium, in a traditional horseshoe shape, that seats 1,400 people (figs. 3–5; see also pp. 206–207). Delinger describes the process as "a collaboration from beginning to end":

> TPC designated the shape and style of the room, which was drawn up by Bassuet, who together with Patel developed the acoustic needs for it. TPC worked to create a three-dimensional room that allows for connections between the performers and [members of the] audience to each other. RPBW pulled all of this together into a vision of the room that will be uniquely Athens.[10]

"Each meeting," Bassuet recalls, "commenced with Renzo's presentation of his idea. This was followed by a long exchange with Bianchi and RPBW associate Vassily Laffineur: Bianchi then made a drawing which was overlaid by my drawing on tracing paper: layers upon layers, sometimes as many as six or seven."[11] Piano responded with equanimity to the question of dealing with the consultants' extensive design recommendations: "Architects live on limitations," he assured me. "Restrictions are part of the game: you don't need to have complete freedom to create."[12]

TPC designed stage facilities that would enable the GNO to share productions with opera companies in Europe and the United States. In order for them to use the same scenery and stage directions, up-to-date mechanization is critical, as are wagon systems to move the sets, stage lifts, and an adequate backstage area (which in Athens is six times larger than the auditorium). Facilities for building maintenance, adjustments to the sets (such as painting), and costume storage and maintenance are accommodated on-site; prop and scenery shops are in Western Attica and may in the future be moved closer to the SNFCC.

Initially, nine hundred rooms and a worker population of five hundred were projected for the building; six stages would have allowed morning rehearsals for evening performances. As the design progressed, the number of rooms and stages was reduced: the main theater ended up with three separate backstages, isolated acoustically by massive doors, which also allow stage-size sets to move on and off the main stage. Even with these cutbacks, the 3,050-square-foot

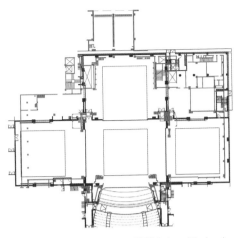

6   Theatre Projects Consultants, SNFCC stage (blue) and
    Metropolitan Opera stage (red), comparison drawing

7   Myron Michailidis

backstage area remains large (as is typical in Europe), almost as large as that at
the Metropolitan Opera in New York (fig. 6).

In sharp contrast with the presence of so many consultants was the absence
of an artistic director at the GNO, the user-client essential to the success of
every architectural undertaking, and the main contact for everyone involved
with the design.[13] Not until February 2011, at which time the design had been for
all practical purposes completed, was Myron Michailidis (b. 1968; fig. 7) named
artistic director of the opera. One Greek newspaper describes him as having a
"methodical, gentle, and creative manner";[14] my impression is of a man with an
iron fist in a velvet glove. Michailidis is an accomplished conductor who has led
orchestras worldwide.[15]

Michailidis believes that "the only hope for opera is to give the feeling that
it is for the people."[16] Possibly Piano anticipated this intention in his handling
of the soaring lobby. Granted it is paved in marble—a common material in
Athens—but the interior walls eschew expensive materials in favor of smooth,
poured-in-place concrete. Balconies are enclosed by RPBW's signature prag-
matic metal railings, painted dark gray, and are complemented along stairs and
other open areas by simple glass balustrades topped by oak handrails.

Restrooms are located next to the box office and cloakroom on the ground
floor and repeat on every level. Three of the opera house's seven public elevators
and several strategically placed stairways take visitors to all levels of the lobby
balconies and to the restaurant. There are also two public scenic elevators in the
agora to the lighthouse on top of the opera house (and two similar elevators to

8   RPBW, La Valletta City Gate, Malta

the park) and seven staff elevators. An east-facing VIP entrance at the lobby's south end leads to a private lounge and to an elevator that goes directly to the restaurant and school of dance.

Within the auditorium, acoustics are the first priority, as they must be for any space in which music is performed. But the creation of a space for natural acoustics (i.e., unamplified sound) is one of the most daunting of all design tasks. As it turned out, seven years of research, experimentation, and exchanges of ideas went into making what one of the consultants calls the auditorium's "transformative experience."[17] During this time, Piano's original quarry concept for the building, which was to have used marble both inside and out, was also evolving. (In 2016, RPBW realized a more literal reinterpretation of a quarry for the parliamentary chamber near the Valletta City Gate in Malta; fig. 8.)

Thousands of years of trials with acoustics in every conceivable context—in caves, hill formations, ritual spaces, religious buildings, and concert halls—have not led to absolute certainty in the design of an auditorium. Not even today's

Opera made its way from Italy to Greece via the Ionian Islands. In the eighteenth and part of the nineteenth century, the provincial Nobile Teatro di San Giacomo di Corfù played an important role in the musical life of the country. At the time Corfù surpassed Athens in this respect. Built as a loggia for the island's Venetian nobility, the structure was converted into a theater in 1720, with the first known opera performance taking place there in 1733. The five-hundred-seat Apollo opera house (left) in Ermoúpolis on the island of Syros, the chief town and administrative center of the Cyclades Islands, was inaugurated in 1864 and operated until 1953. Designed by the Italian architect Pietro Sampo, it is the oldest surviving modern theater in Greece.

unprecedented technological innovations guarantee perfect sound. Architectural acoustics is a relatively young profession. Its inception is credited to physicist Wallace Clement Sabine (1868–1919), whose acoustical design for Boston Symphony Hall (McKim, Mead & White, 1890) is considered a masterpiece thanks to its clear, live, warm, brilliant, and acceptably vibrant sound.[18] Sabine's successful application of scientific methods to the hall in Boston—for example, a mathematical formula that enabled him to predict the hall's reverberation time before it was built, known as the Sabine formula[19]—paved the way for the mandatory inclusion of acoustical expertise in auditorium design.

Theater consulting is an even more recent discipline, arising in the 1970s to advise on and help coordinate a range of issues specific to performance spaces. These can even extend, at the outset, to the choice of architect and acoustician and, at the conclusion, to transition assistance as users grow into a building and learn to fully exploit an auditorium's capabilities.[20]

Stymied by the absence of an artistic director and ongoing managerial staff for the opera, the Alternative Stage theater, and ballet companies during the design of the SNFCC auditorium, Delinger and Coyne of TPC turned to Sherwin M. Goldman (b. 1941), a former American Ballet Theatre president and New York City Opera executive producer, with whom CR had worked on the New York State Theater (now the David H. Koch Theater) at Lincoln Center. Goldman acted as an interlocutor with whom to discuss operational planning: exactly what an opera house in Athens should be. In their efforts to answer this question, the consultants even asked Joseph Volpe, the formidable former general manager of the Metropolitan Opera, for advice.

Arup acousticians Alban Bassuet and Raj Patel relied on an intriguing research process known as auralization: computer modeling that since the 1990s has made acoustical engineering more predictable. The process re-creates the three-dimensional effect of a sound as it would occur in a real room.

Music is first recorded in an anechoic room — a space devoid of reverberation or reflections. The sounds are then electronically processed to simulate the qualities they would have in a particular space, whether existing, planned, or even speculative. The Arup SoundLab in New York is only 20 by 20 by 15 feet. Even so, the consultants were able to simulate the Musikverein in Vienna and the Royal Concertgebouw in Amsterdam.

9 Amphitheater, Epidaurus

When Michailidis became artistic director of the Greek National Opera, he immediately requested changes to the building program and the design. (A parallel situation would take place at the library when Filippos Tsimpoglou became director general there in 2014.) Among these were moving the voluminous music library and archive from the opera house to the library and adding an ensemble rehearsal room and a moving wagon for the main stage.

Bassuet and Patel started their work on the auditorium's acoustics in spring 2008 with an idyllic week in Greece, doing research. They were amazed to discover that Athens missed out on the beginnings of opera in Florence and Venice during the late sixteenth and early seventeenth centuries because Greece was then a province of the Ottoman Empire. Already in the eighteenth century, however—before independence—an audience for opera began to develop in the Ionian Islands, a group of seven islands off Greece's west coast, which were under Venetian rule from the mid-fourteenth through the late eighteenth centuries. Greek composers living on the islands were aware of Italian opera, sometimes even traveling to Italy to study and to write operas with Italian librettos; operas by members of this Ionian School of music were performed regularly in theaters and small opera houses on several of the islands.[21]

The acoustics team was hard at work every day by sunrise. Mornings were spent studying the 14,000-seat Hellenistic outdoor amphitheater at Epidaurus (4th c. B.C.E., enlarged 2nd c. C.E.; fig. 9), on the Peloponnese, a little over an hour's drive from Athens; the theater's continued use is indebted to its legendary acoustics. Bassuet describes the amphitheater's intimate sound as "a soul-to-soul connection between performer and public."[22] The gentle rake of the seating allows sound waves to reflect back and forth between steps and stage, enveloping the audience and enabling the crucial visual connection between performers and public.[23] Among the details Bassuet and his team applied to the GNO was the sculptural shape of small ledges carved at the top of each stone step. A similar configuration on the ceiling of each balcony in the

10   Stair ledge, amphitheater, Epidaurus

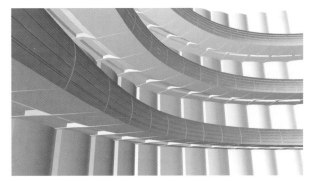

11   Arup/Alban Bassuet, SNFCC, opera house, balconies with soffit detail

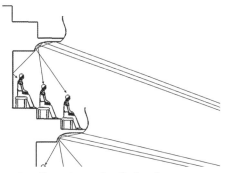

12   Arup/Bassuet, acoustic reflections from undersides of opera house balconies, diagram

13   Odeon of Herodes Atticus, Acropolis, Athens

new opera house catches sound and bounces it to the people sitting beneath[24] (figs. 10–12).

Afternoons were spent examining the 5,000-seat Odeon of Herodes Atticus (161 C.E.; fig. 13), on the southwest slope of the Acropolis, where the GNO performs every summer to sold-out audiences. The rake of this Roman amphitheater is much steeper than that at Epidaurus, with the distance to the stage correspondingly shorter. Consequently, above a certain height, the reflected sound simply dissipates. Based on these observations, Bassuet and Patel specified a moderate floor rake for the new opera house, an angle that would contribute to clarity for the spoken word but at the same time provide enough reverberation to support orchestral and vocal performance.[25]

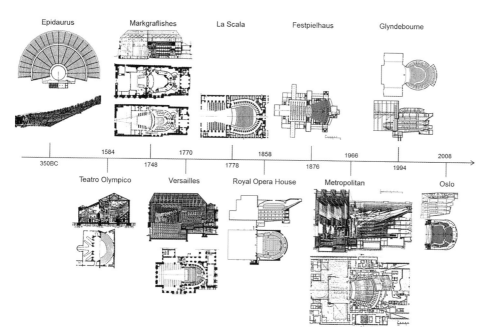

Epidaurus   Markgraflishes   La Scala   Festpielhaus   Glyndebourne

1584   1770   1858   1966
350BC   1748   1778   1876   1994   2008

Teatro Olympico   Versailles   Royal Opera House   Metropolitan   Oslo

14   Arup/Bassuet, timeline of historic opera houses

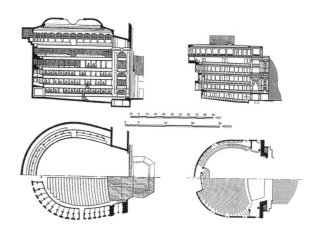

15   Arup/Bassuet, Teatro Colón, Buenos Aires (left), and Semperoper,
Dresden (right), sections and plans, comparison drawing

The acousticians created a timeline of form and design extending from
ancient outdoor theaters such as Epidaurus and the Odeon of Herodes Atticus
to the recently built Oslo Opera House (fig. 14). Their suggestion that an amphitheater might be appropriate for Greece having been overruled by TPC, they designated two opera houses as particular inspirations for the design: the four-tier
Semperoper (Gottfried Semper, 1841) in Dresden and the five-tier Teatro Colón
(Francesco Tamburini, Vittorio Meano, and Julio Dormal, 1908) in Buenos Aires
(fig. 15). In both, limiting the depth to just a few rows in each tier (in Dresden,
only two rows) permits more sound to penetrate the balconies and reflect off the
rear wall. The arrangement of the balconies in these venues, together with curved
walls containing a rich assortment of sound-diffusing ornaments, fixtures,

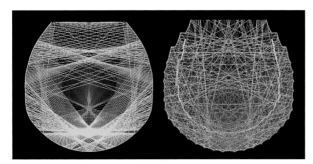

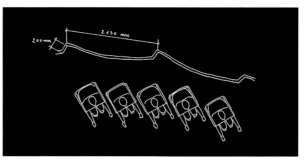

17 Arup/Bassuet, opera house modulated walls, diagram

16 Arup/Bassuet, SNFCC, sound reflections of smooth (left) and
    modulated (right) opera house surfaces, diagram

columns, and door recesses, contributes to an unusually successful balance of
reverberation, intimacy, rich tonal quality, and sound envelopment. To obtain
the best acoustics for Athens, as well as to encourage social interaction among
audience members (a goal the team identified as important to Greek operagoers)
and provide optimum views of the stage, the acousticians combined the horseshoe shape of the Teatro Colón and the semicircular shape of the Semperoper.

Opera house acoustics vary according to local taste. In northern Europe, an
apparent predilection for a greater degree of reverberation calls for an acoustic
design that favors instrumental music (exemplified by the Oslo Opera House's
1.9-second and Dresden's 1.7-second reverberation times); in Mediterranean
countries, less reverberation (1.2 seconds at La Scala in Milan[26]) results in acoustics that favor the clarity of sung or spoken speech. The opera house in Athens was
designed with dimensions that would produce a mid-range reverberation time of
between 1.6 and 1.7 seconds, which many experts feel is ideal for romantic opera.

In the GNO auditorium, three balconies and a parterre ring the orchestra
seats; the modulated profile of the walls at the back of the auditorium and gen-
tler curves at the sides are designed to prevent sound clusters that smooth walls
could produce (figs. 16, 17). In order to ensure complex reflections (for a more
enveloping sound), the walls at the sides and backs of the balconies consist of
convex modules separated by a series of 8-inch-deep ledges (every two to three
seats). The ledges bounce sound waves around listeners' heads in a double reflection referred to as a "cue ball pattern" (it resembles the tracks of billiard balls
after they are hit by a cue ball); the balconies themselves protrude into the auditorium, scattering sound and directing it toward the rear of the room (figs. 18, 19).

The acousticians produced a computer model of the auditorium that was
used in monthly meetings with the architects, and Piano patiently adjusted his
design to take technical considerations into account. At the outset he wanted
to break with tradition by varying the projection of the balconies: each balcony
would overhang the one below, coming closer, horizontally, to the stage. But the

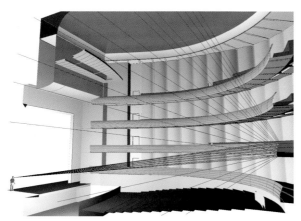

18   Arup/Bassuet, early opera house concept with sound lines, 2009

19   Arup/Bassuet, opera house final concept with ledges visible, 2014

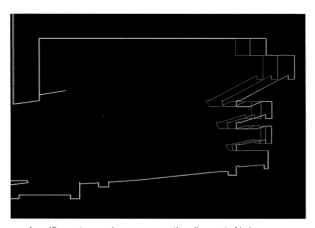

20   Arup/Bassuet, opera house, comparative alignment of balcony fronts, diagram

acousticians pointed out that cutting off reflections above each balcony and reinforcing direct sound from the stage would produce an undesirable acoustic effect besides visually disconnecting the listeners on each balcony from those below.[27]

To demonstrate the superiority of aligned balconies, Arup prepared a sound and sight simulation of three different opera houses: the Oslo Opera House (set back about 20 degrees), the Operaen in Copenhagen (about 10 degrees), and La Scala (0 degrees). It was the first time Piano had experienced Arup's SoundLab acoustic testing facility, and seeing models of the three houses projected onto a large screen with audio was a revelation for him: his team agreed unanimously that the strict vertical lineup was preferable[28] (fig. 20).

Some departures from tradition survived this rigorous analysis. The subtly different sizes and shapes of the balcony fronts, which are slightly separated from one another, create a variety of balcony profiles on each tier. Near the stage they face downward to help project voices to seats at the back of the house, while farther from the stage, they point upward to deflect sound toward the ceiling and help increase reflections.

Having rejected marble for the interior walls, Piano suggested finishing them in gold leaf, an idea that was motivated more by a magazine illustration of a beautiful woman in a shimmering golden swimsuit than by the celebrated Golden Hall at the Musikverein.[29] But by this time the global recession had rendered such extravagant ideas inappropriate, and the architects decided on American cherry wood's natural color for the balcony fronts in the main auditorium and a lighter, hardwood anigré stained red for the back walls. Piano wanted the red walls to darken as visitors penetrated more deeply into the building, so that the color would look like "blood when one cuts oneself."[30]

All the wood used in the SNFCC was milled in Athens. Nikolaos Anastasiou, who with his older brother, Dimitrios, runs the EPEXYL factory, uses a well-known procedure with exceptional success: he scans a room's concrete wall with a laser and inputs the result into a design and manufacturing program, which facilitates the precise cutting of complex geometries. The thin (quarter-inch) veneer required by Greek fire laws is composed of three 32-square-foot pieces of anigré glued together in a giant vacuum press. Piano declared the resulting surfaces so smooth that they felt "sexy!" For his part, Anastasiou, who was subsequently hired to fabricate the library bookshelves as well as much of the furniture in the two wings, calls Piano "the coolest of all the architects."

Seat selection was yet another aspect of the design guided by both acoustic and aesthetic considerations. Because the seats and audience constitute at least 90 percent of the acoustic absorption in a performance space, the choice of seats is critical to a room's acoustics, particularly in terms of reverberation. Upholstery, although it absorbs sound, is needed for comfort, so for an opera house it is confined to the seat and the inside back. The underside and outside back are wood (preferably thick, to avoid absorption) in order to reflect sound. The space under the seats allows sound to flow along the floor. Screens on the seat backs are used for subtitles. TPC specified the size and layout for the seating in order to optimize sightlines and legroom. Arup provided acoustic parameters for the materials and seat thickness. RPBW finalized these guidelines and chose red mohair fabric and, again, American cherry (see pp. 206–207). The seat depth is 3.28 feet in the orchestra level and slightly more in the balconies. The main aisles are about 47 inches wide—a typical width for an auditorium of this size. Bianchi was pleased to see the auditorium develop into a "reinterpretation of the *bonbonnière* opera house, including upholstered red seats and wood floors."[31]

21   SNFCC, opera house, auditorium ceiling with open slice

Illumination of the auditorium was yet another topic subject to a series of heated discussions. Lighting specialist Brian Stacy (b. 1974) of Arup, who collaborated on interior illumination with TPC (and handled exterior illumination as well), wanted the theater to be "wrapped in the warmth of subtly colored light."[32] Here, too, acoustics had to be taken into account, because some parts of a lighting system—the dimmers, for example—produce noise. The lighting design called for long-lived units. But commercial LED bulbs (with a life span of 50,000 hours, or twelve to fifteen years) issue a cold light—contradicting Stacy's preferences—so Arup specified custom fixtures that would improve the hue and facilitate maintenance. During the course of his work on the project— from 2007 until its completion—Stacy ran a race with time, periodically modifying his designs to keep pace with lighting technology, especially that of LED lighting, which evolves every twelve to eighteen months.

Stacy's proposal of a shiny surface for the walls of the auditorium was turned down by the acousticians, who called for some surface texture. Because the walls of an opera house reflect both sound and light, their materiality and illumination must also harmonize with acoustical requirements. In the end Stacy concurred with this specification.

A focal point in the overall lighting design is a giant paper mobile, replacing the traditional chandelier, by the Japanese artist Susumu Shingu (b. 1937), chosen by Piano for its "lightness." David McAllister, a mechanical engineer who was the project manager for Arup, explained the challenge presented by this kinetic sculpture and smaller ones in the opera house and library lobbies. None

22   SNFCC, opera house, double proscenium

of the sculptures incorporates light; rather, distant lighting brings the sculptures to life in an ever-changing spectacle. McAllister explains that not only did the lighting consultants have to illuminate the sculptures effectively and discreetly, but they also had to assure enough air movement to catch the paper squares. Fans with the right airflow were installed in places where the noise they made could not be heard.[33]

In addition, sky effects can be projected onto the ceiling dome, and a so-called ring ceiling covers the bottom of the technical lighting gallery that curves around the auditorium's periphery. In response to the needs of the sound system, an open slice at the center of the ceiling dome allows a portion of the ceiling to be retracted to allow uniform coverage—left, center, and right—from the loudspeaker clusters. This is also where the fans that animate the Shingu sculptures are placed (fig. 21).

Historically, the proscenium, the arch between the stage and the auditorium, has performed different functions at different times and has thus taken on different dimensions.[34] In the Renaissance and Baroque eras, singers performed within the proscenium zone, which could be as much as 10 feet deep. The arch amplified the voices, projecting them into the auditorium. At the end of the Baroque, with the changes in scenery design, the proscenium moved to the front of the stage (with the exception of English Restoration theaters) to enclose the orchestra's sound. Bassuet chose to retain a deep proscenium for the GNO, a more than 9-foot-deep area that helps to project the voices.

23 Opera house, stage with metal structures holding anigré veneer panels for acoustical shell

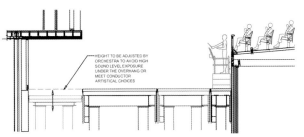

24 Opera house, raised and lowered positions of pit, diagram

Just how important the proscenium and pit designs are is illustrated by the years of dire acoustical issues that plagued Philip Johnson's 1964 New York State Theater at Lincoln Center.[35] Because the arch was initially concave instead of convex, the singers' voices were thrown back onstage instead of out to the audience; and the pit proved too small for the number of musicians needed for grand opera and ballet.

The SNFCC opera house has a double proscenium—one to buttress the singers and a second to buttress the orchestra[36] (fig. 22). The first proscenium—for the singers (roughly 9.5 feet deep, 56 feet wide, and 36 feet high)—is at the sides and above the stage: it projects voices out to the auditorium, back to the singers, and down into the pit. The second, wider proscenium is located at the sides and above the orchestra and reflects sound back to the musicians while also projecting voices into the auditorium. The two frames work together to allow a gentle transition between the stage and the auditorium, avoiding abrupt changes in reflection patterns. For orchestral concerts, thirteen tower-like volumes deployed around the edges of the stage make an acoustical shell (fig. 23).

The stage itself is nearly 97 feet wide and just over 72 feet deep. Balcony fronts are at most only about 79 feet away from the back of the proscenium arch to ensure that the singers' expressions are visible; the distance from behind the arch to the farthest seat in the auditorium is about 102 feet. Ninety percent of the audience has a full view of the stage.

Some performances—Baroque opera, for example—require as few as twenty musicians, whereas others—post-Romantic and many modern operas—call for more than one hundred. To hold both, and everything in between, in Athens the orchestra pit can extend into the audience area by means of four lifts (fig. 24). Moving the pit too far forward from the stage distances the audience from the scene and can also affect the balance between voices and instruments. Conversely, a pit buried too deeply beneath the stage can be claustrophobic

25   SNFCC, opera house, orchestra rehearsal room

and painfully loud for the musicians. The Arup scheme attempts to combine the assets of modern pits that stretch into the audience area (Covent Garden's is one) with Wagner's dream of a completely hidden orchestra (as realized in Bayreuth).

Motorized acoustical curtains at the back of every balcony can be moved remotely to dampen reverberation as necessary. The settings vary according to the type of performance—Baroque, classical, pop, and so on. The curtains are hidden in wall slots when not in use. A similar curtain system is concealed behind the top tier. Video can be projected within the theater, and broadcasting equipment allows performances to be streamed to the Alternative Stage theater and farther afield.

The flat-floored, rectangular Alternative Stage accommodates an audience of 450 people (with movable chairs rather than fixed seating). The higher of its two balconies accommodates technical machinery. Its walls and balcony fronts are a simplified version of the main auditorium's with the same natural American cherry used for vertical cladding (see p. 209). This smaller hall and the practice rooms above it proved as demanding acoustically as the large hall, due to the tricky matter of isolating these spaces' potentially loud activities from the rest of the building (fig. 25). The issue was addressed by building acousticians rather than room acousticians like Bassuet and his colleagues. One of them was Rachid Abu-Hassan (b. 1978), a Lebanese-born sound and vibration specialist who immigrated to the United States in 1996 and joined Arup in 2007. Abu-Hassan describes his job as "making sure that nothing gets in and nothing gets out."[37]

26   Opera house, installation of acoustically isolating box-in-box construction

In addition to protecting the auditoriums and rehearsal rooms from outside noise, the building acousticians had to confront inside background noise from the auditorium's cooling systems. As in many recently constructed theaters, air is supplied to a large plenum beneath the seats and drawn upward by convection, cooling the audience as it slowly and quietly rises. It is finally extracted at an upper level where it can be mixed with fresh air and recirculated to the plenum.

The SNFCC complex as a whole is protected from earthquakes by means of huge seismic isolators; the smaller auditorium, the five rehearsal rooms, and four warm-up rooms that accommodate single musicians are also fully acoustically isolated, each within its own box-in-box construction. No part of the floating inner boxes touches the outer boxes. But the inner boxes had to be restrained to prevent excessive movement and potential damage during an earthquake. An interesting aspect of the box-in-box construction is that the concrete floor slabs for the experimental theater and the rehearsal rooms had to be lifted up to their final positions (nearly 8 inches for some rooms). This was accomplished by unwinding screws within resilient neoprene isolators in cast-iron, bell-shaped housings (fig. 26). Abu-Hassan understates the case when he says that the "details where the isolated and non-isolated must be connected while maintaining the acoustic isolation were fairly challenging."[38]

The seismic isolators are located in the basement, which sits directly on the ground, and allows the floor above to sway almost 2½ feet in either direction, creating a problem of its own. As Abu-Hassan describes it: "You're dealing with flexible joints that can leave a gap sometimes as wide as a foot between a basement partition and the ground-floor slab. Such a gap is an enormous problem in a building, requiring sound isolation, because it would provide a clear path for sound to transmit."

During the elaborate preparations for its sophisticated new theater, the GNO did not sit idly by. Complementing its annual season of productions at the Olympia Theater, the company staged tremendously popular free performances

27   Performance by Opera in a Suitcase in old NLG

with no theater at all. In Athens, the GNO performed in subway stations, at the meat market, in front of the Piraeus port, in the old library building, and, for a 2013 tribute to Maria Callas, in five prominent locations throughout the city. Opera in a Suitcase, a program aimed at younger audiences and funded by the SNF, presents abbreviated versions of famous works in cities across the country (fig. 27). And a new nationwide education initiative in seventy primary schools is fostering opera's future audiences.

The success of these experiments was all the more impressive considering the troubled conditions in Athens when they were carried out. On September 17, 2013, Pavlos Fyssas, a Greek rapper whose music ridiculed extreme right-wing groups, was stabbed to death in a suburban café, apparently by a supporter of the neo-Nazi Golden Dawn party, an incident that provoked massive demonstrations in the capital, in other cities in Greece, and in a wide range of countries. In Greece, the protests turned violent, and on November 1 an anarchist urban guerilla group attacked the local branch of Golden Dawn in a northern suburb of Athens, killing two party members. (In April 2015, sixty-nine Golden Dawn members, including the party leader and several members of parliament, were brought to trial, but the proceedings have stalled.[39])

For the most part, the political unrest characteristic of the 2010s was confined to a few specific neighborhoods, almost completely bypassing the SNFCC. Consequently, Michailidis steadfastly continued to work on plans for the GNO's operations in its new home, planning a mix of opera, operetta, opera for children, ballet, and contemporary works. The director reported in an interview in 2014 that he reduced its debt of $23.5 million in 2010 to $6.5 million in 2013, and cut annual operational expenditures in half.[40] The cost of his productions in the 2012–2013 season was only slightly more than the revenue from ticket sales ($3.9 million compared with revenue of $3.5 million), a balance he hoped to maintain in the new theater, where tickets would be a little more expensive (on average €38 or $41.10—an increase of $2.75 to $4.15 per ticket over 2013 prices) and twice as many seats as at the Olympia would be available. A ticket for a performance at the Alternative Stage will cost €15 ($16.20). The maestro insisted that the opera's monetary problems were due to the financial crisis, not to lack of interest, and he cited the company's successful performances in the Odeon of Herodes Atticus together with attendance of five thousand people at the Callas celebration and of twenty thousand at other free performances.[41]

In contrast to the relatively traditional programming of the large auditorium, the smaller theater, under the leadership of Giorgos Koumendakis, the composer of the opera *The Murderess,* based on a novel by Alexandros Papadiamantis (2014), will be more innovative. Michailidis also planned an opera studio with specialized training for young professionals and an interactive educational program for children. In 2014, he anticipated co-productions with major opera companies in London, Cardiff, Verona, and Vienna.

By April 2015, one and a half years after my initial meeting with Michailidis, he was apprehensive of the new Syriza government's cultural policy, since most opera productions require a long lead time.[42] Because the GNO is funded by the state, it is subject to the policies of rapidly changing governments and ministers of culture. The opera's previous managers had calculated the total costs of running the new house (for fifteen to sixteen productions a year, and for maintenance) at around €40 million ($44.64 million), but the Karamanlis (2004–2009) government in 2007 had agreed to contribute only €24.4 million ($27.23 million). Even though Michailidis, who holds a law degree from Athens University, had managed to shrink these costs drastically, to €17.89 million ($19.32 million), the Samaras government (2012–2015) was willing to contribute a mere €10 million ($10.8 million) annually. With the Syriza victory in 2015, the new government upped the contribution to €12.5 million ($14.09 million), which leaves the annual shortfall just under €4 million ($4.45 million) for 2017 and €4.5 million ($5 million) in 2018. As a result, the €5 million ($5.4 million) transitional grant from the SNF would cover the GNO through at least 2017. The director had mixed feelings about the future; undoubtedly, Michailidis would have been even more concerned had he known that by the end of 2016 he would no longer be artistic director of the GNO.

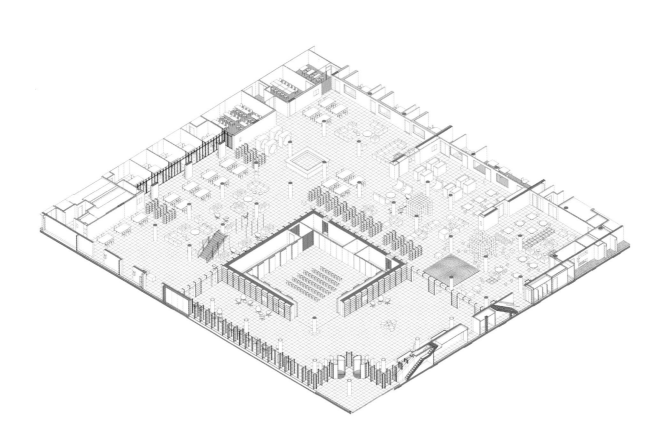

Library

In 2008–2009, when RPBW started to design the new National Library of Greece as part of the SNFCC, the architects faced even greater difficulties than they had for the opera house. The library had been without a director since 2005; there was no complete inventory of its holdings; and no outreach programs were in place. In addition, the SNF planned to expand the NLG—a research institution used primarily by scholars—by adding a lending library and other public services.[1] With no definitive concept for the two different aspects of the new library, the SNF called upon multiple specialists and even flirted briefly with an outside architectural firm in order to clarify the NLG's mission.

Two years of trial and error transformed the aura of the NLG from that of an institution to that of an inviting, family-oriented civic center (figs. 1–4). While the spaces dedicated to the National Library's reading rooms and archives retain the sober demeanor associated with scholarly pursuit, those devoted to services catering to a broader public clearly encourage something different. The walls in those areas are still solid with books, but they have become a background for informal seating areas and a wide variety of amenities. The entire ground floor and half of the second floor (54,000 square feet) are devoted to circulating books.

Piano was well aware of the problems confronting the design of the 247,570-square-foot NLG. "Opera is a given," he says, "You know what it is. Libraries are more problematic: what will their future be?"[2] The architect considers his design, with Richard Rogers, of the Centre Pompidou Library in Paris "a transition between the historical library and open shelves. Then the standard library was a reading room with stacks above and below it. I pulled the stacks and the people together. Now everything is different; the digital library is a new transition."[3]

Both changes cited by Piano are in fact revolutionary, advancing a democratization of libraries that started in the nineteenth century. In the mid-twentieth century, books began to be arranged on open shelves, rather than stored and brought to readers' desks, thus making them more accessible to the public. More recently, the digitization of books goes even further in that direction, contesting

SNFCC, NLG, ground level, isometric

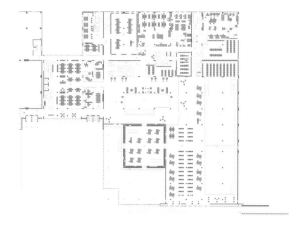

1   SNFCC, NLG, top level plan (with Stavros Niarchos Reading Room)

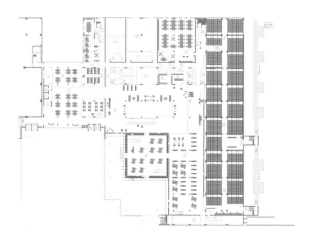

2   NLG, level 2 plan (public library/research library)

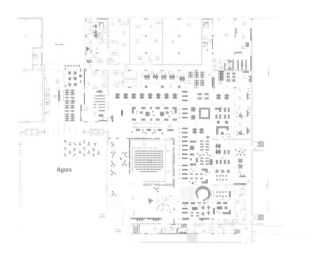

3   NLG, final ground level plan (public library)

4   NLG, section

5   Theophil Hansen, old National Library of Greece, Athens

the very definition of the library by making the contents of books available to users outside the physical building.

The predecessor of the NLG was known as the Public Library when it opened as an independent institution in 1832; this merged with the National University of Athens library in 1842 to become the National Library of Greece in 1866. In 1903 the NLG moved into a 68,400-square-foot building designed by Danish architect Theophil Hansen; it occupied the building until its new home at the SNFCC was completed (fig. 5). The 1903 edifice, funded by the London-based Panayis Athanase Vagliano and his brothers, is yet another example of public philanthropy by diaspora Greeks. A handsome, marble-clad neoclassical building, it is typical of the aloof monumentality characteristic of many national libraries erected in the first half of the twentieth century. Those familiar with Hansen's Parliament building (1883) in Vienna will experience a sense of déjà vu upon seeing the exterior of the NLG.

Even from the institution's inception, however, the administration failed to live up to the impressive symbolic expression bestowed by Hansen. Consider, for example, the fate of the gift received in 1904 from Joannes Gennadius, the son of George Gennadius, a co-founder of the National Library. Gennadius *fils* gave to the library his important collection of 2,904 lithographs and engravings together with a catalogue of the objects. But just three years later, when the catalogue could not be found, the younger Gennadius withdrew the gift. It ended up in a building of its own, the Gennadius Library, at the American School of Classical Studies in Athens.

7   OMA, Qatar National Library, Doha, rendering

6   Joseph Emanuel Fischer von Erlach, Austrian National Library, Vienna

Unlike opera houses, the first of which were created just four hundred years ago—a relatively short period of time—libraries have their origins in the third millennium B.C.E. and have undergone multiple permutations since then. Time and place have produced different requirements for storing and preserving various forms of writing as well as changing attitudes toward their accessibility. In Mesopotamia, books written in cuneiform gave way to the kind of papyrus scroll found in Alexander the Great's famous library in Alexandria, Egypt (3rd c. B.C.E. – 30 B.C.E.). Not until the Christian era did bound manuscripts (codices) similar to the printed volumes produced today come into being, for which magnificent libraries were designed, such as the Hofbibliothek ("imperial library," 1723–1726), today known as the Austrian National Library[4] (fig. 6). Be that as it may, only the switch from illuminated handwritten manuscripts on parchment to type à la Gutenberg was as revolutionary as the twenty-first-century shift from paper to electronic books—the changeover that allows remote computer access to copious online resources.

Since the end of the twentieth century, a great number of libraries have been built in countries newly independent from the former Soviet Union and those in the Persian Gulf and East Asia—an expansion similar to one that occurred around 1900. These archetypal structures—most of them designed by well-known architects, such as OMA's new Qatar National Library in Doha (2015; fig. 7)—are supposed to demonstrate financial capability and cultural wealth.[5] This is hardly the case in debt-ridden Greece, where the prime intention is to make the library's many resources familiar to a public that has the lowest percentage of readers of any E.U. country.[6]

As they had for the opera house, at the very beginning of the project SNF board members and others on the team visited existing institutions: the New York Public Library (1911), the Library of Congress in Washington, D.C. (1897), and New York City's Queens Library (1930; replaced in 1966, expanded 1989).[7] These visits to historic buildings weren't focused on the architecture but on

8   SNFCC, NLG, entrance and book castle

their directors' opinions regarding the purpose of a library in the electronic era. The directors concurred about the importance of digital holdings and the desirability of creating more communal functions for their institutions. In Seattle, the SNF directors bypassed entirely the spectacular new central library designed by Rem Koolhaas and Joshua Prince-Ramus (OMA, 2004), preferring to call on the Bill and Melinda Gates Foundation to garner more information about its efforts through the Global Libraries program to make libraries widely appealing to a greater number of users.

So that there could be no doubt about the building's purpose, Piano designed the NLG's lobby to showcase books that are visible through the glass facade, just as the lobby balconies across the agora signal the opera house. A total of five levels with three full floors and two mezzanines, all containing bookshelves, are tucked into the constructed hill. Piano imagined the walkways at the different levels to be like scaffolding within a quarry.

To make the interior of the library more visually consonant with that of the opera house, Piano changed his original choice of glass to oak for the balcony floors, and all the stairs, including those of the grand stairway (which rises at the east side of the library's large, three-level rectangular skylit atrium). The architect's decision to make timber predominate enhanced the library's warm, welcoming environment, a major goal of the library consultants and the foundation.[8]

Visitors coming into the lobby are greeted by the imposing "book castle" (fig. 8). It is a square, hollow mega-column of books, a 65½-foot-tall structure rising the full height of the building and enclosing a performance space,

9   Gordon Bunshaft/SOM, Beinecke Rare Book
    and Manuscript Library, Yale University, New Haven,
    Connecticut

11   SNFCC, buffer zone between car park and hill

10   Colin St. John Wilson, King's Library Tower,
     British Library, London

entered at its southeast corner. The walls inside the performance area are clad in American cherry, the same wood as that of the opera house's balcony fronts. Oak bookcases wrap the entirety of the castle's exterior walls and, at its southwest and southeast corners, extend to the lobby's peripheral walls, making full-height planes of uninterrupted shelving. Openings in these two extensions of the castle at ground level provide access to the rest of the library.

The book-encased castle resembles similar arrangements in the Beinecke Rare Book and Manuscript Library at Yale University in New Haven (Gordon Bunshaft/SOM, 1963; fig. 9) and the King's Library Tower, the British Library's new space at St. Pancras in London[9] (Colin St. John Wilson, 1997; fig. 10). In Athens, in addition to enhancing the visual presence of the library, the castle fulfills an important structural function. Without this solid and stiff central volume, the library's asymmetrical arrangement of shear walls placed away from the center of the building would cause the building to twist in an earthquake, pulling it apart. The NLG is also protected from earthquakes at the sides: on the north, there is a gap (the buffer zone) between the building exterior and the slope continuing that zone behind the car park (fig. 11); on the south side of the

12 Wolfgang Tschapeller, Ho Fine Arts Library, Cornell
University, Ithaca, New York (unbuilt)

agora, a huge joint separates the two components of the SNFCC so that movement in one does not affect movement in the other.

Seismic considerations affected the design in other ways as well. Stretched
horizontally across the oak bookcases are thin wires that restrain the volumes on
each shelf. The hanging steel structures to which the walkways are for the most
part attached are connected to concrete slabs at each level. Hanging book stacks
appear in several recent library designs. In one such proposal—for the current
redesign and expansion of Cornell University's Ho Fine Arts Library in Ithaca,
New York—the Austrian architect Wolfgang Tschapeller has referred to the
contradiction inherent in weighty books and a weightless hanging bookshelf[10]
(fig. 12). This poetic interpretation applies also to the library at the SNFCC.

George Oates, of Expedition Engineering, who led the team that designed
and completed the structure, asserts that "the library was all about coordinating
the high-load walkways vertically and horizontally. The walkways and stairways
had to feel robust, but at the same time they had to be thin enough to sustain an
element of excitement."[11]

The book castle is undoubtedly an impressive defining element for the
library. But much more was needed to satisfy the master plan's goal of increasing
the number of visitors tenfold, and thereby changing the customs of the country.
The staffing and seating indicated in the master plan give an idea of the magnitude of the envisaged change: it called for 2,000 readers' seats, compared to
956 in the former library building, and 300 staff members, instead of the previous 96. Among the measures recommended by the planners to augment demand
for the library were a separate entrance for the lending library, reading rooms, a
special-events space, a theater research library, a media center, and a café.

In its effort to make the public library a community destination, the SNF
turned to a roster of advisers. A brief relationship with an American library
consultant was followed by an arrangement with the British Library in London.
In 2009, that institution was commissioned to carry out an in-depth study on

13 Clash between officers and protesters, Athens, 2011

the reorganization of the NLG in the continuing quest to render it more user-friendly; in turn, the British Library appointed Joanna Eley (b. 1945) and her colleagues at AMA Alexi Marmot Associates to study the use of space. Eley's principal contact at the British Library was Andy Stephens (b. 1956), then its head of international engagement and board secretary. Stephens, who had worked at the British Library since 1977, was familiar with the architect Colin St. John Wilson's two schemes for a new library building, first in 1962 in Blooms-bury (unbuilt), and then in 1997 at St. Pancras (realized). During the thirty-six years it took to complete the new building, Stephens had ample exposure to the pitfalls that might afflict any major new library, including the Athens enter-prise. As Sherwin Goldman had when he was a consultant for Greece's new opera house, Stephens thought of himself as a stand-in for the library's clients.[12]

In November 2009, Stephens, three of his London colleagues, and Eley went on a fact-finding mission to Athens. One month later, they submitted the first of three reports on their initial response to RPBW's design and location of func-tions. From December 2009 through March 2010, they worked with Piano and project managers Faithful+Gould to provide a final review of the revised plans and an assessment of whether the building would meet the needs of the NLG.

By the time Stephens and Joanna Eley attended a ceremony in Athens in June 2011 to mark the start of foundation excavations for the cultural center, the political climate had heated up significantly. Andy Stephens remembers that as white helium-filled balloons were released at the four corners of the future agora, smoke billowed a short distance away from fires lit by rioters protesting the government's austerity measures. Police wearing face guards were on the scene, lobbing tear gas at the demonstrators (fig. 13).

One recommendation stemmed from the British Library's own struggle to become more user-friendly. There, during the early 2000s, less restrictive registration for a reader's ticket together with expanded exhibition and retail spaces boosted attendance from 400,000 to 460,000 a year by 2005, and to more than 500,000 by 2009. Encouraged by this success, its staffers proposed that the NLG become more of a community attraction, and less a mere container of books.

The London consultants suggested adding more free space for public use on the ground floor and mezzanine, thereby reducing collection storage by 200,000 volumes. They also recommended more flexibility in the design so that the building could be fine-tuned to reflect its operations, readers' reactions, and changes in patterns of behavior that might result from combining a research library and a lending library. In addition, the consultants suggested adding functions and services such as a business center, children's gallery, local and family history facility, and scholars center; events such as concerts and poetry readings in the agora and the library's lobby; and a retail space (to be shared with the GNO). Eley recalls that she saw little of Piano during the year-and-a-half-long project, but that he sent Stephens numerous neatly handwritten comments on her three reports. The third report in particular, which would have dramatic repercussions, pointed out that many earlier proposals—notably a reconfiguration of the ground floor—had not been carried out.

No one was more aware of this oversight than the formidable Ioannis Trohopoulos (b. 1961), who became the de facto client for the library upon his appointment as CEO and managing director of the SNFCC in June 2012. Trohopoulos was made a superstar of the library world when he received a Bill and Melinda Gates Foundation Award of $1 million in 2010 for his direction (1990–2012) of the Central Public Library in his native Macedonian city of Veria. He seemed to be the perfect complement to Dracopoulos, who has stated that "education and libraries are my thing."[13] Trohopoulos was determined to replicate in Athens his twofold success in Veria: the digitization of the library's holdings and transformation of the facility into a community center. Even so, it was a daunting task to apply the lessons of a small neighborhood institution (only 6,200 square feet) in a city of fifty thousand people to the immensely larger new building in Greece's capital of over three million inhabitants.

In January 2013, a little more than seven months after Trohopoulos took office as the director of the cultural center, he gave a speech in which he articulated the center's mission and the objectives of its constituent parts. By then, the fundamental ideas about how the NLG would serve its overlapping communities had been clarified. The public library, he said,

will not just be a place for lending out books or answering queries. It will be, foremost, a place that stimulates human curiosity, that primal force that drives human creativity. The National Research Library will be a meeting place, where citizens will communicate, engage in conversation, broaden their horizons and create.[14]

Soft-spoken and mild-mannered, and with a keen sense of humor, Trohopoulos expanded the functions of the Athens library with as much fervor as scholars and writers in 2011 had opposed the addition of a circulating department at New York's flagship Forty-second Street research library. (In Athens, at the outset, there was similar opposition to adding a lending library with open shelves in the NLG, where books had traditionally been handled only by staff members.)

Early in 2013, after bluntly telling Bianchi that he had not understood the foundation's intentions, Trohopoulos and a member of the SNF staff made the astonishing announcement that they had hired Mecanoo, a Dutch architecture firm, to redesign the public spaces of the NLG. Bianchi reportedly greeted the decision "as if a stake had been driven through his heart."[15]

The idea that work by Renzo Piano—winner of a Pritzker Prize, among numerous other awards—could be corrected by anyone, let alone a far less known firm, would be surprising under any circumstances. What made it especially so is the stark disparity of styles between the two offices. Mecanoo's offbeat assemblages of different shapes, propensity for undulating forms, and use of materials that can appear decorative offer a notable contrast to RPBW's classic, transparent modernism. One of Piano's peers, Rem Koolhaas, deplored the decision as "the pits!"[16]

Trohopoulos thinks big: he describes the SNFCC as the beginning of a "new Greece, a place for the creative juices of the country."[17] He self-assuredly justified his taking on an outside architect with what he considers to be the library's "revolutionary idea for Greece, which requires innovative public spaces at the entry level, with more transparency."[18]

Francine M. J. Houben (b. 1955), one of the founders of Mecanoo, agreed with Trohopoulos, airily dismissing the RPBW design as "still about books. Libraries are no longer about books but about people."[19] Houben's spurning of books is perhaps undermined by two of Mecanoo's own library designs: the library for the Delft University of Technology (1998), Houben's alma mater, and the Library of Birmingham, United Kingdom (2013), both of which feature bound books[20] (figs. 14, 15).

My meeting in September 2013 with Houben and her personal assistant, Carmine Pereira, took place at Mecanoo's office in Delft, in a large, high-ceilinged conference room filled with sunlight within a beautiful historic building (parts of which date to the sixteenth century). Since construction was well under way in Athens, Houben could make only interior modifications to the NLG. One interesting suggestion was to lift above the floor the book wall facing the entranceway, thereby providing clear sight lines to the interior. Another was the addition of self-help desks, kiosks for food and drink (which would be allowed everywhere), increased handicapped access, and more daylight in the reading areas. Conversely, she criticized what she considered excessive, potentially damaging

14　Mecanoo, Delft University of Technology, Netherlands

15　Mecanoo, Library of Birmingham, United Kingdom

sunlight in the areas for book storage. She planned to add amenities for children: a "mess-around area," changing rooms for infants, a room for breastfeeding, plus space for baby carriages and buggies. She also called for less division between the research and public libraries.

Such a connection between zones would have necessitated numerous sound-blocking measures to protect the atrium and adjacent spaces from noise in the children's play area.[21] Houben, however, seemed indifferent to the efforts that had already been devoted to acoustic protection. She disregarded as outdated the silence traditionally maintained in libraries, citing two examples in Amsterdam, each with a piano at the entrance for the public to play.

The interior plans proposed by Mecanoo recalled the flexibility of Cedric Price's layouts in the 1960s (see p. 127, fig. 16). Several of the ideas were similar to concepts that St. John Wilson had applied to his British Library building at St. Pancras, reiterated by Eley. Among these were areas for the study of entrepreneurship, local and family history, and temporary exhibitions on the second level. At ground level were meeting areas and a "youth lab." All of these responded to Trohopoulos's vision for the NLG, and certainly the Mecanoo design for a librarian's desk encircled by visitors' benches was a friendlier entranceway than Piano's somewhat austere design (figs. 16–19).

But it was not to be. For all his savvy as a librarian, Trohopoulos was surprisingly naive about architects. The very idea of asking for more transparency and more flexibility from RPBW, for whom these are hallmarks, and most especially from a completed design, was unthinkable. Having initially greeted Houben with his usual charm, the Italian architect barely glanced at the Mecanoo proposal late in 2013 before rejecting it out of hand.

Piano is no stranger to incursions on his work. At the Centre Pompidou he was without recourse when the government hired Gae Aulenti (in 1981) and Jean-François Bodin (with Piano, in 2000) to convert his exhilarating open exhibition spaces for the permanent collection into traditional white cube galleries—

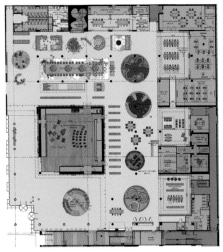

16 Mecanoo, NLG, ground level plan, proposed design

17 RPBW, NLG, initial ground level plan

18 Mecanoo, NLG entrance, proposed design

19 RPBW, NLG, initial ground level, rendering

a regrettable alteration. In 2000, the single entranceway he had designed to the museum and library was modified, and the young Paris-based firm Jakob + Mac-Farlane added Restaurant Georges, on the sixth floor, in a vocabulary unlike Piano's (fig. 20). But in Athens, the Italian architect retained the right of approval for every aspect of the SNFCC design. The foundation therefore had no choice but to accept his decision to start from scratch for the areas in question, despite the time lost and the hefty additional expenses. With Mecanoo out of the picture, Trohopoulos turned to the consultants he had worked with so successfully at Veria.

Bianchi was asked to collaborate with Dimitris Chalkiopoulos (b. 1966), a designer of books and educational interiors, who, with sociologist Irini Vokotopoulou (b. 1964), had organized Veria's children's library. Public lending librar-

20   Jakob + MacFarlane,
     Restaurant Georges, Centre
     Georges Pompidou, Paris

21   Dimitris Chalkiopoulos and
     Irini Vokotopoulou, Magic Box,
     Children's Area, Central Public
     Library, Veria, Macedonia

22   SNFCC, NLG, "magic box" children's area

ies, which began to proliferate in the eighteenth century, first included a separate children's section in 1887, a practice that soon became widespread in the United States and United Kingdom.[22] At Veria, the Magic Box children's space includes features that distinguish it visually from the rest of the library: cozy nooks for solitary pursuits and special places to sit (fig. 21), multipurpose furniture that can be continually reconfigured, and alphabet boxes to help children understand classification and other subjects. They also offer actual boxes in which materials are stored so that opening them is like "magically" discovering a treasure. In addition, the boxes are used to display books and information. Chalkiopoulos believes that "children and adults have the same need for playful, exploratory spaces."[23]

For the cultural center's library, Chalkiopoulos returned to the ideas he had implemented at Veria and at children's libraries in other Greek cities, and developed them further, adjusting interiors of specific areas to their different users. The same elements—reading nests and book exhibitions on specific themes—appear in sections pegged to different age groups, varied by color, size, and form to suit the librarygoers, from six-year-olds, whose space has now become a virtual kindergarten, to youths and adults (fig. 22).

From the outset, Bianchi had questioned what he felt was the "trendiness" of the British Library team's approach, and he had resented Mecanoo's presence as an unfair intrusion, "like two architects with incompatible vocabularies, trying one to design, the other to furnish a space."[24] He fared better with Chalkiopoulos, who articulated Trohopoulos's vision of the library as a place for social exchange and translated it into practicalities.

In September 2014, Bianchi began to redesign the interiors of the public library with Chalkiopoulos's recommendations in mind. At ground level, the public area was enlarged and made into a series of spaces more like domestic interiors than like the monastic layouts of older libraries (see p. 213). Uniform, closely aligned tables and chairs were replaced with looser arrangements of differently shaped tables interspersed with cozy groupings of upholstered couches and easy chairs. The disposition encourages relaxed conversation, and Bianchi concedes that the public library is now more user-friendly.[25] In addition to elements from Italy, Switzerland, and elsewhere, the design team ordered a great deal of costly new furniture made of a durable type of polystyrene in bright colors from a single manufacturer in Belgium, Quinze & Milan. But long waits for approval by the NLG administration held up completion of the interiors.

Chalkiopoulos feels some disappointment with the end results, specifically circulation on the ground floor (where he thinks the young children's zone is too predominant) and the limited flexibility and misplacement of some shelves and furniture. Yet he is convinced that he has made it easier for the public to understand how the spaces work with respect to their functions.

The library consultant was not the only one to effect changes in the cultural center's design. In 2015, the SNF made the lighthouse, the glass box atop the opera house that was intended by Piano to be the public library's reading/meeting room, into a multipurpose event space (see pp. 216–217). The foundation was apparently willing to sacrifice the meditative environment Piano had hoped would be produced by the glass-enclosed room's spectacular vistas and special quality of light. It will be available for hire for independent events with the possibility of catering, and a café will extend outdoors. (These changes entailed some rearrangement of the supporting areas below.) The lighthouse will no longer be managed by the library or the opera house. Together with the bookstore and eating facilities, it is under the jurisdiction of a separate government entity.

The NLG is among many new libraries that have had questions raised about their design, both conceptual and physical. Like the SNFCC, the 285,000-square-foot Dokk1 facility containing the city's main library and citizens' services in Aarhus, Denmark (Schmidt Hammer Lassen, 2014; fig. 23), is meant to revitalize the harborfront and, additionally, to connect with the city's historic centers. Private funding played an essential role for Aarhus as it did in Athens: in Aarhus, the Realdania Foundation contributed a substantial $119.3 million of the $289.8 million estimate.

But at Aarhus, in addition to input from library professionals, the library administration asked the public to participate in establishing Dokk1's programs and in studying user behavior, which resulted in a two-level space connected by a media ramp that features a lively reception area, project room, children's theater, children's lab, café, media area, picnic area, study cells, play areas, and

23   Schmidt Hammer Lassen, Dokk1, Aarhus, Denmark

24   Dokk1, view of media ramp connecting levels 1 and 2

informal open spaces[26] (fig. 24). Trohopoulos explained the absence of compa-rable citizen involvement in the Athens library by noting the lack of precedent in Greece for public participation in this kind of undertaking.[27] Nevertheless, at least one journalist writing articles in *Kathimerini English Edition*, an English-language newspaper distributed in Greece and Cyprus by the *International New York Times*, called for a public dialogue.[28] And *Chronos*, a center-left online mag-azine that shares with Greek leftists a profound suspicion of private foundations engaged in cultural projects, condemned the new library. *Chronos* called the NLG a "pseudo-library...where the authentic role of reading cedes its place to the marketable constant of amusement...and the book's educational value is being transformed into the aggressive consumerism of the ephemeral."[29]

It is likely that Filippos Tsimpoglou (b. 1956; fig. 25) was chosen as library director general—at last, in February 2014—in part to squelch such accusations. For fifteen years (1999 to 2014) he headed the University of Cyprus library; he is a member of many scholarly committees and the author of numerous scholarly publications. Furthermore, he has collaborated for five years with Jean Nouvel on a new 160,000-square-foot library for Cyprus University, whose hill-like exte-rior and interior cone bear a strong resemblance to the Mecanoo library in Delft.

The NLG's spaces dedicated to research were not subject to the multiple reconceptualizations of those for the lending library and other new public ser-vices, but they, too, changed in the course of Bianchi's redesign. On the library's third floor, Tsimpoglou doubled the size of the Manuscripts and Rare Books Department, appropriating space from the scholars' Stavros Niarchos Reading

25   Filippos Tsimpoglou

Room for a dedicated reading room and conservation and restoration laboratories, in addition to storage for the department's growing acquisitions, mostly from Greece's many private collectors. Adjustable shelves throughout were increased according to requirements, replacing display units and cupboards.

The Stavros Niarchos Reading Room at the top level remained as it was designed originally, as did other research spaces. The generous expanse, filled with sunshine pouring in from the skylights, provides the peaceful, well-lit conditions customarily associated with reading and research (see p. 231, fig. 7).

When I met with Tsimpoglou shortly after his appointment, he began by quoting an open letter to the Greek Parliament written in 1888 by the director of the National Library, Emmanuel Rhoides. A historical novelist whose *Pope Joan* (1866) was a runaway best-seller in Greece at the time of its publication, he was pleading with the government for funding. Some 120 years later, Tsimpoglou points out that he faces the same issues.[30] The latter regards his new position "not as a job, but as a mission." He accepted a significant salary cut, hoping instead for the gratification of matching the effective public library system he developed in Cyprus. Given the relatively modest remuneration and long-standing lack of prestige for the position, it is not surprising that the government took so long to hire a qualified person.

Tsimpoglou respects the lively atmosphere of the libraries created by Trohopoulos, but like Rhoides, he is concerned with practical issues. The move from the Hansen building to Piano's NLG is a particularly pressing one. In addition to 1,164,678 books, bound journals, and periodicals (thousands of which have been sitting on the floor waiting to be shelved since 2012), there are 5,066 codices containing 5,431 manuscripts and thousands of books acquired since 2009 that remain uncatalogued. No foreign-language books have been purchased for at least twelve years, and the stacks have not been cleaned for more than six years. As a member of the SNF transition team remarked, "Not knowing what the actual collections are is a major problem of the move."[31]

Another problem is restoration of the staff, which, like the opera house's, had been cut by half. Forty trained librarians are needed to operate the new NLG, along with a secondary staff of approximately fifty. In addition to adequate funding for ongoing activities (cutting the electricity to the old building was one of the state's austerity measures), the historic building must be renovated so that it can be used to complement the new facility, the two possibly linked by a shuttle bus. The question of digitization of books and manuscripts, which is central to Trohopoulos's vision, is also of concern to Tsimpoglou. So far only about 15 percent of the codices have been digitized, and the possibility of web archiving has not been fully considered.

Fourteen months after his appointment, I met with Tsimpoglou once more. He greeted me in his book-lined office by stating how difficult his first year had been: "I could cry," he said, "because of the wealth around me that I'd like the public to know—manuscripts, incunabula, about three hundred post-Byzantine codices unique to Athens, and ten thousand rare books that should be digitized for the next generation."[32]

Highlights include a ninth-century parchment manuscript that contains homilies by John Chrysostom, Archbishop of Constantinople (397-403 C.E.), and a tenth-century parchment written in the unique "bouletée" style of that period, decorated with beautiful geometric and floral motifs in blue, deep red, and brown. A thirteenth-century manuscript is the first instance in the Byzantine and Mediterranean world in which paper (bombycin) replaces parchment. Developed in the Middle East, this substance eventually made books cheaper and faster to produce and easier to disseminate (figs. 26–28). For more recent holdings, Tsimpoglou asserts that "experts on the history of books will be surprised about the number of first editions."

He continued, "The foundation has been great, giving €5 million [$5.4 million] over two years for the transition (as it did for the opera), but the state has not matched that contribution." Indeed, the government had at this time made no commitment to a budget, and the director worried about how—even whether—the salaries and operational expenses in the new building, amounting to €8.3 million annually ($9.256 million), as well as annual maintenance costs of €3.07 million ($3.43 million) will be met. Although thirty-six appointments to the library were made in October 2015 (a far cry from the recommended total staff of 300), they were all government employees whose jobs

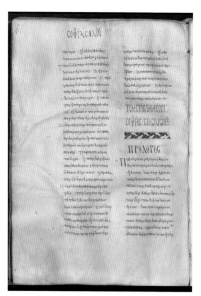

26 Ninth-century manuscript of homilies by John Chrysostom written on parchment

27 Tenth-century parchment codex

28 Thirteenth-century bombycin paper manuscript

were simply reallocated, raising questions about their qualifications for working in a library.[33]

Despite the budgetary limits, Tsimpoglou has managed to arrange for digitization of some NLG texts with the Center for the Study of New Testament Manuscripts in Plano, Texas. The contract calls for putting online three hundred thirteenth- through eighteenth-century codices. He has made similar arrangements with the Institute for Greek and Latin Languages and Literature at the Free University in Berlin for two hundred codices related to Aristotle. These projects as well as creating an "open" library with accessible stacks, digital services, book-lending services, and various forms of free assistance are all part of his agenda.

Like others at the SNFCC, Tsimpoglou regrets that the design process was so advanced by the time he was hired. He would have insisted from the outset that the rare books room be twice as large. By the same token, he feels the library staff should have been involved earlier.

Now that construction of the SNFCC has been completed, the directors of the library and the opera, Tsimpoglou and Michailidis, are fully engaged, although their tasks are quite distinct. At the GNO, an eager, existing audience awaits the inauguration of the building. At the NLG, the public may still be puzzled by the attempt to combine the neglected national research library with what is intended as a popular library open to all, an experiment that will require a major change in Greek habits. The SNF is hard at work to influence this attitude, seeking an increase to at least one thousand a day from the current seventy to one hundred visitors to the NLG, raising the annual number to three hundred thousand, and becoming a prototype for libraries throughout Greece. It is an ambitious goal, but as Dracopoulos repeatedly states, the cultural center is a herald of the social, fiscal, and humanitarian changes that must take place in Greece for the country to function in the twenty-first century. Theodore Maravelias, the SNF's chief technical officer, points out that "the library is Athens's antenna to the world."[34]

Park

Compared with the drawn-out reworking of the library interiors, the design for the 42-acre Stavros Niarchos Park, which occupies the cultural center's roofs and the surrounding land, proceeded smoothly. Starting with a rough sketch hand-drawn by Piano, New York landscape designer Deborah Nevins & Associates developed the park as an oasis of plants. Nevins (b. 1947) followed Piano's lead in discarding the conventional layout in Cooper Robertson's master plan—a round pond and occasional plantings—in favor of dense, largely Mediterranean vegetation arranged geometrically, plus several children's learning playgrounds and other imaginative amenities.

Piano's early decision to place the park on top of the cultural center raised endless questions of structure and maintenance, each one of which had to be resolved with specialists. RPBW and its Athenian counterpart, Betaplan; the Arup civil engineers; the Expedition structural engineers; and Sotirios Mavraganis, a local irrigation designer, were among those who played a part in the decision-making process. Nevins followed the advice of a trusted colleague, mechanical engineer Alistair Guthrie: "When you have many issues, solve each one separately, then put it all together."[1]

The foundation stipulated that the landscape had to be "open, flexible and free…open for easy programmatic use and closed for shade." With his usual promotional flair, Piano elaborated on the program in an early presentation to the SNF: "The park must reflect the soul of Greece—olive trees, pines, native herbs, water, and stone."[2] He also wanted to tie the park into the fabric of the city by aligning paths with adjacent streets and with walkways in the neighboring municipal sports park. He imagined that visitors would meander up the slope of the hill; at the top, they would be captivated by the light and views of Faliro Bay on one side and of the modern city and the Acropolis on the other.[3]

From his earliest works, Piano has taken landscape into account in his architectural designs—for example, the parklike garden designed by Alexandre Chemetoff (b. 1950) for Piano's adaptation of the Schlumberger company's

SNFCC, Stavros Niarchos Park, conceptual sketch

1 RPBW and Alexandre Chemetoff, garden, Pierre Schlumberger Headquarters, Paris

2 RPBW and Desvigne & Dalnoky, garden, Thomson Optronics Factory, Guyancourt, France

factories in Paris (1984; fig. 1); and the various backgrounds for the IBM traveling pavilion (1983–1986), a transparent "tunnel" installed in green spaces in urban parks, and itself reminiscent of a greenhouse, like "a temporary winter garden" (see p. 128, fig. 18). During those years, he sometimes collaborated with garden-focused firms, trained primarily in horticulture, who worked to realize his intentions. But he also began to team up with select landscape architects who participated in decisions regarding site plan and layout as well as in the choice of grading, hardscape, and woody plants. RPBW's Nasher Sculpture Center building in Dallas (2003) is an example of a landscape architect's participation in planning. Faced with three different options, Peter Walker urged the solution that was adopted—placing the structure parallel to Flora Street, so that the center's extraordinary collection, both inside and in the garden beyond, is visible from the street.[4]

In the 1980s and 1990s, Piano executed a series of projects with several of the top French landscape designers: Chemetoff, Michel Courajoud (1937–2014), and the partnership of Michel Desvigne (b. 1958) and Christine Dalnoky (b. 1956), who represented a renaissance in French landscape practice that began in the 1980s. All are associated with the École Nationale Supérieure du Paysage at Versailles, and all have studied with Courajoud. RPBW still works with Desvigne, who, like Bianchi, began his career making sketches in Piano's offices.

The participatory association with Desvigne & Dalnoky (which was formed in 1988 and dissolved in 2002) was operative for the Thomson Optronics Factory in Guyancourt, near Paris (1990; fig. 2), and with Courajoud for the Cité

3   RPBW and Michel Courajoud, Cité Internationale, Lyon, France

4   RPBW and SWA Group, California Academy of Sciences, San Francisco

Internationale redevelopment project in Lyon (2006; fig. 3). Piano and Nevins enjoyed a similarly structured collaboration in Athens. For the Thomson Factory, as for the SNFCC, there was little significant landscape context to take into account, so the designers had considerable latitude in developing a scheme.

The landscaping in Guyancourt began, as it would in Athens, with extensive preparation for drainage (since there was no sewage system). Parallel water channels, the bottoms of which were lined with tiles shaped similarly to those on the RPBW building, alternated with rows of trees and parking and emptied into a pool. One of the most interesting aspects of the project was the anticipated takeover of the 50-acre site by the park, which was expected to outlive the optronics factory. In Desvigne & Dalnoky's landscape, the natural life-cycle of plants became the park's system of construction.[5]

Among RPBW's recent landscape partnerships, a more limited mode of collaboration was its work with the SWA Group on the design of the California Academy of Sciences' new headquarters and museum building (2008; fig. 4), in San Francisco's Golden Gate Park. The SWA Group, a large international landscape architecture and urban design firm, created a landscape around the

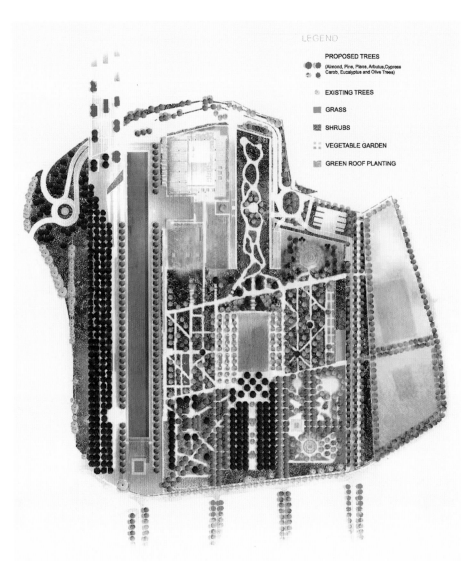

5   Deborah Nevins & Associates, Stavros Niarchos Park, plan

building, but the firm's work on the 2½-acre "living roof" was limited to exe-
cuting the Italian architect's design. The self-sustaining planted roof (created in
consultation with Rana Creek Design), which creates the illusion of the building being completely enveloped within a natural landscape, played an important
part in the project's bid for LEED Platinum certification. The added insulation
provided by the roof's vegetation decreases heating and cooling loads, thereby
saving energy. In both the California project and the SNFCC, nature is lifted up
and sits atop the building.

The garden for the SNFCC offers a new type of open area to serve the surrounding middle-class residential area of Athens (fig. 5). Imported models have
always played an important role in the capital city, since urban parks as they are

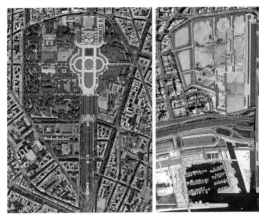

7   Comparison between Jardin du Luxembourg, Paris, and Stavros Niarchos Park

6   National Garden, Athens

known today did not exist in ancient Greece, and in modern Greece there is little or no tradition of professional landscape architecture or even professional garden design.[6] The park differs even more radically than the agora from Syntagma Square, the city's most well-known public space. Together with the agora, the park could well offer an alternative arena for communal expression.

One of the few local gardens is the 38-acre National Garden, founded in 1840 by Queen Amalia (fig. 6). Next to the former royal palace and almost abutting the crowded, touristy Syntagma Square, the National Garden offers a refuge of nature in the center of the city.[7] However, the plantings don't accurately represent the local flora (of the more than 500 species, only about 100 are from Greece); and until a 2015 proposal by a private foundation for renovating the park's pathways, lighting, and drainage is carried out (at the end of 2016, it still awaited government approval), the garden will remain underused and poorly maintained.

The international green spaces studied by RPBW were Millennium Park in Chicago (2004), the Tuileries in Paris, and especially the 55-acre Jardin du Luxembourg (fig. 7), also in Paris, which is closest in scale to the Athens park.[8] Although Nevins insists that the Jardin du Luxembourg served only as a model for how parks are used, it is in fact a good design precedent for the SNFCC garden in its combination of characteristically Italian, French, and English forms. Bianchi told me, "The cultural center's park is more of a garden than a park."[9] In this chapter, I use the two designations—park and garden—interchangeably.

Nevins's role in Athens was not limited to planting out Piano's scheme, his sketch for which simply indicated the park's spatial direction—a dramatic axial movement toward the sea. Rather, she participated in the overall organization of the site, the conceptualization of a Mediterranean park, the movement of people through the park, the intricate grading that would facilitate such movement, and the provision of vistas, framing, and the occasional surprise.

Like architecture, landscape has become increasingly interdisciplinary. Data such as the amount of rainfall, wind speed and direction, aquifer depth, and soil temperatures, some of which have been tracked over decades, together with specialized input from civil and structural engineers, architects, and irrigation experts, are used to guide the design. Landscape urbanist James Corner (who participated in the design of Manhattan's remarkably successful High Line Park, 2009) considers the urban condition itself to be an aspect of ecology, adding political, social, economic, and demographic factors to the usual ecologies of water, air, and vegetation.[10]

Despite the limited landscape tradition in Athens, Nevins discovered one particularly important local precedent: a walkway spiraling through a simple planting of olive trees (*Olea europaea*), oaks (*Quercus*), and cypress (*Cupressus sempervirens*) between the Acropolis and Philopappos Hill (fig. 8). A rare exception to the city's mainly urban recreational spaces, this enchanting parkscape was created between 1954 and 1958 by Dimitris Pikionis (1887–1968), a highly original architect who believed in the interdependence of culture and nature. Also part of the project was his renovation of a church and construction of a neighboring pavilion. Together, buildings and park form a monastery-like enclosure intended to be a place of repose away from the bustle of the city.[11]

Pikionis's design process was largely improvisatory, and to pave the wide footpaths, he placed—apparently at random amid irregular bands of concrete— diversely shaped fragments of marble and clay recovered from nineteenth-century Athens.[12] The whole harmonizes mysteriously with the Parthenon, where the path peaks.

Efforts to protect the world's crop biodiversity are increasingly common. Crop Trust, an organization based in Germany, maintains one of the most ambitious: the Svalbard Global Seed Vault, buried in a permafrost mountain on a remote island in the Arctic Circle, has the capacity to store 500 seeds from each of 4.5 million varieties of crops (i.e., a maximum of 2.25 billion seeds). The vault is intended to safeguard samples even in case of the worst natural or man-made catastrophe. As of 2016, it holds seeds from almost every country in the world, more than 860,000 types.

8   Dimitris Pikionis, Acropolis park walkway, Athens

Nevins's approach to planting the SNFCC park resonates with Pikionis's principles. She committed "to being philosophically true to the region, using the silvery, drought-tolerant plants that speak of the Mediterranean."[13] The use of such plant materials is particularly important, since Greece, in converting arable land to agriculture and more recently developing the country's recreational potential, has eliminated or at least endangered many native species. The Stavros Niarchos Park's great lawn is the one exception to the use of indigenous planting, adopted to provide an open space that would be cooler than pavement for public activities, and more practical for storm drainage. Nevins explains: "I see the plant palette as a pendant to the library collection. The National Library is a resource for all and a repository of Greek and Mediterranean culture. I see the park as a repository of the botanical culture of the region."[14]

This attitude harmonizes with the local cultural context, as the scientific study of plants originated in Greek-speaking Ionian cities at the end of the fourth century B.C.E. It also reflects the urgency of preserving the country's endangered vegetation. Other contemporary organizations in Greece, such as the Peliti Seed Bank (named after the Greek word for "oak tree") and Organization Earth, are beginning to collect and disseminate the seeds of such threatened species.[15] The SNFCC landscape designers are likewise creating a seed bank that will provide broader knowledge about local plant material and its propagation, which it is hoped will increase public interest in the park. Nevins says that, through an arrangement with Dr. Eirini Vallianatou, a plant taxonomist and sociologist in charge of the Diomedes Botanic Garden at the University of Athens, "We are introducing little-known Greek species, that are being used in a public place there for the first time."

Among the focal elements in Nevins's design are a Mediterranean garden, a splash pool/amphitheater (which accommodates performances when it is drained), a labyrinth, the great lawn, nine children's playgrounds, and a stairway

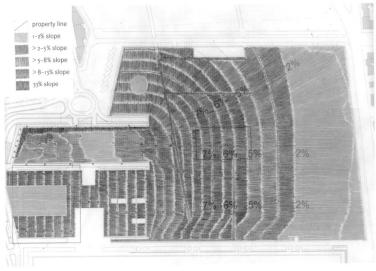

property line
1–2% slope
> 2–5% slope
> 5–8% slope
> 8–13% slope
33% slope

9   Deborah Nevins & Associates, SNFCC, park grading, diagram

that provides access to the canal from the esplanade, with treads that can serve as seating (see p. 63, fig. 26). She also built up the esplanade into a gentle slope rising toward the sea and landscaped it with deference to the protected views of the Parthenon.

The design includes several entrances along the park's edges. Straight paths and diagonals that are more manageable for visitors with special needs are at an incline that is usually only 5 percent and never more than 8 percent (fig. 9). However, this configuration posed formidable grading problems—every diagonal path had to meet paths on the same level—and also required an accessible design that was both practical and aesthetically pleasing. For the pavement, Nevins stipulated a locally sourced mix of natural ingredients called Prolat, which includes ground ceramic tile and other materials. The result is an unbound, rustic-looking substance that is loose enough for water to pass through but not so loose that it erodes.

She wanted the plantings on the library's roof to look like a Greek hillside, with typical grasses and a mix of Mediterranean plants. Among the landscape designer's long-standing convictions is her opposition to the fashion for non-native plants that she sees in flower shops and garden centers all over Athens, among them chrysanthemums (*Dendranthema x morifolium*) and roses (*Rosa*): their year-round color is foreign to the local flora, which bloom only once annually. Her aversion to this vogue recalls that of Irish gardener and journalist William Robinson (1838–1935) to the Victorian era's garish colors and rigid, repetitive designs. His own garden, Gravetye Manor in Sussex, exemplifies the

10   William Robinson, Gravetye Manor, Sussex, United Kingdom

more naturalistic plantings he favored, with formal parterres next to the house transitioning to wilder areas in the outlying countryside (fig. 10).

Nevins has been similarly influenced by Jens Jensen (1860–1951), a Danish immigrant to the United States who founded the Friends of Our Native Landscape in 1913. A strong proponent of the Prairie style, Jensen led the movement in the Midwest to use native plants in garden design. Also of interest to Nevins is Jensen's repeated use of circular stone benches with fire pits at their center, which he called council rings (similar to the open plazas where the Pueblo tribe held council fires). Many of Jensen's numerous parks included open green spaces for the performing arts, just as the cultural center's great lawn does.[16]

The landscape designer traces her own interest in plants to her childhood visits to the Brooklyn Botanic Garden and to her mother's interest in wildflowers. She graduated from Boston University in 1968, where she attended classes with Elisabeth Blair MacDougall (1925–2003), who helped make landscape history an academic discipline as a teacher from the 1960s through the 1980s and as director of the program of Garden and Landscape Studies at Dumbarton Oaks from 1972 to 1988. Nevins's studies in the history of medieval and modern architecture at Columbia University have continued to influence her work and viewpoint. She has organized and contributed to exhibition catalogues such as *200 Years of American Architectural Drawing* (with David Gebhard) in 1977, and she was among the first to rediscover the work of noteworthy female landscape architects such as Gertrude Jekyll (1843–1932) and Beatrix Jones Farrand (1872–1959).[17]

While still at Columbia, Nevins began to try her hand at horticulture. She worked one of about fifty tiny garden allotments set aside by the city on the west side of Broadway and West Ninety-sixth Street in Manhattan, on the site of two demolished Beaux-Arts theaters. To improve the rubble earth there, she periodically drove her small Honda to Central Park's stables to collect manure.

Of the people at Columbia during that time, Nevins says, "No one was interested in landscape history; I had to teach myself."[18] She was soon teaching

11 Deborah Nevins & Associates,
    private estate, Dominican
    Republic

12 Deborah Nevins & Associates, farm,
    midwestern United States

others: she offered survey courses at Barnard College and at the Cooper-Hewitt Museum, where her talks so impressed Sandra Brant, former publisher of *Art in America, Interview,* and *Antiques* magazines, that she gave Nevins her first important commission: adding perennial borders and trees to a Connecticut garden for which the great landscape designer Russell Page designed but did not finish the master plan. She founded her firm, Deborah Nevins & Associates, in 1990.

Much of Nevins's work has centered around private gardens for the wealthy and famous, generally in collaboration with such prominent architects as Thomas Beeby, Annabelle Selldorf, and Robert A. M. Stern. These designers work in a relatively restrained, conservative style, as indeed does Nevins. Her projects include a house in the Dominican Republic (1993), a farm in the Midwest (2006), a private park for a Beverly Hills residence (2007), and a garden for Margot and Thomas Pritzker's vacation home (2010) in Aspen, Colorado (figs. 11–14). It was in the course of her work as landscape consultant for the Colorado house that she first encountered Piano and Bianchi. That large single-story residence is the only private house Piano has designed.

Nevins was an unexpected choice for creating a public park, given her previous concentration on luxurious private gardens. And the master planners had, in fact, recommended more widely known practitioners such as Laurie Olin, Peter Walker, Alain Provost, and Kathryn Gustafson. But because of their successful working relationship in Colorado, Piano selected Nevins for the Athens project. She, in turn, chose Helli Pangalou, an independent practitioner, as her Athens associate. Though firm in her demeanor, Nevins never questions Piano's lead.

13   Deborah Nevins & Associates, private park, Beverly Hills

14   Deborah Nevins & Associates, garden of Margot and Thomas Pritzker residence, Aspen

The SNFCC is the biggest job that Nevins has had to date.[19] Working in an unfamiliar region, she has faced a variety of new challenges. Among these are climatic extremes: between June and September, the temperature often climbs higher than 90 degrees Fahrenheit; there is little rain between April and September; and in the winter, heavy downpours produce violent flash floods (fig. 15).

The region's unforgiving sunshine and heat during the summer would seem to make it a hostile environment for plants, when in fact the Mediterranean Basin—a mere 2.2 percent of the earth's land mass—contains 20 percent of the world's flora (25,000 plant species).[20] Olivier Filippi, author of *The Dry Gardening Handbook* (originally published in French, and focused primarily on gardening in southern Europe), describes in captivating detail how drought-resistant plants survive. To escape dry conditions, he writes, annuals and bulbous plants "disappear when the going gets tough": annuals die in the summer and bulbs remain hidden underground.[21] This book is a bible of sorts for those interested in the subject.

Despite the insistence of Filippi and other enthusiasts of dry gardens that watering is unnecessary, Nevins followed the usual procedures of irrigation, although in this case the efforts were directed at starting plant growth rather than at regular maintenance; in case of drought, the drip method will direct water specifically to the roots. She was aided by Simon Delves (b. 1974), a civil engineer at Arup, who prepared the site for utilities, irrigation, drainage, grading, structural paving, and the canal. Delves is a specialist in water infrastructure and flood risk management and has overseen projects in many areas of the world, from Tanzania and Qatar to the United Kingdom.

Delves explained to me that the main problem in the park was the absence of a steady and reliable source of water; like great gardens throughout history— Hadrian's Villa, for example—a feat of hydraulic engineering was required. The local potable water supply (the only one made available to the site by the city) was insufficient, and in any case the government considered it unacceptable

15   Flash flood, Athens, February 22, 2013

for the SNFCC to draw from this supply for irrigation. Nor was it acceptable to use the citywide treated sewage effluent system, which was already operating at full capacity. Gray water from the opera house is recycled for the toilets, leaving a limited supply for the park. And despite the sometimes heavy winter rainstorms, the usually sparse and infrequent rainfall ruled out storing enough water from precipitation in holding tanks, which would have had to be huge.[22]

Consequently, the engineers decided to use aquifer water (groundwater) channeled up through boreholes—as if from a well—as the main source of irrigation, and to recharge the aquifer by infiltrating storm water throughout the park (via gravel infiltration trenches and geocellular attenuation tanks). However, the groundwater is too salty to use for plants, so it must first pass through a reverse osmosis (desalinization) plant located in a small maintenance pavilion at the western side of the park. To build resilience into the watering system, and to provide water during the hottest summer months, a second source of irrigation water is furnished by the canal, its saline water pumped to a second, specialized part of the desalinization plant before it is used for irrigation. Reverse osmosis produces a brine waste that can be discharged into the canal where it is diluted before being released into Faliro Bay. While it is recognized that desalinization is expensive and usually an irrigation method of last resort, it was the most appropriate option for the SNFCC.

The landscape designers have made other commendable efforts to respond to the environment and the climate. Water is conserved by employing drip irrigation, a low-pressure, low-volume watering system. Gravel mulch keeps roots cooler, reduces evaporation in summer, and discourages the germination of weeds. Storm water is directed to concrete channels running along the paths and to the splash pool, then through pipes to the underground soakaway system, which slowly releases it to help recharge the aquifer.

The canal's 460,000 cubic feet of water offers not only a back-up source of irrigation in exceptionally dry conditions but also an area for runoff in case

16   Robert Irwin, Central Garden, Getty Center, Los Angeles

of flooding. Water is pumped from the bay into the northern part of the canal, streams the length of the channel, and is then returned to the bay. Delves recalls that Piano wanted the waterway to look like a canal, not a swimming pool; he was therefore comfortable with some natural discoloration.

Even after solving the essential issue of a water supply sufficient in volume and quality for irrigation, Nevins had to deal with the problem of soil, since the hill was built of components unsuitable for plant growth. The site conditions (see "Structure" chapter) required careful preparation for successful planting: a soil mixture of base loam (topsoil of various depths), sand, and compost. The soil for the great lawn is a special mix, consisting of the same components in different proportions; the substrate on the roofs is a lighter-weight mixture.

The complex readying of the SNFCC site invites comparison with the equally intricate development of the Los Angeles site of the Getty Center (1997). Both properties are hills overlooking a seascape, and both required cutting away, relocating, and stabilizing an enormous amount of terrain.[23] In contrast with the SNFCC, for which the hill was constructed artificially, the Getty's natural mount was evened out to accommodate various buildings and hollowed out to make a 3-acre area for a garden designed by the artist Robert Irwin (fig. 16).

One of the dominant features of the Athens garden is a prevalence of trees, particularly olive (*Olea europaea*) and carob trees (*Ceratonia siliqua*), Oriental plane trees (*Platanus orientalis*), cypress (*Cupressus sempervirens*), pomegranate (*Punica granatum 'Ermioni'*), bitter orange (*Citrus x aurantium*), flowering almond (*Prunus dulcis*), umbrella pine (*Pinus pinea*), redbud (*Cercis siliquastrum*), and kermes oak (*Quercus coccifera*). Nevins was inspired by the Greek landscape, which has been characterized by olive trees, fig trees (*Ficus carica 'Kalamata'*), and grapevines (*Vitis*) since early classical antiquity, as well as by the iconic role of trees in villages in ancient Greece, in the Far East, and in England, France, and Italy, where centrally placed "sacred" trees evoke a feeling of perpetuity. Not only were certain trees considered sacred in ancient Greece, but the olive tree was

17   Van den Berk Nursery, Eindhoven, Netherlands

consecrated to Athena. Another source of inspiration was Italo Calvino's novel *The Baron in the Trees*, which tells the fantastic story of an Italian nobleman who, as a child, decides to live his life perched in the branches, refusing ever to return to earth, and finding various ways to adapt to such a life.

Nevins observes that arbors are missing from Athens's few parks and says, "People love to be under trees that provide shelter and a feeling of rootedness, besides being a point of attraction."[24] In the SNFCC park, the garden designers have positioned the trees, as is common in landscape plans, to mark the terminals of paths, but without blocking the view behind them. Bowing to the cultural importance given to olive trees, Nevins uses them as focal points (see pp. 39 and 112). Throughout, insets in the pathways for benches—including a seating area with chess tables—will benefit from the small shadows cast by the olive trees in the park, but these may never grow tall enough to screen a standing adult from the sun.

All the plants chosen for the park are typical of Greece; they are low maintenance, being drought-tolerant and wind-resistant to ensure against damage by the prevailing gusts at the park's crest. But acquiring the 1,400 trees and approximately 310,000 shrubs and perennials was no mean task. The massive amount of plant material required meant that trees had to be collected as early as 2012, as soon as the contractors had been chosen, even though construction of the SNFCC precluded planting the first trees until 2014. By 2013, Nevins was traveling to Europe to locate and acquire material nine or ten times a year rather than the two or three times a year she had come to Greece during the design process. Because tree species cultivated in Attica are frequently more attractive elsewhere, the search took her to Italy, the Netherlands, Spain, and Portugal, in addition to Greece.

In general, Nevins prefers to import mature tree specimens from abroad, which is also where she finds trees with a more natural appearance. Almond trees in Greece are trained so radically that Nevins feels they "look like lollipops";[25]

18   André Le Nôtre, Tuileries, Paris, engraving by Gabriel Perrelle, 1680

olive trees were easily acquired in Greece (she purchased as many as 110 in two days, a number of which were at least one hundred years old), but they must be drastically cut back to facilitate transportation. Nevins describes her procedure as "almost like looking at sculpture." The town of Grosseto in Tuscany is particularly rich in nurseries containing what she is looking for: trees that are free of worms, disease, ground branching, and too many stubs.

However, her favorite nursery is Van den Berk in Eindhoven, the Netherlands, whose owners run a vast operation that, like most Dutch and German nurseries, supplies thousands of trees as far afield as Moscow and Uzbekistan (fig. 17). Because Greece and the Netherlands are located in the same horticultural zone, transporting plants from one to the other presents no problem. In the impressive loading yard of the Dutch facility, a huge crane is used to hoist trees and load them onto a flatbed truck for shipment through Germany and Austria and down through Bulgaria to reach Greece—admittedly a non-green procedure.

It was at Van den Berk's that the designer found a source for Oriental plane trees. Nevins uses them throughout the park, planted at fairly standard 26-foot intervals, to provide shade. In addition, a double allée along the western side of the esplanade will shelter events such as a farmers market. The allées and parterres share a scale and typology with André Le Nôtre's 1671 design for the Tuileries Garden (fig. 18). Niarchos would have loved the regal effect.

The trees that were selected for the park were held in a facility in Viotia, about 70 miles northwest of Athens, because of its cooler climate. The root balls were enveloped using the Air-Pot system, which consists of a plastic container

19 Trees in Air-Pot containers

20 Jean-Claude Nicolas Forestier, Jardines del Teatro Griego, Montjuïc, Barcelona

with tiny perforations; the apparatus allows air to penetrate and prevents the roots from growing around themselves, a condition known as girdling (fig. 19). This hydroponic system facilitates tree maintenance and transportation and allows small roots to grow, which helps with transplanting. After the Air-Pot is removed, the root ball re-forms and is held in place by thin-gauge metal mesh.

When I visited the site of the cultural complex in April 2015, almost all the trees and more than half the shrubs had been planted. I entered through the main entrance at the northeast corner and proceeded with Nevins and Panga-lou down one of many allées of olive trees. The olive trees, bordered by densely planted lavender (*Lavandula*), extend to the Mediterranean Garden at the east, and are surrounded by plants that were selected for their scent and texture rather than year-round blooming: spurge (*Euphorbia*), wormwood (*Artemisia*), sage (*Salvia*), rockrose (*Cistus*), mastic (*Pistacia lentiscus*), and boxwood (*Buxus*). A vast array of species contributed to various color themes. The air was fragrant with sage, oregano (*Origanum*), thyme (*Thymus*), lavender, and rosemary (*Rosmarinus*). The sound of falling water from the splash pool in the northwest corner of the park contributes to the sensory experience. This is clearly one of the parkscape's apogees, each season offering a new bloom: in winter, bulbs, Jet Trail quince (*Chaenomeles x superba 'Jet Trail'*), and pineapple sage (*Salvia elegans*), for example; in early summer, other sages; in mid-summer, gaura (*Gaura lindheimeri*), blue spire Russian sage (*Perovskia 'blue spire'*), and chaste tree (*Vitex agnus-castus*); and in late summer, Western Hills California fuchsia (*Epilobium canum 'Western Hills'*).

21   OAB, Barcelona Botanical Garden

The adaptation of native plants into a formal European idiom recalls the extensive use of color and fragrance in the works of Jean-Claude Nicolas Forestier (1861–1930), a French garden and urban designer as well as park manager whose books (among them *Gardens: A Notebook of Plans and Sketches* and *Grandes Villes et Systèmes de Parcs*) had considerable influence on landscape design. Forestier worked internationally as far afield as Casablanca, Havana, and Buenos Aires, even serving as a planning consultant for the city of New York, and set a precedent for the importation of foreign landscapes. His projects for Andalusia, Catalonia, and southern France distilled the essence of the Mediterranean, which he called the "climate friendly to the orange blossom"[26] (fig. 20).

The Stavros Niarchos Park also forms an interesting contrast with the Barcelona Botanical Garden (1999) designed by OAB's Carlos Ferrater, Bet Figueras, and Josep Lluís Canosa (fig. 21). The multidisciplinary team superimposed a triangular grid over the 34-acre site, located in Montjuïc Park, and sowed plants from five regions around the world having Mediterranean climates. This garden shares Nevins's intentions to conserve, document, and promote the region's natural heritage; unlike the SNFCC park, however, it is designed in a wholly modern idiom.

The Mediterranean Garden in Athens culminates in a wide stairway that climbs southward to the library's green roof, extending the main north–south path where large slabs of gray stone cover a metal rainwater drainage canal. To reach the library roof, the walkway bridges the 36-foot-wide void that acts as a buffer zone separating the cultural center from the hill if an earthquake or a landslide were to cause a cave-in. The landscape covering the roofs of the bridge, library, and garage posed tricky problems, including how much soil could be loaded, where the engineers would allow trees to be planted, and how the areas would be irrigated and drained. The large green roofs absorb water (unlike hardscape roofs), and a system of drainage components and filter sheets allows proper runoff and prevents roots from penetrating the substructure; at the edges, the sheet is integrated with a parapet and waterproofing so that water does not seep

22   SNFCC, grasses and a poppy on NLG roof

23   Sanctuary of Apollo Pythios, Argos

below the protection materials onto the roof itself or rise up over the roof in extreme weather.

For the library roof, the narrow area above the buffer zone, and the south end of the park, Nevins again used, among other plants, mastic, thyme, rosemary, and lavender. Grasses on the library roof move with the wind and reflect weather changes. Poppies (*Papaver rhoeas*) and spring bulbs also adorn the roof, intensifying the local identity of the planting program (fig. 22). These grasses, bulbs, and wildflowers, mixed in some areas with shrubs and perennials like phlomis (*Phlomis*), form a continuous fabric, although the substrates are all different. They also demonstrate how native plants can be used on a large scale. As many as 165,000 plugs of grasses propagated by local nurseries from seeds collected by the Diomedes Botanic Garden were planted by hand in the library roof's thin layer of soil (like the edges of the opera house roof, only 5 inches deep to keep the weight light), as were wildflower seeds, all irrigated by low-volume spray heads. Large-scale roof gardens are part of an increasingly common trend: Chicago's Millennium Park (2004) and the nearby Maggie Daley Park (2015) are both built over a subterranean parking structure.

The vast area on top of the opera house is a terrace devoted primarily to strolling and seating, with only the perimeter planted with perennials such as various species of rosemary and trailing rosemary, and hanging vines of winter jasmine and English ivy. The entire outdoor area (accessible from ground level via two dedicated scenic elevators and a glass-protected passageway on the terrace) and the enclosed lighthouse offer spectacular panoramic views of Athens, including the Acropolis, the surrounding mountains, and the sea. In another historical recall, the broad concrete stairs with marble curbs at both sides of the opera house roof can be used for seating, just as the monumental processional steps of ancient Greek sanctuaries once were[27] (fig. 23).

The sloping roof slab of the two-level, 1,000-car garage is different again (like the buffer zone cover, its soil is in parts nearly a foot and a half deep). Its

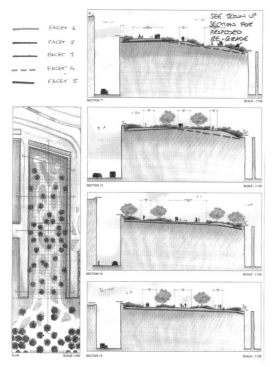

25 Expedition Engineering, garage's faceted roof slabs, diagram

24 Expedition Engineering, SNFCC, garage's faceted roof, diagram

26 Parking garage with roof garden

meandering pathways (the only ones that break the linearity of the walkways elsewhere) bring visitors to the park's highest place, the viewpoint at its southern edge. The shorter plants here are especially wind-tolerant: lavender, oregano, myrtle, rockrose, and even olive trees.

To acknowledge the city's natural surroundings, the opera house beside it at the east, and the architects' wish for a curved roof, the structural engineers shaped the garage roof like a faceted stone (figs. 24–26). Figuring that "air is cheaper than fill," this design balanced the cost of constructing the structure with the cost of the fill, limiting the maximum depth and landscaping above the slab.[28] "I would have liked more trees in the park," Nevins said, "but we couldn't afford much weight on the rooftops."

West of the Mediterranean Garden is the great lawn, intended by the SNF to be the conceptual and literal center of the park. This vibrant gathering place can host a variety of activities, including film projections, concerts, and performance art. If the celebratory event staged in June 2015 can be taken as an indication of future success, it should be noted that thirty-five thousand people in three days attended an installation of nine videos by Robert Storr, then dean of the Yale University School of Art, plus jazz concerts by the Wayne Escoffery Quartet (see pp. 222–223). The lawn is planted with drought-tolerant turf (Platinum TE Paspalum). Because the non-indigenous lawn is particularly vulnerable, drip irrigation is supplemented by overhead spray rotors.

The playgrounds, labyrinth, and splash pool are located in what Nevins calls the "western walks." Marble cobblestones, their tops roughened by deep chisel marks (again, to recall the quarry theme), define the labyrinth's narrow walkways. The circular maze, intended by Nevins as "a meditation tool" (like Pikionis's monastery-like church and pavilion near the Acropolis), is bordered by olive trees (fig. 27).

To the north of the labyrinth are the splash pool and the playgrounds, both shielded from the sun by plane trees. Also in this northern part of the park is a dense pine grove. The visitors center at the north end of the canal was originally intended to house a permanent exhibition of archaeological finds from the site; instead, in 2015 it was made into the main reception area and café, replacing a visitors center on the esplanade. The archaeological artifacts were, in mid-2016, entrusted to the Inspectorate of Antiquities, and most of the 1,500 skeletons, at least temporarily, to the American School of Classical Studies in Athens.[29]

When I expressed surprise at the design's classicism, Nevins cited archetypal agricultural forms: hedgerows and groves. She called my attention to the ordered grids of Greek orchards, where pistachio and pomegranate trees are planted in

There are nine playgrounds in the SNFCC park. Highlights of the play equipment for the larger play areas are the Balance Blocks and the Jumping Discs, both made by Richter Spielgeräte. The smaller play areas feature wooden animals, slides, and, at one site, equipment that responds to its use with music. All are suitable for children four years and older. The surface of both small and large playgrounds consists of either sand or wood chips, which minimize skidding as well as the accumulation of broken glass and other detritus.

27   SNFCC, labyrinth

28   Pomegranate trees, Greece

straight, parallel rows[30] (fig. 28). In my opinion, more relevant is the neoclassicism of early-nineteenth-century urban plans for modern Athens, which established the rectangular grid to which the park's paths relate (see "Athens" chapter).

In 2013 Joseph Volpe, former director of the Metropolitan Opera, told me he was convinced that the park "would play as big a role as the opera house or the library in the evolution the cultural center could bring about."[31] Certainly, the children's playgrounds will help support the foundation's determination that the facility be welcoming to all. Nevins's designs respond to the limited number of high-quality play areas in the United States. Since the mid-twentieth century, a number of distinguished artists, architects, and landscape architects—including Isamu Noguchi, Louis Kahn, and M. Paul Friedberg—have created interesting playground spaces with aesthetically pleasing equipment, but too few of them have received the attention they deserve (figs. 29, 30).

European playgrounds are generally more fanciful and better integrated with their neighborhoods than their United States counterparts.[32] Nevins contacted a German company, Richter Spielgeräte, which has had success with playgrounds around the world. The company was founded in Germany at the end of World

29   Isamu Noguchi, Noguchi Playscape, Piedmont Park, Atlanta

30   M. Paul Friedberg, Buchanan School Playground, Washington, D.C.

War II, when there was no place for children to play. Instead of the endlessly replicated plastic and metal equipment found in U.S. recreation grounds, Richter's head designer, Peter Heuken (b. 1965), uses solid, unpainted wood (much of which comes from the company's own black locust forest in Hungary), which ages gracefully over time. The fact that Richter equipment is more expensive than other brands has not deterred its many clients. Each piece is custom-made, and an engineer's three-dimensional model is mocked up before the life-size version is built.

The Richter concept owes much to the adventure playground, which was introduced in 1931 by Carl Theodor Sørensen, a Danish landscape designer. His "junkyard playground," consisting of an empty lot with arrays of wood, bricks, and other found materials replacing the traditional static equipment in an asphalt-covered playground, fostered creative activities in a newly built housing development in Emdrup, outside Copenhagen, in 1943.[33] The notion eventually spread globally, as, for example, in a playground in St. John's Wood, London[34] (fig. 31). The common purpose of these play areas is to let young people—as young as two and as old as twenty—handle materials as they wish in a free setting and encourage them to explore and create.[35]

31 Carl Theodor Sørensen, St. John's Wood Adventure Playground, London

32 Aldo van Eyck, Vondelpark playground, Amsterdam

From 1947 to 1978, Dutch architect Aldo van Eyck designed and constructed more than 700 such open places throughout Amsterdam, as well as equipment for them, including slides and igloo-shaped jungle gyms; in all these spaces, children adapted incidental elements to their own needs[36] (fig. 32). However, the wide geographical distribution of this network in the city of Amsterdam exacerbated the playgrounds' vulnerability to poor maintenance, loss of equipment, and infrequent replacement; today only seventeen of van Eyck's recreation areas remain intact—a cautionary tale for the SNFCC playgrounds.[37]

After much of the planting was in place, Dracopoulos decided to add athletic facilities at the western edge of the park on the advice of Dr. Panagiotis Koulouvaris, an orthopedic surgeon and an elite athlete, together with Giannis Psarelis, a triathlon expert.[38] Two running tracks (one 985 feet long with four lanes, the other 656 feet long with six lanes) were added, together with a bicycle path and exercise equipment, and lighting was installed for nighttime use. Such changes so late in the game can necessitate a considerable effort. This was indeed the case for the cultural center, with redesign in this part of the park that included reworking the grading, irrigation, and walking and driving paths, and removing fifty-eight trees, as well as some shrubs and perennials.

In making these additions, the foundation's director may have been responding to a trend that began in European and American parks from around 1900 through the 1930s, one that favored active recreation over the scenic design characteristic of earlier, large pleasure gardens such as New York's Central Park. More recently, multiple activities, including sports, were offered in Bernard Tschumi's competition-winning scheme for the 125-acre Parc de la Villette in Paris (1998; fig. 33). Program-centered innovations have become expected elements of public parks, even central parts of the design concept in several high-profile instances.

But this is not the case in the 42-acre Greek garden, where the largest area is devoted to lush, spectacularly beautiful vegetation. Nevertheless, the areas

33 Bernard Tschumi Architects, Parc de la Villette, Paris

34 Alain Provost, Parc André Citroën, Paris

that include attractions such as playgrounds, installations, and performances, in addition to panoramic views, acknowledge the contemporary need for something more than aesthetics in a public venue of this sort.

Sustainability and ecological performance are a current focus in the design of large urban parks.[39] In her plan for the Stavros Niarchos Park, Nevins has been mindful of its cultural sustainability as well as its environmental sensitivity: the garden fosters community and a sense of cultural identity, offers social interaction, provides work, and is open to all. In the final analysis, the park's popularity will be the best indicator of its social and ecological contributions.

Like several recently created public parks in Europe and the United States, the SNFCC park, working in tandem with the architecture, also improves the urban environment. This has been accomplished by other, less formally designed parks that occupy obsolete industrial zones. The Parc de la Villette and Parc André Citroën in Paris; the nearly 570-acre Duisburg-Nord Landscape Park in Duisburg, Germany (Latz + Partner, 2002); and Brooklyn Bridge Park in New York City all fit this category, in which Paris's Parc des Buttes-Chaumont was a pioneer (figs. 34–36; see also p. 69, fig. 38).

35   Latz + Partner, Duisburg-Nord Landscape Park, Germany

36   Michael Van Valkenburgh Associates, Brooklyn
     Bridge Park, New York

The 35-acre Parc André Citroën (1992), designed by a team led by Alain Pro-vost and constructed on the site of the former eponymous automobile plant, offers an interesting comparison with the SNFCC. The outstanding impression of the Athens garden is a comprehensive display of Mediterranean plants paired with a medium-size lawn (originally 253 feet by 148 feet, less than 1 acre; extended at the client's behest in 2016 almost 100 feet to the north). In contrast, the Citroën park boasts an enormous lawn (900 by 280 feet, nearly 6 acres), whose large scale is highlighted by contrast with six small thematic gardens at one side.

Michael Van Valkenburgh Associates' 85-acre, 1.3-mile-long Brooklyn Bridge Park (2016), formerly a series of working docks on the shore of the East River near the bridge, was inaugurated with the 9½-acre Pier 1 (2010). Like the Athens park, it offers magnificent vistas, in this case of New York Harbor and its bustling barge and ferry traffic. Views of the Statue of Liberty are the American equivalent of views featuring the Acropolis.

Unusual as the SNFCC park is for the capital, the rapid adaptation of its local vegetation to the site (already home to a varied bird population) suggests a sense of permanence. Piano calls the hill and building *topos* (Greek for "place"). In reference to this designation, technical advisor Theodore Maravelias remarks that a place cannot be created, but rather becomes. Nowhere is this better illustrated than in this elegant park, which has captured the spirit of this part of the world.

Preceding pages: SNFCC, "Metamorphosis" celebration, June 23–26, 2016

Atrium, pop-up magic show by David Shiner

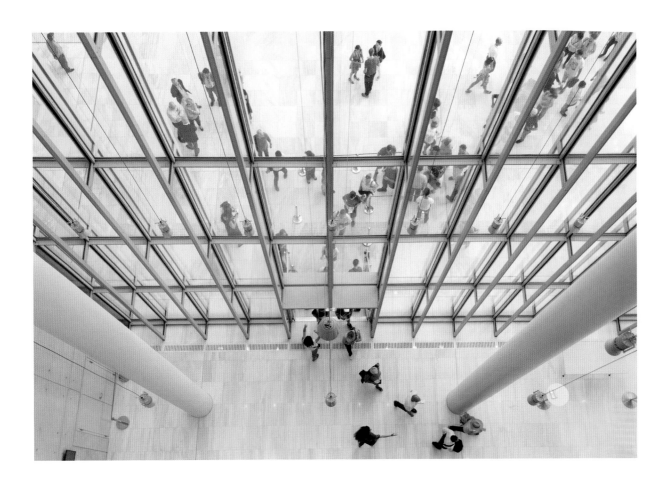

Opera house, lobby

Opera house, auditorium

Opera house, Cellia Costea on stage

Alternative Stage, *Piano I* and *The Strychnine Lady*, music by Jani Christou;
Whale art installation by Alexandros Psychoulis

NLG, glass facade

NLG, reception area

NLG, atrium stairway

NLG, atrium with seating areas

Overleaf: Opera house roof and bridge to lighthouse terrace

Lighthouse and terrace, with "umbilical cord" transferring energy from solar panels and converters on roof to storage

Stavros Niarchos Park, Mediterranean Garden

Stavros Niarchos Park, color-themed plantings

Stavros Niarchos Park, playground with Richter Spielgeräte equipment

Stavros Niarchos Park, splash pool with water jets and street dance show
with Funky Habits and Waveomatics

Stavros Niarchos Park, great lawn, Demy and Friends concert

Metamorphosis

"Metamorphosis: The SNFCC to the World" was the title given to four days of festivities celebrating completion of the cultural center's construction (June 23–26, 2016). "Metamorphosis" is an appropriate word for the process that rendered a flat, abandoned lot into a 100-foot-high hill and gave a dead area, in Andreas Dracopoulos's words, "a soul."[1] The building became an instant symbol of faith in Greece's ability to survive; its finalization offered a joyful respite to the country's woes.

The SNFCC is an extraordinary achievement in many ways. It is a triumph of design and construction that adds a significant landmark to the roster of must-see architecture worldwide. It is a triumph of environmental sensitivity, earning, among other honors, LEED Platinum certification. It is a triumph of responsible management in having been completed nearly on time and amazingly close to the original budget estimates. And it is a triumph of belief in the future of Greece despite near constant economic and social turmoil. As for Renzo Piano, whose career has been a series of triumphs, the Athens cultural center is among the most noteworthy.

That weekend in June, with the opening of the Stavros Niarchos Park and tours of the opera house and library offered in advance of their operational opening, anticipated for 2017, I joined the 115,000 men, women, and children who thronged the SNFCC, undeterred by temperatures that soared into the high 90s Fahrenheit or by the meager public transportation to that area of Athens. In addition to these major attractions, plentiful free food and varied programs of entertainment and activities were provided—games and sports, showings of films and art, concerts, and dance.

The huge canopy and its gently swaying 130-foot-high mast conspicuously signal the presence of the $842 million, over 1-million-square-foot cultural center. They are clearly visible from Syngrou Avenue east of the center, as well as from the north and west. From the south—the waterfront and Poseidonos

Regatta on SNFCC canal during "Metamorphosis"

Avenue—the building appears more massive and fortresslike, defined by the freestanding, self-supporting "cliff" wall.

Below the canopy's glossy, reflective underbelly, the extensive, marble-paved outdoor terrace on the opera house's roof is the most spectacular of the complex's public spaces (see pp. 216–217). Not only are the views breathtaking, but constant breezes are a welcome relief from the nearly year-round heat at ground level. The architects have taken every opportunity to provide locations in which to enjoy Attica's clement climate, and this high point offers panoramic vistas of the sea and the city, including views of the Acropolis.

There is only one discordant element in the complex: the vaulted, steel-truss roof of the glass-enclosed lighthouse. Its curved form seems like an effort to echo the subtle arch of the canopy, but its aluminum top is heavy-looking—the single exception to the complex's fine overall detailing.[2] In contrast, the whimsical curved tube outside the lighthouse, which brings energy from the solar panels and converters to energy storage spaces, provides a welcome variation to the building's predominant horizontality.

While the canopy soars in the sky, at ground level the 1,300-foot-long, 100-foot-wide canal stretches toward the sea, reinforcing the relationship with the latter. Seeming to extend to infinity, the canal reflects the complex along its full length and visually ties together its components.

The long promenade to the agora beside the canal was brutally hot in June (see pp. 6–7). Five years hence, when newly planted Oriental plane trees are tall enough to provide adequate shade, this walkway will be another pleasurable public space. Other tree-lined areas will require comparable time before they offer protection from the sun.

Entrance to the cultural center is from the northeast, by the visitors information building, on axis with the canal (fig. 1). The walkway to the NLG and the opera house is bordered at the west by the man-made hill, to the east by the canal. The eastern facades of the building are impressive. The monumental outer walls of the stairways that rise diagonally beside the opera house and library recall the ziggurats of Mesopotamia, which were also built on flat land. The slender columns are an ephemeral modern interpretation of the Parthenon's sturdy Doric order. The towering, transparent curtain walls are Piano at his best.

Regrettably, visitors arriving by car forgo this visual excitement. (While bus access to the center was being improved in 2016, it is now estimated that, if renewed, an extension of the subway to Kallithea would require ten years to complete.[3]) Automobile passengers will debark instead in the aptly named "canyon" between the stark concrete walls of the parking garage and those of the back of the library and opera house. The small agora leads from this drive to an indoor reception area before finally opening to the large agora (fig. 2).

1   SNFCC, visitors information building

2   "Canyon" between garage and backs of library
    and opera house

Entered from the agora, the lobbies of the opera house and the library have a pleasing homogeneity. The materials of the balconies, suspended from the concrete ceiling slab in both institutions, are the same—white-painted steel, glass balustrades, and oak floors, ceilings, and handrails. Both lobbies (and many areas in the library) are animated by fluttering, brightly colored paper mobiles by Japanese artist Susumu Shingu; these alternate with RPBW's Le Perroquet light fixtures, which are white at the opera, gray at the library (fig. 3). Whereas the relatively narrow opera house lobby is intended to be boisterous and lively when filled with people, the library's spacious ground-level entrance area is serene, though brightened by the vividly colored easy chairs and sofas that are also used on the library's upper floors, together with pieces from Vitra in Switzerland (see p. 213).

The exposed concrete of the opera house lobby's walls and structural columns conveys an informal feeling while retaining a stylish juxtaposition with its floor of gray-veined white marble (a very Greek divergence from the carpeting usually found in opera house lobbies). In the auditorium, informality gives way to the plush elegance of a traditional opera venue, with red-upholstered seats

3 SNFCC, opera house lobby

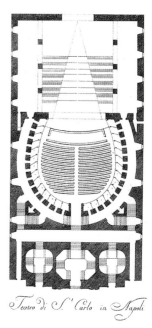

4 Giovanni Antonio Medrano,
   Teatro di San Carlo, Naples, plan

and a wood floor that departs from the marble floor at ground level (as does the Artigo rubber floor in the upper levels of the library). And the few, narrow steps up to the orchestra level, which curve to the right and left at the entrance to the auditorium, recall those in the eighteenth-century Teatro di San Carlo in Naples (fig. 4).

An obvious difference from the typical Italian opera house is the open slice at the center of the ceiling dome, described by Bianchi as "a natural smile"[4] (see p. 148, fig. 21). This element allows a portion of the ceiling to retract in order to provide a uniform sound from the variously spaced loudspeaker clusters for non-classical music. Different shades of the dominant red tonality create a warm, intimate feeling that is enhanced by the space's moderate size. Cellia Costea's performance of the aria "Vissi d'Arte" from *Tosca*, accompanied by a piano, promised excellent acoustics, an impression that was confirmed during a series of tryouts in September (see p. 208).

The soprano voice has a specific range—no bass content below certain frequencies—and, accompanied by a percussive instrument, gives a good sampling of the sound for a particular type of acoustics. But the real test of a hall comes from listening to different kinds of concerts—featuring a broad range of music types and performance groups, including classical chamber music, a full orchestra in the pit or on stage, and amplified popular music—from various parts of the hall.

In late September 2016, a first set of acoustic trials based on a wider spectrum of singers (two sopranos and a baritone) and an orchestra of twenty-five to thirty musicians in the pit took place at the opera house, the Alternative Stage theater, and the orchestra rehearsal room—one of five rehearsal rooms (for orchestras, choral groups, ballet, and so forth, together with warm-up rooms for soloists). Two months later, there were trials of the entire orchestra onstage once the removable orchestra shell with its side and back towers rising the full height of the proscenium was installed (see p. 151, fig. 23). Carl J. Rosenberg, a principal consultant at Acentech Acoustics in Cambridge, Massachusetts, attended the September tryouts, offering an unofficial but highly informed report on the acoustics.

Listening to successive performances of Mozart's opera music from seats in several areas of the orchestra level and in the four balconies of the main auditorium, Rosenberg judged both the sightlines and the acoustics to be excellent. The sound is warm and balanced, with brilliance in the high frequencies (the trebles, without which the sound would be muffled and gloomy), even distribution between sections of the orchestra, and good tonal balance. The quality of acoustic envelopment that Bassuet worked so hard to capture is present everywhere, perhaps most intensely in the balconies.

Flexibility characterizes both the opera house and the Alternative Stage. The main stage of the former has twelve lift wagons (13 by 52½ feet); at each side stage there are four such wagons (13 by 39 feet); and at the back stage, a larger one (52½ square feet). These allow for the stage's complete reconfiguration. Likewise, the size of the orchestra pit can be modified by means of lifts (see p. 151, fig. 24). Loudspeakers at the front and at either side of the opera house stage are available when microphones are used to boost the volume of speech, and for amplified popular music. Thick, sound-absorbing curtains can moderate reverberation in all three spaces.

The smaller, more modern-looking Alternative Stage theater is a rectangular room with two narrow galleries. Lifts can raise the flat floor to different heights in different areas. With the help of retractable seats, the whole theater can be recomposed. In addition to its excellent acoustics, this 450-seat theater provides the excitement of placing the audience close to the performers.

The orchestra rehearsal room, due to its large size and exceptional height, is unusually successful. It is more than ample enough for a full orchestra, and its nearly forty-foot-high ceiling evenly distributes reflections around the room, an effect that is helped by the diffusive wall and ceiling panels, which have various sound absorption values at different frequencies (see p. 152, fig. 25). There seems

6 NLG, book castle, upper level

5 SNFCC, NLG, book castle, black box theater

to be no background noise in any of the three spaces tested, and sound-lock vestibules protect each location from undesirable exterior sound.

Rosenberg applauds the absence, at the opera house, of adjustable overhead reflecting panels: found in many music venues, they are rarely changed. The wide proscenium, which helps reflect sound evenly; the shallow balconies, which make the entire audience acoustically part of the main space; the balcony faces, which are positioned to help disperse and distribute sound evenly; and the horseshoe shape of the room and contour of the walls, which also help diffuse sound—all of these contribute to the stunning success of the auditorium's acoustics for the musicians as well as for the audience. Performances offering a wider vocal range, and with an audience and scenery in place, are unlikely to affect the acoustics significantly.

It is more difficult to assess the library before it has opened, with its miles of empty shelving, and without the color and materiality that the books will provide. As might be expected from RPBW, the atrium, located to the west of the book castle and extending the full height from ground level to roof, is awash in natural light, as are the library's many spacious reading rooms (and also the opera house's support spaces, such as the rehearsal rooms). Bordered at one side by a delicate staircase, the atrium furnishes circulation to all levels and spaces within the library (see p. 212).

Among the library's many features is the full-height, multilevel book castle with its ground-level performance space, which is designed like a black box theater (fig. 5). Heavy curtains shield the entrance from sound and light; and walls

7   NLG, Stavros Niarchos Reading Room

8   Morgan Library and Museum, Sherman Fairchild
    Reading Room, New York

9   NLG, rare books reading room

10   New York Public Library, Brooke Russell Astor
     Rare Books Reading Room

are lined with movable panels backed by acoustic fabric that can be adjusted according to what is being performed. Books wrap around the outer walls of the book castle; the interior walls on levels above the performance space will also be lined with books, but these cannot be experienced as a continuous vertical movement because not all levels are connected (fig. 6).

On the library's top level is the sizable, skylit Stavros Niarchos Reading Room for scholars, bordered on three sides by a mezzanine, with a fine quality of daylight comparable to the Morgan Library and Museum's Sherman Fairchild Reading Room (figs. 7, 8). The equally daylight-filled rare books reading room (2,820 square feet) is larger than the Brooke Russell Astor Rare Books Reading Room (1,800 square feet) in the much larger New York Public Library (figs. 9, 10); and the NLG's restoration laboratory is adjacent to its rare books reading room, whereas the NYPL's restoration laboratory is off-site. Practical Italian-made furnishings for the study areas—Tolomeo desk lamps by Artemide, De Padova tables and chairs—fit the working requirements of these elegant spaces.

The enormous rooms in the library, built to accommodate 100,000 visitors in the first year, with a prospect of 300,000 annually, may be overly ambitious.

11   SNFCC, Stavros Niarchos Park, meadow and path on library roof

Nearly 2,000 seats in the new building are more than double the 956 seats in the old building. As a point of comparison, the Gennadius Library in Athens, focused on Greek subjects, is visited by only 6,000 researchers annually (see "Library" chapter).

With neither the opera house nor the NLG fully functioning in 2016, only the Stavros Niarchos Park (which opened to the public full time in late August 2016) can be assessed fully in terms of how it works. Judging from the crowds that mobbed the area in the cooler early-evening hours of the "Metamorphosis" event in June, Joseph Volpe's prediction about the park's importance to the center's success seems prescient (see "Park" chapter). The park clearly fulfills the foundation's hope that it will be a destination for families, and similar demographics are projected for the people who will visit the rest of the SNFCC.

A stroll through the completed park revealed the importance of the many slaloming cross-paths in helping to ascend the hill, which is quite steep. Designed with wheelchair accessibility in mind, for which they work well, the diagonal pathways are also helpful for the able-bodied. A central, 22⅜-foot-wide main road (required by law to accommodate vehicles such as fire trucks) is an unfortunate, if unavoidable, departure from the narrower paths elsewhere[5] (fig. 11). Also out of scale are two disproportionately deep ferro-cement roofs similar to the canopy (and used to test it)—one protecting the outdoor café, one atop the visitors center (figs. 1, 12). The Prolat path covering, however, is an inspired choice, creating an impression of tamped earth that is discreet and eminently appropriate to the natural setting.

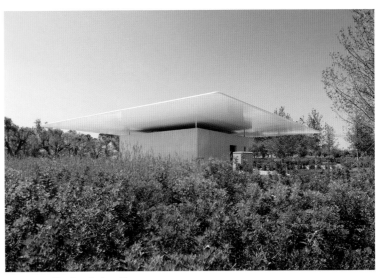

12 Stavros Niarchos Park, café

The park displays two distinct identities. One is apparent in the formal, botanically intense Mediterranean Garden and other areas planted in similarly geometrical beds; the second is the more casual design of the park's western-most areas, which include the labyrinth at the south, the interactive splash pool at the north, the playgrounds in between, and to the east of these, the meadow that covers the library roof. In a category of their own are the curvilinear paths of the parking garage rooftop, which also offer a fanciful alternative to the strict rectilinearity elsewhere. The formal and more casually designed sectors are equally popular. Older visitors, some in groups led by horticultural societies, have been attracted to the 160-odd species of the Mediterranean Garden. Young parents and their wards were obviously delighted with the playgrounds, where the Richter equipment was a tremendous success.

Deborah Nevins and Helli Pangalou again accompanied me, explaining Nevins's intentions. Among the most stunning are the color themes she created. More than a dozen planting beds, each limited to a single color, or closely related colors, produce a vivid impact. In one of the first beds of the Mediterranean Garden are Twickel Purple lavender (*Lavandula angustifolia 'Twickel Purple'*), blue spire Russian sage (*Perovskia 'blue spire'*), chaste tree (*Vitex agnus-castus*), and sage (*Salvia*), all flowers in various shades of purple; nearby, mountain marigold (*Tagetes lemmonii*) and anthyllis (*Anthyllis cytisoides*) burst into a bright yellow area (fig. 13).

Nevins's interest in trees is evident in the 2,593 that have been planted here, with a range of nearly thirty species. Aged olive trees (*Olea europaea*) predominate, but pencil thin cypress (*Cupressus sempervirens*), carob (*Ceratonia siliqua*),

13   SNFCC, Stavros Niarchos Park, purple and yellow color-theme planting beds

and a variety of Italian umbrella pines (*Pinus pinea*) are also prominent reminders of the Mediterranean.

Given the inspiration exerted by the Jardin du Luxembourg, it is not surprising that the powder-blue metal chairs (from the French company Fermob) are similar to the ones found in that Parisian park. They are amply distributed throughout the Athens garden, together with benches (from the Italian firm Etere). Many of the pathways are lit by handsome RPBW-designed lights, manufactured by Fratelli Guzzini in Italy. Restrained, easy-to-understand signage by Atelier Martine Harlé, a French designer of environmental graphics, orients the public in the park as it does in the opera house and library (fig. 14).

These are the physical accomplishments, which are an unequivocal success. But how will they work? How satisfactory will the acoustics, sight lines, and general comfort of the three performance spaces be? How easily will each production be mounted? How will the library function in a country with no tradition of using such an institution, where students are accustomed to libraries that specialize in specific subjects? How will the planners' vision work for what Scott Newman of Cooper Robertson described as "not just a new home for the library, but a whole new way of serving the public"?[6] Will the park remain popular if the many activities envisaged for it are slow to materialize? Will the trees, in time, provide the shade that is needed in this sunny climate? And how will the cultural center be affected by the uncertainty and the dire economic conditions in this politically volatile country? What will happen when the SNFCC is entrusted, as agreed, to the Greek state? The arbitrariness of changing governments in the area

15　Giorgos Koumendakis

14　Atelier Martine Harlé, Stavros
Niarchos Park, signage

of culture has recently produced failures, resignations, replacements, removals, and expulsions that make for ongoing instability and unexplained policy reversals.[7] One of many such instances was the replacement of Michailidis as artistic director of the GNO by Giorgos Koumendakis, artistic director of the Alternative Stage theater (fig. 15). The switch was made by a newly appointed minister of culture, Lydia Koniordou, an actress with no political experience.[8] A similar switch could conceivably occur for Tsimpoglou at the NLG.

Indeed, the future holds many imponderables.

The question of who will in fact pay for the SNFCC's maintenance and programming is paramount. Already, almost a year before the "Metamorphosis" celebration, the issue that haunted the project from the beginning was addressed in public. In August 2015, the online art news site Blouin Artinfo headlined an interview with the SNFCC's director, Ioannis Trohopoulos, with the question "Can the New Stavros Niarchos Cultural Center Survive in Greece?"[9] His response was a plan to create a European network that would contribute to the cost of running the SNFCC.

Both Michailidis at the opera and Filippos Tsimpoglou at the library were concerned about their ability to carry out the plans they had devised. The GNO's artistic director had planned to be in the new theater by the end of November 2017. But this plan and the budget for it were called into question when Michailidis was replaced. During his tenure at the opera, Michailidis had pointed out that the proposal by the previous government (Samaras, 2012–2015) to make an annual contribution of €10 million ($11.14 million) to run the GNO was no longer sufficient. The GNO's current estimates show costs of €14.5 million ($16.15 million) the first year (2017), rising to €16.4 million ($18.27 million) in the second year, and €17 million ($18.94 million) the third year. The annual increase is due to the rising cost of what the GNO must contribute to the SNFCC. Even the SNF donation of €5 million ($5.4 million) would meet these expenses only for 2017.[10]

Tsimpoglou is more optimistic. What he calls the building's "magic" has vanquished the tearful frustration he felt a year ago. He is now "more than happy, I'm flying." He says, "For the first time, the best people are applying for jobs; there are already promised gifts of rare books and manuscripts; and after a fifteen-year hiatus, the NLG was represented at the prestigious European Council of Libraries that was held this year in Vienna."[11]

The library director considers the move to the new building to be generational as well as geographical—part of the digital revolution. He dreams of a human "chain" of "ordinary people" to pass books from the old to the new building or, he says playfully, possibly just one individual carrying a USB drive. But he cautions that, because of its complexity, the move will take at least six months.

Before that can happen, the library's spotty cataloguing must be completed, and then books and other artifacts must undergo the cleaning that was neglected when the library was without a director. A radio-frequency identification (RFID) tag will be affixed to each object before it is wrapped and packed in a box or tube. Possibly most tricky of all, outdoor temperature and humidity have to be monitored to avoid environmental shock, which can create dampness and insect infiltration. This is particularly important for the rare books that will be moved first and placed in one of the NLG's four vaults (the other three are for manuscripts, maps, and archives).

For Tsimpoglou, the library's strength is its unique collection; its weakness is the lack of personnel, part of the overall problem of insufficient state funding for salaries, preservation, microfilming, digitizing, bookbinding, and public services, as well as maintenance. In its Needs Analysis report back in 2008, CR had called for a staff of 300 for the NLG (an increase of 204 from the 96 then employed).[12] In 2016, there were only sixty-nine permanent librarians with fifty-four temporary staff who belong to other educational organizations; at least sixty-three more are needed for the library to begin functioning. (Presumably the goal of 300 would be met as new services and technologies are installed and working.)

As for the park, the number of gardeners needed varies according to the season, ranging from four to fifteen, with the most required in autumn, when leaves fall. Its maintenance costs are estimated at between €4.58 million ($5.10 million) and €10 million ($11.14 million), depending on the number of commercial activities and the amount of special programming. My guess that the vegetation would survive without care for at best one year makes funding even more crucial here than for the rest of the cultural center.

16   Migrant camp, Athens, 2016

The question posed by Blouin Artinfo in 2015 was timely, given that cultural institutions throughout Greece were suffering from insufficient financing, and even closing down; it came shortly after the forced merger of two museums of contemporary art in Thessaloniki. Equally unsettling as the deficient budgets was the failure to open to the public the National Museum of Contemporary Art in Athens more than two years after its lengthy renovation was completed in 2014. Even the SNF withdrew the grant of €3 million ($3.34 million) it had offered to the institution at the time, because the museum and the Culture Ministry failed to meet the agreed deadlines for completing the supporting studies.[13]

In February 2016, various calculations of the cost of running the cultural center (maintenance, security, and so on)—made by the SNF and Boston Consulting Group, among others—came to about €15.54 million ($17.31 million) annually. This estimate did not, however, include the general operating costs, such as staff salaries, production costs, and marketing of the opera house and the library—approximately €22.5 million ($25.07 million) for the former and €8.3 million ($9.25 million) for the latter, for a grand total of €46.34 million (nearly $51.62 million).[14]

Compounding Greece's financial problems was the influx into the country of refugees from the Middle East, which in 2015 rose to monstrous proportions: more than eight hundred thousand that year (fig. 16). In addition to the E.U.'s intransigency about the Greek debt, the other member states began to criticize Greece's handling of the flow of migrants, even threatening to exclude the country from the Schengen Agreement boundaries—an area of twenty-six European countries without internal border controls. The border checks on sea and air access to Greece that such a move threatened would handicap tourism and would further worsen the nation's relationship with the rest of the E.U.[15]

The situation revealed the lack of unity in the E.U. and reopened fears of its possible dismantling.[16] By January 2016, in response to the flood of asylum seekers from the Middle East, six of the member countries—Austria, France,

Denmark, Germany, Norway, and Sweden—had imposed border controls for two years (only six months is allowable by the group's rules), thereby paralyzing traffic and raising the prospect of commercial losses in excess of $108 billion should the checks continue.[17]

In July, the failed coup d'état by the Turkish military threatened that country's ability to carry out its agreement, made in March with the E.U., to stem the flow of migrants into Greece and accept the return from Greece of migrants ineligible for asylum.[18] By August, 57,000 people were still trapped in a distressing limbo.[19] And in September, the waning hope of visa-free travel to Europe for Turkish citizens made the likelihood of Turkish cooperation with regard to the migrants even more unlikely.[20]

Greece's repeated threats to leave the Eurozone and eventually the E.U., first heard in the summer of 2012,[21] brought to the fore differences between north and south, advanced and developing economies, lenders and debtors, and the nineteen member countries of the Eurozone and the nine member nations outside the zone.[22] The refugee crisis created further divisions among those countries. On June 23, 2016—the first day of the SNFCC "Metamorphosis" celebration—the U.K. vote to leave the union reinforced such fears.[23]

By early 2016, schisms in the Greek parliament had increased considerably. The most troubling of these concern the crucial privatization arrangements inherited from previous governments and a major condition of Greece's second bailout, amounting to €130 billion ($144.82 billion). Left-wing members of Syriza passionately voiced their long-standing opposition to privatization, while leaders of the party tried desperately to persuade foreign investors to come to Greece to kick-start the economy. Even Tsipras is torn between the two factions.

On February 6, 2016, Prime Minister Alexis Tsipras toured the SNFCC. The visit, on which he was accompanied by his ministers of culture, Aristides Baltas, and state, Nikos Pappas, was seen as a vote of confidence. But as is so often the case in Greece, appearances can be deceptive. Just three months later, on May 6, a minister in Tsipras's Syriza coalition party gave the Ministry of Justice the use of the volleyball facilities near the SNFCC for high-profile court trials over the next twenty years. Such trials would impose security measures and traffic congestion on the cultural center, a possibility that elicited an immediate, and successful, protest from high-ranking members of parliament and mayors of local boroughs.

His waffling on deals to privatize, among other properties, the container terminal at the port of Piraeus, and—with a long-term lease—the site of the old Hellinikon International Airport is hardly reassuring for potential investors[24] (see "Athens" chapter).

Yet amid all this contention, it was heartening to see the protectiveness with which the SNFCC is widely regarded when the government briefly considered turning over the nearby volleyball facility to the justice department. Kyriakos Mitsotakis, who had been elected head of the opposition New Democracy party in January 2016, joined the protesters, referring to the cultural center as "this jewel of Athens, which should be the starting point of the Athenian Riviera."[25] The plan was subsequently withdrawn.

At about the same time in 2016, Greece's economy showed signs of a slight improvement (as it had in 2014): shrinkage was only 0.7 percent; 1.9 percent growth seemed possible in 2017; and the nation's credit rating had been upgraded.[26] But the government was slow to respond to additional conditions for the July 2015 loan agreement and enacted fiscal measures that produced lower revenues than anticipated. At this moment, the SNFCC had yet another reminder of its uncertainty. In a public interview with Trohopoulos on April 6, TV anchor Maria Houkli exclaimed "God help us" after he mentioned the government takeover of the cultural center, whereupon the audience burst into laughter. Trohopoulos resigned nine days later and was replaced, six weeks later, by Dimitris Protopsaltou, then chief operating officer of the SNFCC.[27]

In May, two events had opened a much-needed window of optimism for the country. The first was Tsipras's announcement that construction would begin on the Trans Adriatic Pipeline. The $45 billion joint project is the biggest foreign investment ever to have taken place in Greece, with shares held by six major oil companies.[28] The deal would bring €33 to €36 billion ($36.76 to $40.1 billion) to the Greek economy over a period of fifty years, generating during that time between 4,300 and 4,800 jobs per year.[29]

The second was the Greek parliament's passage of legislation that allowed the release of €10.3 billion ($11.47 billion) for the nation's third bailout. Despite the opposition to it, this included a go-ahead for the government's wide-ranging privatization program. At the same time, E.U. ministers agreed to consider a plan that would ease Greece's mountain of debt.[30]

As considerable as the pipeline's revenue projections seem to be, they in fact amount to less than a billion euros a year in an economy of $195.3 billion in 2015—and the third bailout was greeted with skepticism.[31] Greece's debt of more than $345.5 billion, the highest in Europe, is about 177 percent of its gross domestic product.[32] If debt relief were to take place only in 2018, as suggested by Greece's lenders, it would come too late to be meaningful for an economy whose arrears could reach 250 percent of GDP by 2050.[33]

Since the bailouts go primarily to servicing Greece's external debt—they are not invested in the economy—they do nothing to improve the financial situation.[34] The nation is caught in a vicious cycle: the government cannot begin to pay its staggering obligations unless a recovery takes place, but the way in which the loan payments are structured impedes a recovery.

This Sisyphean challenge leaves Greece at an impasse. Between 1998 and 2007, Greece's annual economic growth per person was in fact 3.8 percent—the second fastest in Europe. Its booming economy, with its growing government deficits—which was also the case in Ireland and Spain, but in Greece hidden from view—caused prices to rise, wages to increase, and exports to become more expensive. So when the financial crisis hit, these countries were competitively weak, and their debts unsustainable. Says Matthias Matthijs, an assistant professor at Johns Hopkins University School of Advanced International Studies, "It's when the tide goes out that you see who's swimming naked."[35]

Enter the involvement of the International Monetary Fund in May 2010 regarding plans for a Greek bailout, which its directors, under the leadership of Dominique Strauss-Kahn, knew were seriously flawed. New information in 2016 revealed continuing turmoil and divisions within the fund. IMF officials under Strauss-Kahn's leadership bent the fund's rules to lend to Greece knowing that the resulting debt would be unsustainable rather than pushing for a debt restructuring that could have given the economy a fresh start.[36]

In contrast to the SNFCC festivities taking place at Kallithea in the summer of 2016, Athens's working-class neighborhoods exuded a feeling of quiet resignation (fig. 17). Athens has in fact become a city of extremes, with little change in the wealthier areas, but with the edges becoming frayed by the homeless, panhandling, and political protests. Incongruously, the disarray produced in Turkey by the attempted coup d'état in July made Greece the West's last bulwark of security and stability against potential political upheavals to the east. This seemingly strengthened the case for providing that nation with meaningful long-term debt relief, thus enabling the IMF to make restructuring the debt a new requirement for any deal over repaying its creditors.[37]

Tsipras's deep-seated faith in publicly run institutions and the bolstering of Greece's international political and financial status were reflected in his announcement on August 30, 2016, that the first year's running costs for the SNFCC had been secured, along with an exceptional €3 million ($3.34 million) to help cover the transition to the new facilities (even though, contrary to the prime minister's promise, the GNO budget had not yet been approved).[38] His statement to the press recalled the hopes that Andreas Dracopoulos had expressed in November 2015 that the cultural center could represent "a new beginning" for Greece.[39] To make sure that this belief would be a reality, in December the foundation announced its intention to continue actively supporting the SNFCC, at least for

17   Working-class neighborhood, Athens

18   SNFCC, remarks by President Obama, November 16, 2016

the next five years, with grants of up to €50 million ($55.7 million).[40] Most of the grant comes from the VAT taxes that the Greek government returned to the SNF. Dracopoulos admits that from the beginning of the project he had anticipated this donation as a necessary endowment.

Certainly the SNFCC needs all the help it can muster in order to function satisfactorily. The prime minister's statement, on September 10 at the opening of an annual trade fair in Thessaloniki, that "Greece [is] turning the corner" was greeted with ridicule by the approximately fifteen thousand people in attendance, who threw firecrackers and scuffled with police to protest new pension cuts and increased taxes. Furthermore, Greek television was unable to broadcast the prime minister's speech because of a twenty-four-hour strike staged by journalists and technical staff to demonstrate opposition to expected job cuts.[41]

At the SNFCC opera house, in November, just two months later, U.S. president Barack Obama gave a speech that received a very different reception (fig. 18). The packed audience applauded enthusiastically throughout the nearly hourlong delivery. Generously sprinkled with Greek words, and opening with a reference to the hospitality of the Greek people to the refugees who have flooded their country, the address went on to express Obama's trust in democracy, justice, and hope over fear.[42] The event was a vivid reminder of the belief, expressed by Renzo Piano at the beginning of the project, that the cultural center would be a place "where fear disappears and people can share."[43]

Afterword

In the course of my forty-plus-year friendship with Philip Johnson, I often heard him say that great architecture can be achieved only under a dictatorship. The Stavros Niarchos Foundation is markedly undictatorial: the unusual transparency with which it carried out the creation of the SNFCC, and its pursuit of innumerable professional opinions over the ten years of the center's gestation and development are but two examples. However, the organization did keep its Athens undertaking uncompromisingly on track, avoiding the self-serving political maneuvering and the obfuscation that divert many such projects from their intended goals. The ability of Andreas Dracopoulos to maintain an even keel—with the help of Faithful+Gould's Martin Hirko, the lead construction supervisor—has been especially remarkable given the chaotic conditions in Greece during the construction period.

Neither public protests nor significant labor strikes held up work on the SNFCC. There were no unresolvable disputes between the Greek and Italian contractors or between the various consultants. The foundation went out of its way to keep the public informed: it made available the terms of its agreement with the government and the estimated cost of construction; built a temporary observation bridge overlooking the site; and set up a temporary pavilion to provide information about the project. In addition, the SNFCC website streamed a continuous 24-hour video of work on the site, and also furnished regular updates. Although the project's entire financing by the SNF was an exceptional advantage, the history of the enterprise from beginning to end offers important precedents for any significant future public building.

Lessons Learned

Neil Clemson, of F+G, says, "The hardest part of every construction project is identifying the objectives, laying them out simply with their respective funding, and controlling them. Conflicts often arise between the users, designers, clients, funders, and the public on the priorities and interpretation of these objectives. You need to balance these views and wish lists with how much to spend on each part to maximize value."[1]

Clemson's statement points up the importance of thoroughly preparing every aspect of a project. In Athens, after the foundation's initial meetings with the master planners and early consultants, nearly four years of preparation passed before any excavation began. In contrast, construction of the Acropolis Museum by Bernard Tschumi Architects was held up for three years by conflicts between archaeologists and preservationists, and by the politicians who exploited that antagonism for their own ends. Investigation of the potential problems before construction was scheduled to begin might have tempered the difficulties. Once they were resolved, the museum was built in three years with no other disruptive incidents.[2]

The expediency with which the SNF approached its project illustrates the importance of establishing a construction budget that is manageable for the client and of ensuring that it is adhered to. Hirko notes that "Renzo Piano isn't used to someone telling him things are too expensive. F+G was constantly keeping the architects within the budget. The SNF is strong, but fair."[3] Once construction costs were established, change orders were kept to a minimum. The availability of the required financing avoided the budget cuts that often compromise architectural quality. Not the least of this remarkable project's accomplishments is the ongoing friendship that developed between Piano and Dracopoulos. The foundation director never thinks of Piano "just as an architect, but as a phil-Hellene."[4]

It is equally important that the costs of maintenance and programming be established at the same time as the cost of construction, and with the same precision and transparency. Between 1994 and 2008, various institutions in the United States spent a total of between $24 and $25 billion on building and equipping cultural facilities. The authors of the 2015 book *Building Better Arts Facilities* describe the result as "a cultural landscape awash with arts organizations struggling to stay afloat."[5] An organization that constructs a building it cannot afford to maintain and program faces certain trouble.[6]

Greece's dire economic situation at the time the cultural center rose had the perhaps unexpected effect of favoring its construction conditions. Because it was the only project of its scale in the nation's capital, the SNF had its pick of first-rate contractors and workers. To successfully pull off such an undertaking, Hirko says, you need "people who listen and believe in you." He reports that "many workers love coming to work here because they feel the client cares about them and they are proud of what they have done. The project logged only seven minor accidents, a record low for such an enterprise in Greece."[7] As a point of comparison, fourteen deaths occurred during construction of the 2004 Olympic Games facilities in Athens.[8]

Furthermore, the thousands of jobs required to build the SNFCC, with the prospect of thousands more to administer it, deterred critics from condemning both the SNF and the government for spending millions on art rather than on humanitarian aid. These facts would have made such criticism politically disadvantageous, especially since the foundation also maintained a generous grant program to improve living conditions in Greece.[9] From its inception the cultural center has, in fact, served as a beacon of hope in the midst of Greece's despair.

Prospects for the cultural center once it has been completed are somewhat less secure. The foundation early on expressed its willingness to provisionally subsidize maintenance and programming if necessary, but its much publicized commitment to hand over the facility to the cash-strapped Greek government has raised uncertainties that have been seized upon and amplified by the local press. Not only was the government slow to allocate sufficient funds to properly maintain and program the facility, but its well-known failure to successfully administer cultural institutions—museums, for example—has undermined the people's trust. In January 2016, an article called attention to the "turmoil in the area of culture…establishing an extensive party politics that stymies creative energy for society and culture."[10] And in August an article in *Kathimerini English Edition* called for more "capable management" of the cultural center in partnership with the SNF "outside the power-sharing process…Such a move would signal that something is changing in this country."[11]

This kind of political *and* practical change, modeled on the transparency and efficient methods used to create the cultural center, is exactly what the foundation had hoped to bring about. Rather than wanting to eliminate the government's involvement in the project, Dracopoulos and the board hoped to help reform the state's methods.[12] It was a tall order. Even before the center became a reality, the government's failure to ensure the hiring of directors for the opera and library was a breach of the public trust.

Comparisons

Building for culture has been booming worldwide for decades now, and numerous major projects in different parts of the world have been embarked upon more or less contemporaneously with the design and construction of the SNFCC. Several of these have fallen drastically behind their scheduled completion dates and gone astronomically over budget. Although four of these cultural buildings offer examples of distinguished architecture, they also reveal just how painful the construction process can be, especially when compared with that of the Athens venue.

2　Philharmonie de Paris, Grande Salle Pierre Boulez

i　Ateliers Jean Nouvel, Philharmonie de Paris

When the Philharmonie de Paris by Ateliers Jean Nouvel opened early in 2016, the architect sued the French government for inaugurating the hall in what he considered to be an unfinished state. Taiwan's National Taichung Theater (originally called the Metropolitan Opera House) by Toyo Ito premiered in November 2014, shut down shortly thereafter, and did not open until September 2016. Also in 2016, the Elbphilharmonie Hamburg by Swiss architects Herzog & de Meuron, begun in 2007, delayed its opening until January 2017 despite an initial completion date of 2010. And construction of the Ciudad de la Cultura (City of Culture), the cultural center in Santiago de Compostela by Eisenman Architects, begun in 2001, was halted in 2012 and finally terminated in 2013 after only four of the six buildings planned had been completed.

The Philharmonie de Paris and the SNFCC bear little similarity to each other in function or architectural style. One is a concert hall; the other an opera house, library, and park. The Nouvel building's aggressively fragmented, asymmetrical forms are the opposite of RPBW's classic, rectilinear modernism (figs. 1, 2). Likewise, the processes of design and construction utilized for each were radically different.

Originally planned in 1982 as part of the French government's Cité de la Musique complex on the city's northeastern edge (which opened in 1995), the Philharmonie de Paris was delayed until an architect, Ateliers Jean Nouvel, was chosen by competition in 2007. Nouvel supplied an unrealistically low cost estimate of €173.1 million ($192.8 million) for construction of the 2,400-seat reconfigurable hall; he later argued that the government would not have pursued

4   National Taichung Theater

3   Toyo Ito, National Taichung Theater, Taiwan

the endeavor if an accurate sum—at least twice as much—had been given. As it turned out, costs peaked at €534.7 million ($595.7 million).[13]

The architect's subterfuge led to endless haggling about expenditures among the national, regional, and city governments who footed the bill. Value engineering changed many aspects of the design and contributed to three more years of construction.[14] However, despite the painful struggle in France to pay for building the concert hall, the federal and city governments affirmed their commitment to subsidizing its operating expenses, in contrast to Athens. For 2016, the cost is expected to be €27.8 million ($30.97 million), of which nearly €15 million ($16.71 million) is public subsidy: €9 million ($10.03 million) from the French state and €6 million ($6.68 million) from the city of Paris.

In Taichung, Taiwan's third-largest city, politics were responsible for the premature opening of the National Taichung Theater, which contains three separate auditoriums (figs. 3, 4). This building, too, was designed by a world-renowned architect. When Ito was chosen for the project in 2005, completion was expected to take four years and cost $60 million; but ground was not broken until 2009, at which time the cost estimates rose to $110 million, to be paid for by the city and national governments. In 2015, the costs had escalated to $141 million.

A week before the nationwide municipal elections were held on November 29, 2014, Jason Hu, the mayor of Taichung at the time, rushed to claim credit for the novel performance venue by expediting a much-publicized inauguration of the unfinished building. The interiors had not been completed, the building's infrastructure had not been inspected for safety, and the staff had not been

5   Herzog & de Meuron, Elbphilharmonie Hamburg

6   Elbphilharmonie Hamburg with NDR–Elbphilharmonie Orchester
    on stage

trained. Visitors to the theater in October 2015, nearly a year later, found work continuing throughout the building.[15] Hu lost the election to Lin Chia-lung, who closed the venue immediately after taking office on December 25, 2014; the grand theater opened at last on September 30, 2016.

The Elbphilharmonie Hamburg is a spectacular example of a flawed process (figs. 5, 6). When the municipal senate approved the project for a 2,150-seat concert hall, two smaller auditoriums, and a commercial development in 2001, the price tag for construction was €186 million ($207.2 million) and completion was anticipated for 2010. At the time the city finally signed the construction contract in 2006, the cost had been recalculated at €351.8 million ($319.9 million), an estimate that by 2013 had risen to €798 million ($889 million), with completion postponed until 2017.[16]

From the outset, disputes among the architects, the city, and a construction consortium led by the giant Hochtief company plagued the project: areas of responsibility were not clearly defined, and there were ongoing change orders. When Pierre de Meuron was questioned by *Spiegel Online* in 2013 about the enormous rise in costs, he blamed "scheduling delays, project disputes, and even shutdowns" for pushing the price up. "What we lacked at the time was enough time for careful planning."[17]

In April 2013, the regional government of Galicia threw in the towel on two of the six cultural buildings designed in 1999 by Eisenman Architects for the Ciudad de la Cultura in Santiago de Compostela. Initially estimated to cost $146.4 million, construction was to begin in 2001 and be completed by 2004.

7   Eisenman Architects, Ciudad de la Cultura, Santiago de Compostela, Spain

8   Ciudad de la Cultura

In 2011, when only the first four buildings were inaugurated, the price tag had risen to $600 million (figs. 7, 8). The disproportionately large size—1 million square feet—for a cultural complex in this modest pilgrimage town of 100,000 inhabitants (the size of Hartford, Connecticut) stemmed from the newly elected Conservative government's attempt to compete with its Socialist predecessor's modernization plan. Another factor was the effort to match the successes of the Guggenheim Museum in Bilbao (Gehry Partners, 1997) and the Ciudad de las Artes y de las Ciencias in Valencia (Santiago Calatrava, 1998). The results were disastrous, due to a program driven by these political and regional rivalries rather than by the needs of the local population and of the twelve million pilgrims who make their way to Santiago de Compostela each year.

"Within chaos there are opportunities."
—*Andreas Dracopoulos, October 10, 2014*

In 2016, the year the SNFCC was completed though not yet inaugurated, Athenians continued to stay fervently involved with art despite their miserable living conditions. In April, local artists protested their perceived exclusion from the upcoming Athens and Epidaurus Festival—the annual May-to-October arts festival in these two cities on the Saronic Gulf—and effected the ouster of Jan Fabre, the Belgian director, and the appointment of a Greek director, Vangelis Theodoropoulos.[18] At the Benaki Museum in March and April, "As One," a show of performance art, tapped into the nation's feelings of fear, entrapment, discomfort, and control. Performance pieces by Greek artists, under the direction of the Marina Abramović Institute, acted out these very emotions in presentations that lasted eight hours a day, seven days a week for seven weeks. The collaboration between the institute and the underwriter, NEON (the Greek word for "new"), a three-year-old Athens-based nonprofit arts organization, attracted 22,000 visitors in the first three weeks despite most Greeks' unfamiliarity with this art form.[19] Even more ambitious is Athens's commitment to co-host, with Kassel, Germany, the esteemed Documenta art exhibition in 2017.

A belief in the "therapeutic power of beauty," as cited by Renzo Piano in 2014 as part of "Dance of the Cranes," has a long history. During World War II, noontime classical music concerts offered in London's National Gallery were considered a sign of the nation's recovery. The SNFCC is not alone in sharing Piano's conviction. For example, despite Lebanon's political and financial instability, at least five new museums are planned or under construction in Beirut. One of these—the Aïshti Foundation for contemporary art (David Adjaye, 2015) is already operational, and RPBW has been commissioned to design the Beirut City Museum as well as a master plan for Martyrs' Square.

In 1999 Argentinian-Israeli conductor Daniel Barenboim and Palestinian-American academic Edward Said implemented a new approach to the seventy-year-old Israeli-Palestinian conflict. The West–Eastern Divan Orchestra (a youth orchestra named for a collection of poems by Johann Wolfgang von Goethe) has provided a workshop in Seville, Spain, for young musicians from countries throughout the Middle East with the goal of promoting an intercultural dialogue between Arabs and Israelis. In March 2017 these musicians will move to their own dedicated concert hall, Pierre Boulez Saal in Berlin, a former warehouse renovated by Gehry Partners.

In Birzeit, in the West Bank, the Palestinian Museum opened in May 2016 in a handsome new $24 million building designed by Heneghan Peng, a firm based in Dublin. The museum intends to celebrate and redefine Palestinian art, history, and culture; regrettably, due to a disagreement between the board and the director, its inauguration took place without any exhibitions after the long-planned opening show, "Never Part," was suspended. Omar Al-Qattan, the museum's chairman, announced that "Palestinians were 'so in need of positive energy' that it was worthwhile to open, even an empty building."[20]

In Brazil in 2006, Bernardo Paz, the mining magnate and art collector, inaugurated a 5,000-acre art park, the Centro de Arte Contemporânea Inhotim, in the impoverished Belo Horizonte area in the southern part of the country. The park employs 1,000 people and attracts nearly 500,000 annual visitors, giving a tremendous boost to the region's economy.[21]

In the wake of repeated terrorist attacks in France, which have taken hundreds of lives since November 2015, François Pinault, the French luxury-goods billionaire, announced his intention to open a private museum in 2018 in central Paris to display his collection of contemporary art. To this end, he is spending $55 million to restore and renovate the eighteenth-century Bourse de Commerce, and has hired Japanese architect Tadao Ando to work on the project with a French team. Says the art collector, "In the face of this barbarism, the only possible reaction is to move forward."[22]

Just as the architects of the SNFCC have stretched the boundaries of form and materials for the cultural center in Athens, the SNF directors are trying to expand the boundaries of the Greek way of life. Within the chaos of the nation's crisis, the foundation is pinning its hopes on help from the redemptive power of culture.

Acknowledgments

Chaos and Culture is a detailed account of the intricate ten-year process of designing and constructing the Stavros Niarchos Foundation Cultural Center in Athens. Throughout that time, I maintained a conversation with an astonishing number of individuals who conceived, supported, planned, designed, and built the complex. The extraordinary generosity, in time and patience, of those with whom I talked made this book possible.

Among the most noteworthy are the Renzo Piano Building Workshop architects, especially Renzo Piano himself and Giorgio Bianchi, the partner in charge of the project; their Betaplan senior partner in Athens, Eleni Tzanou; the SNF's chief technical officer, Theodore Maravelias; the landscape designer, Deborah Nevins, and her Athens associate, Helli Pangalou; the Cooper Robertson master planners, chiefly Scott Newman; Neil Clemson and Martin Hirko of Faithful+Gould, who oversaw construction; the Expedition Engineering team, especially director Bruce Martin and associate director Chris Wise, with contributions from associates Jared Keen and Pete Winslow; Patrick Jennings, the civil and structural engineering consultant; the facade consultants, Marc Simmons and Leo Henke at Front; the Arup team for services in mechanical, electrical, plant, information/communication technology, security, and lighting engineering, especially George Oates in structural engineering, Simon Delves in civil engineering, David McAllister, project manager, in building services engineering, and Raj Patel, Alban Bassuet, and Rachid Abu-Hassan in acoustics; the Theatre Projects consultant Benton Delinger; the library specialists Andy Stephens, at the British Library during the time he consulted on the project, and Joanne Eley at AMA Alexi Marmot Associates; and the library consultant Dimitris Chalkiopoulos.

From the very beginning, Andreas Dracopoulos, co-president and director of the SNF, together with chief operating officer Vasili Tsamis and Stelios Vasilakis, director of programs and strategic initiatives, encouraged this book project and went out of their way to facilitate it. Ioannis Trohopoulos, director of the SNFCC undertaking from 2012 to 2016, together with Myron Michailidis, artistic director of the Greek National Opera from 2011 to 2016, and Filippos Tsimpoglou, director general of the National Library of Greece since 2014, were also tremendously helpful.

I am grateful to the following friends and colleagues who read the manuscript and made valuable factual corrections and editorial suggestions: Yannis Aesopos, Jean-Louis Cohen, Joanne Gonchar, Alex Gorlin, Mildred Schmertz, and Suzanne Stephens. Asimina Grigoriou, Alexander Kitroeff, and Georgia Nakou commented on political events; and Kitroeff also contributed the timeline of recent Greek governments. Additional readers generously reviewed individual chapters: Rafi Segal, associate professor of architecture and urbanism, MIT, and Ioanna Theocharopoulou, assistant professor of interior design, School of Constructed Environments, Parsons the New School for Design (and author of the book *Builders, Housewives, and the Construction of Modern Athens*), on my description of the growth of Athens; Guy Nordenson on structural engineering; Sam Omans on the agora; Raphael Mostel and Carl Rosenberg (who also offered an acoustical evaluation) on the opera house; Joanne Eley and Andy Stephens on the library; and Dorothée Imbert, as well as Justin Parscher and Eleanor McPeck, on the park.

Most of the photography of the SNFCC was provided by Yiorgis Yerolymbos, courtesy of the SNF, and expedited by the ever-patient Asimina Koutroumpousi at the foundation in Athens. Aerial views of the SNFCC and some ground-level images are the work of Iwan Baan, who realized our commission despite multiple strategic complications. Sarah Rafson's diligent photo research produced the contextual illustrations.

My long-time editor, Andrea Monfried, refined the text with the help of copy editor Stephen Robert Frankel and Sophia Ma, my personal assistant, both of whom diligently researched, tracked, and verified innumerable details. Lars Müller introduced the design approach; Yve Ludwig and Julie Fry developed the scheme and executed the final presentation. Elizabeth White did an excellent job of producing the book. As usual, I am greatly appreciative of Gianfranco Monacelli's faith in me. I owe the work's concept and ongoing guidance to Robert Gottlieb.

Notes

Introduction

1 Joanna Woronkowicz, D. Carroll Joynes, and Norman M. Bradburn, "Two Case Studies: Chicago and Philadelphia," *Building Better Arts Facilities: Lessons from a U.S. National Study* (London and New York: Routledge, 2015), 22–23.

2 Andreas Dracopoulos, co-president and director of the SNF, in conversation with the author, November 5, 2015.

3 The music critic and historian George B. Monemvassitis attested to the relatively good conditions for the performance of opera at the Megaron, in conversation with the author, December 10, 2015.

4 Artists now also rely on a host of specialized collaborators to help them realize their work; see Joann Gonchar with Zachary Edelson, "The Engineering of Art," *Architectural Record,* August 2004, 122–27.

5 "Lever House, New York: Glass and Steel Walls," *Architectural Record,* June 1952, 130–35.

6 Pierluigi Serrano, "Genesis of Genius," *Architectural Record,* May 2016, 113.

7 Renzo Piano, in conversation with the author, June 24, 2015.

8 This description of Piano is based on remarks by Eleni Tzanou, a senior architect with the Greek firm Betaplan, in conversation with the author, November 11, 2015.

9 "The Stardust Factor," *The Art Newspaper,* April 2016, 11.

10 Guido Guerzoni, *Museums on the Map 1995–2012* (Turin, Italy: Umberto Allemandi & Co., 2014), 71.

11 Renzo Piano, conversation with the author, May 6, 2015.

12 Sylvie C. Davis and Ian M. Johnson, "The Mitterrand Library in Context: The Bibliothèque Nationale de France and Library Provision in France," *Libri,* 48, no. 4 (December 1998), 187–211.

13 Bruno Giussani, "European Politicians' New Mantra: Wiring Up Schools to the Internet," *Cybertimes,* April 1, 1997.

14 Robert McG. Thomas Jr., "Stavros Niarchos, Greek Shipping Magnate and the Archrival of Onassis, Is Dead at 86," *New York Times,* April 18, 1996; online at ‹www.nytimes.com/1996/04/18/world/stavros-niarchos-greek-shipping-magnate-archrival-onassisis-dead-86.html›.

15 Perry Anderson, "The Italian Disaster," *London Review of Books,* May 22, 2014, 5 (for youth unemployment statistic).

16 Piano, SNFCC press conference, June 29, 2011.

17 This and the following summary of modern Greek history is based on Thomas W. Gallant, *Modern Greece* (London: Hodder Education, 2001), chapter 3.

18 Carmen M. Reinhart and Christoph Trebesch, "The Pitfalls of External Dependence: Greece, 1829–2015," *National Bureau of Economic Resources Working Paper No. 21664,* 2015, online at ‹http://www.nber.org/papers/w21664›, 8–10.

19 John S. Koliopoulos and Thanos M. Veremis, *Greece: The Modern Sequel from 1831 to the Present* (New York: New York University Press, 2002).

20 Koliopoulos and Veremis, *Greece: The Modern Sequel,* introduction and chapter 2.

21 Richard Clogg, *A Concise History of Greece* (Cambridge, U.K.: Cambridge University Press, 1992), 6.

22 David H. Close, *Greece since 1945: Politics, Economy and Society* (London: Longman, 2002), 4, and Clogg, *Concise History of Greece,* 65.

23 Alexander Kitroeff, in conversation with the author, June 2, 2014.

24 "The Tax-Exemptions of the Contract with the SNF for the Transfer of the National Library and the National Opera in Faliro," *Alfa Vita,* July 26, 2013; online at ‹https://www.alfavita.gr/node/103905›.

Client

1 Michael Demarest, "Shipping: The New Argonauts," *Time,* August 6, 1956, 57.

2   Tom Bergin, "The Great Greek Shipping Myth," *Reuters.com*, November 25, 2016; online at ‹http://www.reuters.com/investigates/special-report/eurozone-greece-shipping/›.

3   Gelina Harlaftis, *Greek Shipowners and Greece, 1945–1975: From Separate Development to Mutual Interdependence* (London and Atlantic Highlands, N.J.: Athlone Press, 1993), 73–75. "U.S. Gets $16-Million Judgment against Niarchos Lines for Tax," *New York Times*, April 27, 1966, 1, 61.

4   Bergin, "Great Greek Shipping Myth."

5   "Special Report: Greek Shipowners Talk Up Their Role to Protect Tax Breaks," *Reuters.com*, November 25, 2015; online at ‹http://www.reuters.com/article/us-eurozone-greece-shipping-specialrepor-idUSKBN0TE1I520151125›. See also Niki Kitsantonis, "A Promise to Protect Pensions Will Test Greece's Red Line on Austerity," *New York Times*, September 18, 2013, B-10; online at ‹http://www.nytimes.com/2013/09/19/business/global/testing-greeces-red-line-on-austerity.html›.

6   The two Niarchos sons, Philip and Spyros, are also co-presidents; and there are two additional trustees: George Agouridis and Heini Murer.

7   Vasili Tsamis, SNF chief operating officer, e-mail to the author, October 15, 2015.

8   An SNF board member (who wishes to remain anonymous), e-mail to the author, October 13, 2014.

9   Robert McG. Thomas Jr., "Stavros Niarchos, Greek Shipping Magnate and the Archrival of Onassis, Is Dead at 86," *New York Times*, April 18, 1996; online at ‹www.nytimes.com/1996/04/18/world/stavros-niarchos-greek-shipping-magnate-archrival-onassisis-dead-86.html?pagewanted=all›.

10 Doris Lilly, *Those Fabulous Greeks: Onassis, Niarchos and Livanos, Three of the World's Richest Men* (New York: Cowles Book Company, 1970), 2.

11 Peter Evans, *The Life and Times of Aristotle Onassis* (New York: Charter Books, 1986), 3.

12 Murat Çizakça, *A History of Philanthropic Foundations: The Islamic World From the Seventh Century to the Present* (Istanbul: Boğaziçi University Press, 2000) 1, 43, 45, 71.

13 Demetrios J. Constantelos, *Byzantine Philanthropy and Social Welfare* (New Brunswick, N.J.: Rutgers University Press, 1968).

14 Dimitris Arvanitakis, ed., *To Phenomeno tou Evergetismou sti Neoteri Ellada* [The Phenomenon of Donorship in Modern Greece] (Athens: Benaki Museum, 2006).

15 This and other quotes and facts from statements by Andreas Dracopoulos are from his conversation with the author, April 2, 2013, and from an e-mail by Stelios Vasilakis, programming officer of the SNFCC, to the author, May 4, 2016.

16 Anthony Marx, in conversation with the author, February 1, 2013.

17 Andreas Dracopoulos, in conversation with the author, October 10, 2014.

18 "Andreas Dracopoulos, Co-President, Stavros Niarchos Foundation," *Philanthropy News Digest*, March 7, 2012; online at ‹http://philanthropynewsdigest.org/newsmakers/andreas-dracopoulos-stavros-niarchos-foundation›.

19 Simon Shuster, "Exclusive: Greek Shipping Magnate Urges Tycoons to Pull Their Weight," July 9, 2015; online at ‹http://time.com/3951086/dracopoulos-shipping-magnate›.

20 Melissa Eddy, "Greece Slips in Survey on Corruption," *International New York Times* (INYT Europe), December 6, 2012; online at ‹http://www.nytimes.com/2012/12/06/business/global/06iht-corrupt06.html›.

21 Transparency International, accessed online on May 4, 2016; online at ‹https://www.transparency.org/country/#GRC›.

22 Zoe Lanara, "Trade Unions in Greece and the Crisis: A Key Actor under Pressure," *International Policy Analysis*, Friedrich Ebert Stiftung, April 2012; online at ‹http://library.fes.de/pdf-files/id/ipa/09012.pdf›.

23 George Agouridis, SNF chief legal counsel, in conversation with the author, October 24, 2013.

24 The Gates Foundation, for example, discovered that its massive funding of global health programs, while helpful, eliminated the need for poor nations or other funders to retain interest in disease management.

25 The Niarchos Foundation reserves in perpetuity the right to use the theaters when they are not being used for performances of the NGO.

26 "Cultural Center 'Stavros Niarchos': Governmental Obeisance to the Capital," *Rizospastis*, July 27, 2013.

27 Stavros N. Papastavrou, the Greek prime minister's staff secretary, in conversation with the author, October 23, 2013.

28 Gerard Mortier, in conversation with the author, June 18, 2013.

29 "Performance Cancellations of the National Opera due to Strike," *Tovima.gr*, November 23, 2015; online at ‹http://www.tovima.gr/culture/article/?aid=756228&wordsinarticle=%CE%BB%CF%85%CF%81%CE%B9%CE%BA%CE%B7%3b%CF%83%CE%BA%CE%B7%CE%BD%CE%B7›.

30 Vasili Tsamis, e-mail to the author, August 21, 2016.

31 "Greece Signs Host Government Agreement with TAP Consortium," *Athens News Agency*, June 26, 2013; online at ‹http://www.amna.gr/english/article/3297/Greece-signs-host-government-agreement-with-TAP-consortium›. Katerina Sokou, "Greek Premier Promotes the Country as 'Bastion of Stability,'" *Washington Post*, August 8, 2013; online at ‹https://www.washingtonpost.com/business/economy/greek-premier-promotes-country-as-bastion-of-stability

/2013/08/08/9ec6f6a4-ffc0-11e2-96a8-d3b921c0924a_
story.html›.

32 "Greek Civil Servants Start 2-Day Strike," *New York Times*,
September 24, 2013; online at ‹http://www.nytimes.com
/2013/09/25/business/global/greek-civil-servants-start-2
-day-strike.html›.

33 The enormously high number of pensioners in Greece—
1 for every 1.3 workers—made reductions in their receipts a
major issue throughout the government's efforts at reform,
according to Paschos Mandravelis, "Lies, Damn Lies and
Pension Reform," *Kathimerini*, October 7, 2014; online at
‹http://www.kathimerini.gr/786985/opinion/epikairothta
/politikh/yemata-megala-yemata-kai-asfalistiko›.

34 Suzanne Daley, "So Many Bribes, A Greek Official Can't
Recall All," *International New York Times* (INYT Europe),
February 8, 2014, A1, 6; online at ‹http://www.nytimes.
com/2014/02/08/world/europe/so-many-bribes-a-greek
-official-cant-recall-all.html›.

35 Helena Smith, "Corruption Still Alive and Well in Post-
Bailout Greece," *The Guardian*, December 3, 2014; online at
‹http://www.theguardian.com/world/2014/dec/03/greece
-corruption-alive-and-well›.

36 Andreas Dracopoulos, in conversation with the author, January 22, 2014.

Beginnings

1 Scott Newman, in conversation with the author, March 11,
2015.

2 See Victoria Newhouse, *Site and Sound: the Architecture
and Acoustics of Opera Houses and Concert Halls* (New York:
Monacelli Press, 2012), 144–47.

3 This and the following quotes and references to the choice
of an architect are based on Andreas Dracopoulos, in conversation with the author, April 2, 2013.

4 Renzo Piano, *Log Book* (New York: Monacelli Press, 1997).

5 Piano, in conversation with the author, May 6, 2015.

6 Unless otherwise indicated, this and the following description and quotes from Piano come from his conversations
with the author, June 24 and November 10, 2013.

7 Placing the building within the hill saves as much as 7 percent of the energy required for cooling it. Alistair Guthrie,
civil engineer, e-mail to the author, November 21, 2014.

8 Piano, in conversation with the author, May 7, 2015. Borges,
in his short story "Funes the Memorious," describes a char-
acter who, after a fall from a horse, remembers every detail
of everything he experiences but is incapable of abstract
thinking; he has only memories devoid of thought.

9 Giorgio Bianchi, in conversation with the author, October 17,
2014.

10 Technologies have been developed that allow direct communication between architect and tradespeople, bypassing the
need for a contractor; one example is Gehry Technologies.
"Interview with Frank Gehry," *Perspecta 47: Money* (Cambridge, Mass.: MIT Press, 2014), 66–67.

11 The discussion of Piano's drawings and models is based on
his conversation with the author, May 6, 2015. Piano also
collects images and newspaper cuttings, which he pastes
into books that he keeps in different places; "Book in Progress," *Abitare* 497, no. 11 (November 2009): 117.

12 "In Conversation: Peter Schjeldahl with Jarrett Earnest," *Brooklyn Rail* (July–August 2015), 40; online at ‹www.brooklynrail
.org/2015/07/art/peter-schjeldahl-with-jarrett-earnest›.

13 The responsibility began to be a legal obligation in the
United States on a state-by-state basis in the last decade
of the nineteenth century. See Branko Mitrović, "Leon Bat-
tista Alberti, Mental Rotation, and the Origins of Three-
Dimensional Computer Modeling," *Journal of the Society of
Architectural Historians* 74, no. 3 (September 2015), 312–22.

14 Mario Carpo, "Craftsman to Draftsman: The Albertian Paradigm and the Modern Invention of Construction Drawings,"
in *The Working Drawing: The Architect's Tool* (Zurich: Park
Books, 2013), 278–80.

15 W. H. S. Jones, trans., "Pausanias 1.17–29," *Description of
Greece* on Theoi.com, accessed August 5, 2016; online at
‹http://www.theoi.com/Text/Pausanias1B.html›.

16 Raj Patel and Alban Bassuet, both acousticians at Arup, in
conversation with the author, March 26, 2013.

17 Eleni Tzanou, Betaplan architect, "SNFCC Construction
Update Report for November 2013."

18 The discussion of the Athenian Acropolis is based on Vincent Scully, *The Earth, the Temple, and the Gods: Greek Sacred
Architecture* (New Haven and London: Yale University Press,
rev. ed. 1979), chapters 1 and 9.

19 Elizabeth K. Meyer, "The Public Park as Avante-Garde
(Landscape) Architecture: A Comparative Interpretation of
Two Parisian Parks, Parc de la Villette (1983–1990) and Parc
des Buttes-Chaumont (1864–1867)," *Landscape Journal* 28,
no. 1 (January 1, 2009), 22–39.

20 Antoine Grumbach, "The Promenades of Paris," *Oppositions*
8 (Spring 1977), 51–67.

21 This and the following costs are based on Neil Clemson,
F+G project management and commercial director worldwide, in conversation with the author, June 25, 2014.

22 Martin Hirko, in conversation with the author, November
26, 2013.

23 Hirko, in conversation with the author, January 7, 2013.

24 Hirko, e-mail to the author, April 21, 2013.

25 Hirko, e-mails to the author, June 23, 2015, and November 23, 2015.

26 Boston Consulting Group, "SNFCC Impact Study and Business Plan: Impact Assessment," Athens, December 23, 2010.

27 Millennium Park Quadruple Net Value Report, Texas A&M University and DePaul University, summer 2011.

28 Boston Consulting Group, "SNFCC Impact Study," 3. Nikos Rousanoglou, "Athens Rivera Finally Growing Into Its Potential," *Kathimerini English Edition*, August 24, 2016, online at ‹http://www.ekathimerini.com/211442 /article/ekathimerini/business/athens-riviera-finally -growing-into-its-potential›.

29 Dracopoulos, in conversation with the author, October 10, 2014.

Athens

1 Ioanna Theocharopoulou, "Urbanization and the Emergence of the *Polykatoikia*: Habitat and Identity, Athens 1830–1975" (Ph.D. dissertation, Columbia University, May 2007), 125; published in slightly modified form as *Builders, Housewives and the Construction of Modern Athens* (Chicago: Artifice Books, 2016).

2 Lila Leontidou, *The Mediterranean City in Transition: Social Change and Urban Development* (New York, Port Chester, Melbourne, and Sydney: Cambridge University Press, 1990), 47–50.

3 Eleni Bastéa, *The Creation of Modern Athens: Planning the Myth* (Cambridge, U.K.: Cambridge University Press, 2000), 70–82.

4 Yannis Aesopos, *Landscapes of Modernization: Greek Architecture 1960s and 1990s* (Athens: Metapolis Press, 1999), 117.

5 Bastéa, *Creation of Modern Athens, 111.*

6 Gordon E. Cherry, Harriet Jordan, and Kiki Kafkoula, "Gardens, Civic Art and Town Planning: The Work of Thomas H. Mawson (1861–1933)," *Planning Perspectives* 8, no. 3 (1993), 307–32; online at ‹http://www.tandfonline.com/doi /pdf/10.1080/02665439308725777›.

7 See, for example, Aristotle, *Politics*, Book 2, Section 1267b, online at ‹http:www.perseus.tufts.edu/hopper/text?doc= Perseus%3Atext%3A1999.01.0058%3Abook%3D2%3 Asection%3D1267b#note2›.

8 George Seferis, "Mythistorema," in *George Seferis: Collected Poems 1924–1955*, trans. Edmund Keeley (Princeton, N.J.: Princeton University Press, 1995), online at ‹www.poetry foundation.org/poem/181958#poem›.

9 These ethnic Greeks were sent to Greece as part of the Greek-Turkish Exchange of Populations (1923), which stipulated that all (2 million) Orthodox people in Turkey (which had replaced the Ottoman Empire) would be relocated to Greece, and that Greece would send its Muslim population (400,000) to Turkey. Many refugees and exchanged Greeks settled in a ring around Athens.

10 Thomas Maloutas and Stavros Spyrellis, "Vertical Social Segregation in Athenian Apartment Buildings," *Athens Social Atlas*, December 2015, online at ‹http://www.athens socialatlas.gr/en/article/vertical-segregation/›. "History of Athens—Post-War Period—Athens Info Guide," accessed on June 8, 2016, online at ‹http://www.athensinfoguide.com /history/t-9-97-1governments.htm›.

11 Kostas Biris, *Athens: From the 19th to the 20th Century* (Athens: Melissa Publications, 1966), 287, quoted in Theocharopoulou, Builders, *Housewives*, 142.

12 Written report of the architects who did the city analysis, EEST IV.44, Cornelis van Eesteren archive, New Institute, Rotterdam, online at ‹http://collectie.hetnieuweinstituut .nl/en/collection-news/cornelis-van-eesteren-archive- inventoried›.

13 Peter Buchanan, "The City as Natural Habitat versus the City as Cultural Artifact," *Architectural Review* 176, no. 1054 (1984), 64–65.

14 Maloutas and Spyrellis, "Vertical Social Segregation in Athenian Apartment Buildings."

15 Yannis Aesopos, "Polykatoikia as an Urban Unit," in *Bauwelt* 29 (Berlin: Bertelsmann, 2004). Yannis Aesopos and Yorgos Simeoforidis, *Contemporary Greek City* (Athens: Metropolis Press, 2001), in which growth of Athens is discussed in several essays.

16 T. Pagonis, I. Chorianopoulos, S. Drymoniti, and S. Koukoulas, "Urban Competitiveness and Sprawl as Conflicting Planning Priorities: The Olympic Legacy of Athens," 44th ISO-CARP Congress 2008, online at ‹http://www.isocarp.net/ data/case_studies/1361.pdf›. "Greece: A City Is Dying," *Time*, April 23, 1979, 23.

17 Giorgos Stathakis and Costis Hadjimichalis, "Athens as a World City: From the Anxiety of the Few to the Reality of the Majority," *Geographies*, no. 7 (2004).

18 Accounts of Olympic expenditures vary from study to study; one source for the Barcelona Olympics is Ferran Brunet, *An Economic Analysis of the Barcelona '92 Olympic Games: Resources, Financing and Impact* (Barcelona: Centre d'Estudis Olímpics UAB, 1995), 6.

19 This and the following comments on the problems that plagued the 2004 Olympics are based on Alexander Kitroeff,

Wrestling with the Ancients: Modern Identity and the Olympics (New York: Greekworks.com, 2004), 201, 235.

20 Christopher Rhoads, "The Newest Wonder of the World: The Ruins of Modern Greece," *Wall Street Journal*, June 17, 2010; online at ‹http://www.wsj.com/articles/SB10001424052748 7040253045752848413806683082›.

21 Yannis Aesopos, "Post-Olympic Architecture: An Architectural Tour of Athens," *A10*, no. 15 (2008), 66–68.

22 Renzo Piano, in conversation with the author, November 26, 2012.

23 Andreas Dracopoulos, in conversation with the author, April 2, 2013.

24 Kristina Killgrave, "Archaeologists to Study Shackled Skeletons from Ancient Greece to Understand Rise of Athens," *Forbes*, March 24, 2016, online at ‹http://www.forbes.com /sites/kristinakillgrove/2016/03/24/archaeologists-to-study -shackled-skeletons-from-ancient-greece-to-understand -rise-of-athens/#2b91ef703591›.

25 Stella Chryssoulaki, in conversation with the author, October 22, 2013.

26 Quotes and information about the site are based on my conversation with Theodore Maravelias, October 22, 2013.

27 As relayed by Martin Hirko, Faithful+Gould construction manager, in conversation with the author, October 23, 2013.

28 All paints, carpets, and wood-based materials specified for use within the building meet stringent environmental performance requirements to safeguard indoor air quality. Also, more than 10 percent of the complex's 970 parking stalls are designated as preferred parking for carpooling and low-emission, fuel-efficient vehicles, and there is a secure area for two hundred bicycles. I am indebted to Gable Bennett, Faithful+Gould, LEED coordinator, for the LEED certification information related to the SNFCC.

29 The pilot version, LEED New Construction (NC) v1.0 in 1998, led to LEED NC v2.0 in 2000, LEED NC v2.2 in 2005, and LEED 2009 (also referred to as LEED v3). LEED v4 was introduced in November 2013.

30 Eirini Matsouki, in conversation with the author, March 24, 2014.

31 No author, "Hellinikon Upgrade Project on Its Way To Becoming A Reality," *Greek Travel Pages: Headlines*, June 7, 2016; online at ‹http://news.gtp.gr/2016/06/07/hellinikon-upgrade-project-reality/›.

32 Lefteris Papadimas, "Greek PM Tsipras Freezes Privatisations, Markets Tumble," *Reuters News Agency*, January 28, 2015; online at ‹http://www.reuters.com/article/us-greece -politics-idUSKBN0L10VP20150128›.

33 Kerin Hope, "Athens Approves Fund to Speed Up Privatization Programme," *Financial Times*, September 27, 2016; online at ‹www.ft.com/content/81dc1d54-84f5-11e6-8897 -2359a58ac7a5›.

Structure

1 Martin Hirko, Faithful+Gould construction manager, in conversation with the author, November 23, 2015.

2 Sylvie Deswarte and Bertrand Lemoine, *L'architecture et les ingénieurs: deux siècles de réalisations*, 2nd ed. (Paris: Le Moniteur, 1997), 28.

3 Giorgio Bianchi, in conversation with the author, October 17, 2014.

4 Bianchi, in conversation with the author, October 23, 2015.

5 Earthquakes of magnitude 5 or higher on the Richter scale are considered potentially damaging; Sandra S. Schulz and Robert E. Wallace, "The San Andreas Fault," *U.S. Geological Survey*, 1992, online at ‹http://pubs.usgs.gov/gip/earthq3 /endnotes.html›. In 1994, the Northridge earthquake in Los Angeles, which measured 6.6 on the Richter scale, killed 60 people, injured 7,700, and rendered 5,000 buildings unsafe; "On this Day," *BBC News*, online at ‹http://news .bbc.co.uk/onthisday/hi/dates/stories/january/17/newsid _4079000/4079741.stm›.

6 Kenneth Chang, "Staying Ahead of Quakes in Nepal and Elsewhere," *New York Times*, May 6, 2015, 8.

7 This and the following quotes and information from Bruce Martin come from his conversation with the author, September 17, 2013.

8 Jared Keen, e-mail to the author, July 31, 2013.

9 Eleni Tzanou, Betaplan architect, in conversation with the author, October 14, 2015.

10 Joachim Krausse and Claude Lichtenstein, eds., *Your Private Sky: R. Buckminster Fuller—The Art of Design Science*, trans. Steven Lindberg and Julia Thorson (Baden: Lars Müller, 1999), 226.

11 This and the following quotes from Chris Wise come from his conversation with the author, May 3, 2013.

12 Piano, in conversation with the author, May 6, 2015.

13 Extensive research was devoted to finding a material that would satisfy Piano's requirement that the slender 130-foot mast (diameter 16 in. at the base, 3 in. at the top) respond to varying wind conditions as well as to stress, fatigue, and other factors; the final choice was composite fiberglass (GFRP).

14 "Ferro-Cement and Reinforced Concrete," *Concrete Construction*, July 1, 1971; online at ‹http://www.concreteconstruction .net/how-to/ferro-cement-and-reinforced-concrete_o›; and the concise definition of ferro-cement in V. A. Ducatti,

R. C. Lintz, and J. M. Santos, "Comparative Study with Alternative Materials for Manufacture of Machine Tool Structures," in *Proceedings of the 17th International Congress of Mechanical Engineering* (November 10–14, 2003), 2; online at ‹http://www.abcm.org.br/anais/cobem/2003/html/pdf/COB03-0310.pdf›.

15 Patrick Jennings, in conversation with the author, October 23, 2013 and email to the author, November 8, 2016.

16 J. M. Pemberton, "Ferrocement—An Insight and Review—So What Is New?" in *Ferrocement 6, Lambot Symposium: Proceedings of the Sixth International Symposium on Ferrocement*, ed. A. E. Naaman (Ann Arbor: University of Michigan, 1998), 75–83. Rowland Morgan, "Saint Budoc and Lambot's Washerwomen," in *Ferrocement: Proceedings of the Fifth International Symposium*, ed. P. Nedwell and R. N. Swamy (New York: CRC Press, 2010), 28–29, 31.

17 Tullia Iori and Sergio Poretti, "Pier Luigi Nervi's Works for the 1960 Rome Olympics," in *Proceedings of the Congreso Nacional de Historia de la Construcción, Cádiz* (January 27–29, 2005), 205 and 209; online at ‹http://www.sedhc.es/biblioteca/actas/CNHC4_058.pdf›.

18 Pete Winslow, Expedition Engineering expert in roof structures, e-mail to the author, Febuary 18, 2014.

19 Winslow, in conversation with the author, Sept. 17, 2013.

20 Queen Alia Mausoleum in Amman, Jordan (Halcrow, 1980); APICORP headquarters in Al Khobar/Dammam, Saudi Arabia (DEGW, 2000); Yanbu Cement Company in Yanbu, Saudi Arabia (Francesco Audrito & Athena Sampaniotu, 2000).

21 Winslow, e-mail to the author, Febuary 18, 2014.

22 Neil Clemson, e-mail to the author, Jan. 28, 2016.

23 Winslow, e-mail to the author, April 17, 2013.

24 Ove Nyquist Arup, "The Engineer Looks Back," *Architectural Review* 166, no. 993 (November 1979), 315–21. *Philosophy of Design* (Munich, London, New York: Prestel, 2012), 207.

25 Ove Nyquist Arup, "The Engineer and the Architect," speech at the Institution of Civil Engineers, in *Proceedings of the Institution of Civil Engineers* 13, no. 4 (August 1959), 503–10.

26 Kieran and Heidi Rice, "It's Not Just Architects Who Make Great Buildings," *The Guardian*, October 18, 2007; online at ‹http://www.theguardian.com/commentisfree/2007/oct/19/comment.architecture›.

27 Ian Volner, "The Sky's the Limit," *Metropolis*, September 13, 2013, 58.

28 See Joe Morgenstern, "The Fifty-Nine-Story Crisis," *New Yorker*, May 29, 1995, 45–55.

29 Even discounting human error, a recent book by Henry Petroski, professor of civil engineering at Duke University, is indicative of the profession's uncertainties: *To Forgive Design: Understanding Failure* (Cambridge, Mass., and London, England: Belknap Press of Harvard University Press, 2014), 41.

30 Peter Rice, *An Engineer Imagines* (London: Artemis, 1994), 25–46.

31 "Bridge 'Wobble' Blamed On Walkers," *BBC News*, December 24, 2008; online at ‹http://news.bbc.co.uk/go/pr/fr/-/2/hi/uk_news/england/london/7785421.stm›.

32 Chris Wise, "Build with an Eye on Nature," *Nature* 494, no. 7436 (Febuary 14, 2013), 173.

Agora

1 Comments by Renzo Piano quoted in this chapter are from his conversations with the author on May 6 and 7, 2015.

2 Richard Sennett, in the 1998 Raoul Wallenberg Lecture "The Spaces of Democracy" (Ann Arbor: University of Michigan College of Architecture + Urban Planning, 1998), 8–21; online at ‹http://taubmancollege.umich.edu/pdfs/publications/map/wallenberg1998_richardsennett.pdf›.

3 Mohhamed Elshahed, "Occupied Spaces," *Architectural Record*, December 2011, 34–36.

4 Marc Simmons, in conversation with the author, April 25, 2014, and February 17, 2015. Front currently employs forty staff people around the world.

5 To avoid confusion between what is referred to alternatively as a structural glass curtain wall and as a structural glass facade, I use throughout this text the simpler term "glass facade," which possesses attributes of both systems.

6 Neil Clemson, in conversation with the author, April 21, 2015.

7 The choice of subcontractors by the general contractors was a consequence of the SNF's insistence on a 100 percent budget guarantee on the finished building before subcontractors were selected by competitive bidding.

8 Comparative industry costs were supplied January 20, 2016, by the Tocci Group, a New York City–based cost-estimating company.

9 Front was also responsible for the east-facing glazing of the agora, the frameless glass (also protected by blinds) of the lighthouse, and the expanded metal cladding of the garage (similar to the metal skin fabricated by Front for the New Museum in New York).

10 Giorgio Bianchi, in conversation with the author, October 17, 2014.

11 Concrete Network, "Properly Curing Concrete Slabs," online at ‹http://www.concretenetwork.com/concrete/slabs/curing.htm›.

12 Bianchi, in conversation with the author, April 22, 2015. The description echoes the distinction made by Colin Rowe and Robert Slutzky in their 1956 article "Transparency: Literal and Phenomenal," *Perspecta* 8 (1963), 45–54: the Menil Collection's building displays phenomenal transparency; the SNFCC, literal transparency.

13 Mark di Suvero, "Renzo Piano," *Interview Magazine*, May 13, 2015; online at ‹http://www.interviewmagazine.com/art /renzo-piano/#_›.

14 Ruth Eaton, *Ideal Cities: Utopianism and the (Un)Built Environment* (New York and London: Thames & Hudson, 2002), 164.

15 Jean-Louis Cohen, *Ludwig Mies van der Rohe* (Basel: Birkhäuser, 2007), 30.

16 Diana M. Bush, "The Dialectical Object: John Heartfield 1915–1933" (Ph.D., Columbia University, 2013), online at ‹Bush_columbia_0054D_11592.pdf›, 62. See the abstract of this thesis online at ‹http://academiccommons.columbia .edu/item/ac:177556›.

17 Scott Murray, "New Directions and New Priorities," *Contemporary Curtain Wall Architecture* (New York: Princeton Architectural Press, 2009), 48–63.

18 The facade description is based on Simone Medio and James Murphy, Paper No. 342: "Aesthetic Vision and Sustainability in the New York Times Building Ceramic Rod Façade"; online at ‹http://architecture.ucd.ie/Paul/PLEA2008/content/ papers/oral/PLEA_FinalPaper_ref_342.pdf›.

19 Pranksters who used the rods to climb the building shortly after its completion were deterred when existing glass canopies were extended over the street to make the rods inaccessible.

20 Bruce Fowle, in conversation with the author, July 22, 2015.

21 Suzanne Daley, "Greeks' Patience with Austerity Nears Its Limit," *New York Times*, December 30, 2014, A1, A8. Paul Krugman, "Ending Greece's Nightmare," *New York Times*, January 26, 2014, A21.

22 Niki Kitsantonis and James Kanter, "Europe Braces for Economic Fallout as Greece Heads to Early Elections," *New York Times*, December 30, 2014, A8.

23 James Kanter, in his news article "After Talks, Eurozone and Greece Fail to Settle Differences Over Debt," *New York Times*, Feb. 12, 2015, B3, described Varoufakis as "characteristically casual in a tieless, untucked shirt" and declared that Lagarde's "black leather jacket seemed to signal her readiness to take an approach as tough as Varoufakis's." Five months later, in a news article for Agence-France Presse, "Varoufakis: Scourge of Greece's Creditors" (online at ‹https://www.yahoo.com/news/yanis-varoufakis-greeces -erratic-marxist-090341195.html›), Sophie Makris called him "Greece's maverick finance minister," stating that he "achieved near-celebrity status with an urban-cool image and visceral attacks on the country's international creditors" and "refuse[d] to bow to convention." She referred to his "abrasive style," "unconventional manner," and the way he dressed: "His look immediately set him apart from the pinstriped world of finance ministers. His jacket collar was turned up to his shaven head, his shirts were sometimes flowery, and away from meetings he preferred a motorbike to a chauffeur-driven limo."

24 "Give Greece Room to Maneuver" (editorial), *New York Times*, Febuary 17, 2015, A20; online at ‹http://www .nytimes.com/2015/02/18/opinion/give-greece-room-to -maneuver.html›.

25 James Kanter and Niki Kitsantonis, "Greece's Leaders Face a Revolt at Home as They Try and Appease Creditors," *New York Times*, Febuary 23, 2015.

26 Alison Same and Jim Yardley, "Language of Greek Crisis Shifts from Financial Jargon to Humiliation," *New York Times*, March 13, 2015, A8.

27 On February 10, 2016, the Greek government announced its intention to nationalize the Megaron Mousikis; Thanasis Koukakis, "The State Passed the Building and the Debts of the Athens Concert Hall," *CNN Greece*, February 10, 2016; online at ‹http://www.cnn.gr/money/story/21222/sto -dimosio-perna-to-ktirio-kai-ta-xrei-toy-megaroy -moysikis-athinon›.

28 Aristides Baltas, press release, Stavros Niarchos Foundation website, May 7, 2015, online at ‹http://www.snf.org/en /newsroom/news/2015/05/visit-of-the-minister-of-culture, -education-and-religion-at-the-snfcc/›.

29 "Donation of Niarchos in Faliro Is Ready, Searching for Resources in the Ministry of Economy to Run the Facility," *Proto Thema News* (Greece), March 25, 2016; online at ‹http://www.protothema.gr/greece/article/564615/etoimi -i-dorea-niarhou-sto-faliro-psahnoun-porous-sto-upour geio-oikonomias-gia-na-leitourgisei/›.

Opera

1 Suzy Hansen, "Divide," *New York Times Magazine*, May 24, 2015, 38.

2 Hansen, "Divide," 52.

3 Eric Maurice, "Greece Ready to Pay Debts, But Flirting with Moscow," *EUObserver*, April 7, 2015; online at ‹https://eu observer.com/news/128248›.

4 "Greek Prime Minister Tsipras Announces Bailout Referen-

dum," Reuters News Service, June 27, 2015, text of national address given that day by Tsipras; online at ‹http://www .reuters.com/article/2015/06/27/us-eurozone-greece-tsipras -text-idUSKBN0P700T20150627›.

5   Herodotus of Halicarnassus, *The Histories*, trans. Robin Waterfield (Oxford: Oxford University Press, 2008), 337; online at ‹http://www.paxlibrorum.com/books/histories/›.

6   Niki Kitsantonis, "Greek Government Unveils Tough Draft Budget for Next Year," *New York Times*, October 6, 2015, B2.

7   Nikoleta Papazoglou, "They Transferred to Faliro and Greek Migrants from 2300 Idomeni," *CNN Greece*, December 9, 2015, online at ‹http://www.cnn.gr/news/ellada/story/14328 /metaferthikan-se-faliro-kai-elliniko-2-300-metanastes -apo-eidomeni›. Ioanna Zikakou, "Refugee Crisis in Athens Is Out of Control," *Greek Reporter*, December 30, 2015; online at ‹http://greece.greekreporter.com/2015/12/30/refugee -crisis-in-athens-getting-out-of-control-refugees-sleeping -outside-in-the-cold/›.

8   This and other comments by Dracopoulos quoted in this chapter are based on his conversation with the author, November 5, 2015.

9   Arup has expanded its expertise to encompass a broad variety of disciplines, making it today one of the largest engineering firms in the world. Its staff of 11,000 occupies 90 offices in 35 countries. Engineers are regularly reassigned so that they can familiarize themselves with one another. Since 1978, Arup employees and charitable trusts have owned all equity in the company; profits are distributed according to shareholdings.

10 Benton Delinger, e-mail to the author, November 1, 2015.

11 Alban Bassuet, in conversation with the author, November 7, 2015.

12 Renzo Piano, in conversation with the author, May 7, 2015.

13 For the havoc wrought on Lincoln Center's New York State Theater by the absence of client input, see Victoria Newhouse, *Site and Sound: The Architecture and Acoustics of Opera Houses and Concert Halls* (New York: Monacelli Press, 2012), 82–88.

14 Nikos Vatopoulos, "The 'Political' Project of the National Opera," *Kathimerini Newspaper*, September 28, 2013; online at ‹http://www.kathimerini.gr/737002/opinion/epikairothta /arxeio-monimes-sthles/to-politiko-egxeirhma-ths-lyrikhs›.

15 The facts about the GNO director and the information about new initiatives for the GNO are from Myron Michailidis's conversation with the author, October 23, 2013.

16 This statement and information on the opera house's current finances are based on Myron Michailidis's conversation with the author, April 23, 2015.

17 "The big room needs to give a transformative experience" is among the statements made by Brian Stacy, the lighting leader for the GNO, in conversations with the author on November 7, 2013, and Febuary 6, 2014.

18 Leo Beranek, *Concert Halls and Opera Houses: Music, Acoustics, and Architecture* (New York, Berlin, Heidelberg: Springer, 1996, 2nd ed., 2004), 47.

19 Leo L. Beranek, "Analysis of Sabine and Eyring Equations," *Journal of the Acoustical Society of America* 120, no. 3 (September 2006), 1399, online at ‹http://www.leoberanek.com /pages/sabineandeyringeq.pdf›. Heinrich Kuttruff, *Room Acoustics*, 5th edition (New York: Taylor & Francis, 2009), 98, 131; online at ‹http://197.14.51.10:81/pmb/ARCHITECTURE /Room%20Acoustics.pdf›.

20 Typically, for a large project such as the Athens opera house, TPC charges a flat fee based on the scope of the project and an assumed budget total that also includes elements unrelated to the performance spaces.

21 See Konstantīnos Kardamis, "Nobile Teatro di San Giacomo di Corfù: An Overview of Its Significance for the Greek Ottocento," paper presented during the XI Convegno Annuale di Società Italiana di Musicologia (Leece, Eng., October 22–24, 2004); online at ‹http://www.academia .edu/185488/_Nobile_Teatro_di_San_Giacomo_di _Corf%C3%B9_an_overview_of_its_significance_for_the _Greek_ottocento_›. I am indebted to George B. Monemvassitis, a music critic and historian, for his comments about the evolution of interest in opera in Greece in a conversation with me on December 10, 2015.

22 Bassuet, in conversation with the author, March 26, 2013.

23 Alban Bassuet, "The New National Opera House for Greece: Reflections from an Acoustical Design Practitioner," *Opera Quarterly* 27, no. 4 (Autumn 2011), 483–94.

24 Unless otherwise indicated, the acoustical discussion of the GNO is based on Alban Bassuet, "The Acoustical Design of the New National Opera House of Greece," *Building Acoustics* 18, no. 3–4 (December 2011), 313–28; also delivered as a paper at the ISRA conference in Sydney, August 29–31, 2010; online at ‹http://www.acoustics.asn.au/conference _proceedings/ICA2010/cdrom-ISRA2010/Papers /O4a.pdf›.

25 Bassuet, in conversation with the author, February 6, 2013.

26 Beranek, *Concert Halls and Opera Houses*, 624.

27 Bassuet, in conversation with the author, February 6, 2013.

28 Bassuet, in conversation with the author, February 6, 2013.

29 Bassuet, in conversation with the author, September 12, 2013.

30 Eleni Tzanou, Betaplan architect, "SNFCC Construction Update Report for January 2014."

31 Giorgio Bianchi, in conversation with the author, May 20, 2014.

32 Brian Stacy, in conversation with the author, Febuary 6, 2013.

33 David McAllister, email to the author, July 29, 2016.

34 Bassuet, "Acoustical Design of the New National Opera House," 317–18.

35 Newhouse, *Site and Sound,* 82–88.

36 Bassuet, e-mail message to the author, November 27, 2015.

37 This and other quotes from Rachid Abu-Hassan are based on his conversation with the author, September 5, 2013.

38 This and the following information about sound isolation are from Abu-Hassan and Ryan Biziorek, "Building Acoustics," in "SNFCC Preliminary Summaries of Key Arup Design Contributions." The two boxes are connected for access, services, and restraint of the inner walls, which are free to move on their seismic isolators.

39 Paris Ayiomamitis, "Trial of Far-Right Golden Dawn Leaders Starts in Greece," *The Guardian,* April 20, 2016; online at ‹http://www.theguardian.com/world/2015/apr/20/greece-far-right-golden-dawn-nikos-michaloliakos-trial-start›. Omaira Gill, "Greece's Golden Dawn Trial Going Nowhere Fast," *Deutsche Welle,* April 20, 2016; online at ‹http://www.dw.com/en/greeces-golden-dawn-trial-going-nowhere-fast/a-19197580›.

40 Luiz Gazzola, "The Exclusive Opera Lively Interview with Maestro Myron Michailidis from the Greek National Opera," *Opera Lively,* January 11, 2014; online at ‹http://operalively.com/forums/content.php/914+The-Exclusive-Opera-Lively-Interview-with-Maestro-Myron-Michailidis-from-the-Greek-National-Opera›.

41 Gazzola, "Interview," *Opera Lively,* January 11, 2014.

42 Michailidis, in conversation with the author, April 23, 2015.

Library

1 In Greece, unlike in the United States, there is less understanding of the need and use of public libraries. Consequently, scholars have become accustomed to using other libraries in Athens for their research.

2 "Press Conference with the SNFCC architect, Renzo Piano," Stavros Niarchos Foundation website, June 24, 2015; online at ‹http://www.snf.org/en/newsroom/news/2015/06/press-conference-with-the-snfcc-architect,-renzo-piano/›.

3 Renzo Piano, in conversation with the author, November 26, 2012.

4 Matthew Battles, "Burning Alexandria," chap. 2 of *Library: An Unquiet History* (New York and London: W. W. Norton, 2003).

5 Daniel Rauchwerger and Noam Dvir, "Facades of Nations:

National Libraries as Knowledge Icons," *Harvard Design Magazine,* no. 38 (Spring/Summer 2014), 84–89.

6 Only 22 percent of the Greeks interviewed by the Boston Consulting Group as part of their impact study said they had read a book within the last year, as compared with 37 percent in the E.U. The Boston Consulting Group, *Final Impact Study Report* (Athens, February 22, 2016); online at ‹http://www.snfcc.org/about/impact-study-(bcg)/›, 23.

7 Queens Library director Thomas Galante was subsequently accused of improperly using money earmarked for improving the library's sixty-two branches and steering construction contracts to an acquaintance; Al Baker, "Hint of Scandal Embroils Queens Library's Leaders," *New York Times*, August 21, 2014, A17.

8 At the same time, in early 2014, Piano briefly toyed with, and subsequently dropped, the idea of replacing marble with wood for the floor of the agora; Eleni Tzanou, Betaplan architect, e-mail to the author, February 16, 2014.

9 In the New Haven and London libraries, this central place of honor is reserved for rare and valuable volumes with distinguished old leather bindings that need special care.

10 Wolfgang Tschapeller, e-mail message to the author, October 28, 2015.

11 George Oates, in conversation with the author, April 8, 2015.

12 This and subsequent facts about the participation of the British Library in the Athens design are based on Andy Stephens's conversation with the author, November 27, 2012.

13 Dracopoulos, in conversation with the author, October 10, 2014.

14 "Speech by the CEO and Managing Director of the SNFCC," Stavros Niarchos Foundation website, January 2013; online at ‹http://www.snf.org/media/3001934/Iioannis-Trohopoulos-EN.pdf›.

15 Martin Hirko, F+G construction manager, in conversation with the author, July 30, 2013.

16 Rem Koolhaas, in conversation with the author, May 8, 2013. Another similarly unfortunate juxtaposition of opposing styles was that of the classical interiors by Thierry Dupont and the modernist exteriors by Richard Meier at the J. Paul Getty Museum in Los Angeles.

17 Ioannis Trohopoulos, in conversation with the author, May 14, 2013.

18 Trohopoulos, in conversation with the author, May 14, 2013.

19 This quote and references to Francine M.J. Houben's ideas come from her conversations with the author, May 7 and September 19, 2013.

20 The New York Public Library's hiring of Mecanoo in September 2015 for the renovation of its Mid-Manhattan Library

and the much-disputed part interior of the main library proposed by Foster + Partners, plus the library commissions it has won in Washington, D.C., and Boston attest to the firm's respect for books.

21 Rachid Abu-Hassan, acoustician at Arup, in conversation with the author, October 29, 2013.

22 Lee Erickson, "The Economy of Novel Reading: Jane Austen and the Circulating Library," *Studies in English Literature, 1500–1900*, 30, no. 4 (1990): 574; Elizabeth W. Stone, *American Library Development, 1600–1899* (New York: H. W. Wilson, 1977); and the entry on "Children's Libraries" in Wayne A. Wiegand and Donald G. Davis, Jr., *Encyclopedia of Library History* (New York: Garland, 1994), 127–28.

23 Dimitris Chalkiopoulos, in conversation with the author, April 23, 2015.

24 Giorgio Bianchi, in conversation with the author, May 7, 2013, and November 19, 2013.

25 Bianchi, in conversation with the author, September 30, 2015.

26 Peter Dalsgaard and Eva Eriksson, "Large-Scale Participation: A Case Study of a Participatory Approach to Developing a New Public Library," Proceedings of the Conference on Human Factors in Computing Systems, January 2013; online at ‹https://www.researchgate.net/publication/253340553 _Large-Scale_Participation_A_Case_Study_of_a_Partici patory_Approach_to_Developing_a_New_Public_Library›.

27 Trohopoulos, e-mail to the author, July 3, 2014.

28 Maria Katsounakis, "The Libraries of Our Future," *Kathimerini Newspaper*, February 25, 2014; online at ‹http:// www.kathimerini.gr/754850/article/politismos/vivlio/oi -vivlio8hkes-toy-mellontos-mas›.

29 Aris Maragkopoulos, "Public Libraries, Not Video Games," *Chronos,* vol. 10, February 26 2014; online (in Greek) at ‹http://www.chronosmag.eu/index.php/gpls-th-sggf.html›.

30 See Peter Mackridge, *Language and National Identity in Greece, 1765–1976* (Oxford: Oxford University Press, 2009), 205.

31 Member of the seven-person board formed in February 2013 by the SNF to oversee the move to the new building, in "Recruitment of 36 Officials for the National Library Positions," *Proson*, October 28, 2015; online at ‹http://www .proson.gr/arthro/℗ροσλήψεις-στην-36-μονίμων-στην- εθνική-βιβλιοθήκη-κατανομή-θέσεων›.

32 All facts presented here regarding the library are based on Filippos Tsimpoglou's conversation with the author, April 21, 2015, unless noted otherwise. Tsimpoglou figures on twenty months for the transition: six months for preparation and transportation, eight months to move, and six months for familiarization; the opera house expects to take only ten months for the move (two months for transpor-

tation, six months for familiarization, and two months for testing equipment).

33 "Recruitment of 36 Officials."

34 Theodore Maravelias, in conversation with the author, April 22, 2015.

Park

1 Deborah Nevins, in conversation with the author, October 31, 2015.

2 "Landscape," in RPBW-Zurich Board Presentation, October 15, 2009, 29.

3 This and other references by Renzo Piano to the park design are from his conversation with the author on May 6, 2015.

4 Peter Walker, conversation with the author, September 9, 2016.

5 Anita Berrizbeitia and Linda Pollak, *Inside Outside: Between Architecture and Landscape* (Gloucester, Mass.: Rockport, 1999), 76–81.

6 One might call the sparse plantings around some temples the beginning of landscape design. See Elizabeth Barlow Rogers, *Landscape Design: A Cultural and Architectural History* (New York: Harry N. Abrams, 2001), 63.

7 In 1913 the King of Greece commissioned Thomas Hayton Mawson (1861–1933), a British garden designer, landscape architect, and town planner, to design the royal gardens and park system in Athens, construction of which was prevented by World War I.

8 The Jardin de Luxembourg keeps 195,000 plants and shrubs stored for maintenance of its flower beds, only 20 percent more than the 150,000 used in Athens. Richard Reeves, "Greeneries: Toy Boats and Pony Rides in the Heart of Paris," *New York Times*, March 15, 1987, section 6, part 2, 59.

9 Giorgio Bianchi, in conversation with the author, May 20, 2014.

10 Peggy Tully, "On Landscape Urbanism," in *The Routledge Companion to Landscape Studies*, ed. Peter Howard et al. (London and New York: Routledge, 2013), 442.

11 Alexandra Papageorgiou, *Dimitris Pikionis, Architect 1887– 1968: A Sentimental Topography* (London: Architectural Association, 1989), 57.

12 Dimitri Philippides and Agni Pikionis, "Dimitri Pikionis in situ," in *Relating Architecture to Landscape*, ed. Jan Birthed (London: E & FN Spon, 1999), 194–204.

13 Nevins, in conversation with the author, September 12, 2013.

14 Nevins, e-mail to the author, August 26, 2015.

15 Stephen Harris, *The Magnificent Flora Graeca* (Oxford: Bodleian Library, 2007), 24.

16 Robert E. Grese, *Jens Jensen: Maker of Natural Parks and Gardens* (Baltimore and London: Johns Hopkins University Press, 1992), 176.

17 Deborah Nevins, "The Triumph of Flora: Women and the American Landscape, 1890–1935," *Antiques Magazine* 127, no. 4 (1985), 904–22.

18 Nevins, in conversation with the author, December 22, 2014.

19 Nevins, in conversation with the author, April 16, 2013.

20 "Landscape," October 15, 2009, 30.

21 Olivier Filippi, *The Dry Gardening Handbook: Plants and Practices for a Changing Climate*, Eng. ed. (London: Thames & Hudson, 2008), 24–25.

22 Simon Delves, in conversation with the author, May 2, 2013, and e-mails to the author, January 12, 2015, February 25, 2015, and January 22, 2016.

23 Richard Meier, *Building the Getty* (New York: Knopf, 1997), 58.

24 Nevins, in conversation with the author, September 12, 2013.

25 This and the following statements are from Nevins, in conversation with the author, October 24, 2013.

26 Dorothée Imbert, "J. C. N. Forestier: Plants and Planning," in *The Modernist Garden in France* (New Haven: Yale University Press, 1993), 11–26.

27 Alex Kitnick, "Giant Steps," *Artforum,* November 2016, 121. Kitnick calls the current popularity of over-scaled step design "the stair as social media."

28 Bruce Martin, Expedition Engineering associate director, e-mail to the author, April 4, 2016.

29 The skeletons became the subject of controversy when a recent discovery hypothesized that many may have resulted from executions in the late seventh century B.C.E. and therefore might be attributed to the conspiracy of Kylon to seize the state. This action ended when the conspirators withdrew to the sanctuary of Athena on the Acropolis, where they were discovered and executed. James Wright, director of the American School of Classical Studies in Athens, e-mail to the author, July 3, 2016.

30 These descriptions of Nevins's philosophy of design are based on her conversations with the author on April 16, 2013; September 13, 2013; and December 22, 2014.

31 Joseph Volpe, in conversation with the author, November 12, 2013.

32 European playgrounds are also just as safe as American playgrounds, despite fostering more active play. About 2007, the New York City Parks Department began to address the deficiencies of its playgrounds, distributing loose objects and, among other initiatives, using the mobile Imagination Playground created by theater set and restaurant designer David Rockwell. See Rebecca Mead, "State of Play," *New Yorker*, July 5, 2010; online at ‹http://www.newyorker.com/magazine/2010/07/05/state-of-play›.

33 Carol Kino, "The Work Behind Child's Play," *New York Times,* July 7, 2013, AR-18; online at ‹www.nytimes.com/2013/07/07/arts/design/carnegie-museums-playground-project-traces-an-evolution.html›.

34 "Junkyard Playgrounds," *Time*, June 25, 1965; online at ‹http://content.time.com/time/magazine/article/0,9171,833789,00.html›.

35 Lady Allen of Hurtwood (Marjory Gill Allen), *Planning for Play* (Cambridge, Mass.: MIT Press, 1969), 54–117.

36 See "Playgrounds by Aldo van Eyck," *ArchiNed,* July 2, 2002; online at ‹www.archined.nl/2002/07/playgrounds-by-aldo-van-eyck›. "Aldo van Eyck (1918–1999)," *Team 10 Online*, accessed on December 1, 2016; online at ‹www.team10online.org/team10/eyck/index.html›.

37 James Taylor-Foster, "Amsterdam's Seventeen Playgrounds: Aldo van Eyck's Neglected Legacy," *Architecture Daily,* May 13, 2016; online at ‹http://www.archdaily.com/787273/amsterdams-seventeen-playgrounds-aldo-van-eycks-neglected-legacy›.

38 Triathlon NZ, "Coaches: Giannis Psarelis," accessed August 25, 2016; online at ‹https://triathlon.kiwi/directory/coaches/giannis-psarelis-2/›.

39 Galen Cranz and Michael Boland, "Defining the Sustainable Park: A Fifth Model for Urban Parks," *Landscape Journal* 23, no. 2 (January 1, 2004), 102–20.

Metamorphosis

1 Andreas Dracopoulos, in conversation with the author, January 22, 2014.

2 Early on in the process, the curved, canopy-like shape of the lighthouse roof was made more square from Eleni Tzanou, Betaplan architect, "SNFCC Construction Update Report November 2013."

3 A view expressed by the local media: "16 May 2016/63rd Regular Assembly of the Special Advisory Committee of the Greek State with the SNF for the SNFCC," Stavros Niarchos Foundation website; online at ‹ www.snf.org/en/newsroom/news/2016/05/63rd-regular-assembly-of-the-special-advisory-committee-of-the-greek-state-with-the-snf-for-the-snfcc/›.

4 Giorgio Bianchi, comments made while touring the SNFCC, June 24, 2016.

5 As a point of comparison, the widest paths in the Barcelona Botanical Garden are 10 feet wide; secondary paths are 5 to 8 feet wide.

6 Scott Newman, Cooper Robertson partner, e-mail to the author, September 7, 2016.

7   An opinion expressed by the local media: Maria Katsou-naki, "Domino Changes in Culture," *Kathimerini Newspaper*, January 12, 2016; online (in Greek) at ‹www.kathimerini.gr/845367/article/epikairothta/ellada/ntomino-allagwn-ston-politismo›.

8   Matoula Kousteni, "I Want the GNO to Be Artistically Restless," *Ephemerida ton Syntakton*, January 2, 2017; online at ‹http://www.efsyn.gr/arthro/thelo-ti-lyriki-kallitehnika-anisyhi›.

9   Mostafa Heddaya, "Can the New Stavros Niarchos Cultural Center Survive in Greece?," *Blouinartinfo*, August 14, 2015; online at ‹www.blouinartinfo.com/news/story/1217318/can-the-new-stavros-niarchos-cultural-center-survive-in›. Trohopoulos left the SNFCC in April 2016; online at ‹https://www.linkedin.com/in/ioannis-trohopoulos-8b94937›.

10   Myron Michailidis, in conversation with the author, June 23, 2016.

11   This and the following comments by Filippos Tsimpoglou were made during his conversation with the author, June 23, 2016.

12   All statistics quoted here for the NLG are from Cooper Robertson's "Needs Analysis" report, October 2007, 19–20, archived at Cooper Robertson and at the SNF in New York City.

13   "Niarchos Foundation Withdraws 3-Million Euro Donation to National Museum of Contemporary Art," *Kathimerini English Edition*, November 19, 2015; online at ‹www.ekathimerini.com/203582/article/ekathimerini/life/niarchos-foundation-withdraws-3-million-euro-donation-to-national-museum-of-contemporary-art›.

14   A. Craig Copetas, "Greece's $473 Billion Debt Mirrors Crisis in Cultural Assets," *Bloomberg Businessweek*, October 18, 2011.

15   Alastair MacDonald and Gabriela Baczynska, "EU Gives Greece Warning To Fix Border 'Neglect,'" *Reuters*, January 27, 2016; online at ‹www.reuters.com/article/us-europe-migrants-greece-eu-idUSKCN0V51JK›.

16   Eric Maurice, "Greek Migration Crisis Enters Worst-Case Scenario," *EU Observer*, Febuary 23, 2016; online at ‹https://euobserver.com/migration/132416›.

17   Lorne Cook, "Refugee Crisis: Six Countries in Schengen Now Have Border Checks in Place," *Independent*, January 4, 2016; online at ‹http://www.independent.co.uk/news/world/europe/refugee-crisis-six-countries-in-schengen-now-have-border-checks-in-place-a6796296.html›.

18   James Kanter, "Turkey Places Conditions on E.U. for Migrant Help," *New York Times*, March 8, 2016; online at ‹www.nytimes.com/2016/03/08/world/europe/europe-migrants-refugees-turkey.html?_r=0›. "Greece, Turkey Take Legal Short-Cuts in Race to Return Migrants," *Kathimerini English Edition*, March 31, 2016; online at ‹www.ekathimerini.com/207503/article/ekathimerini/news/greece-turkey-take-legal-short-cuts-in-race-to-return-migrants›. Alexander Clapp, "Take a Country on the Brink. Now Add 10,000 Asylum Hearings a Week," *Foreign Policy*, March 31, 2016; online at ‹http://foreignpolicy.com/2016/03/31/take-a-country-on-the-brink-now-add-10000-asylum-hearings-a-week-greece-eu-turkey/›.

19   Liz Alderman, "Bleak Times for Marooned Migrants in Greece," *Seattle Times*, August 13, 2016; online at ‹www.seattletimes.com/nation-world/bleak-times-for-marooned-migrants-in-greece/›.

20   Ceylan Yeginsu, "Migrants Pour Out of Turkey Once More," *New York Times*, Sept. 15, 2016, A4, A10; online at ‹www.nytimes.com/2016/09/15/world/europe/turkey-syria-refugees-eu.html›.

21   Julia Kollewe, "How Greece Could Leave the Eurozone in Five Difficult Steps," *The Guardian*, May 12, 2012; online at ‹https://www.theguardian.com/business/2012/may/13/greece-leave-eurozone-five-difficult-steps›.

22   Steven Erlanger, "Greek Debt Crisis Highlights Fractures in European Union," *New York Times*, July 16, 2015; online at ‹www.nytimes.com/2015/07/17/world/europe/greek-debt-crisis-highlights-fractures-in-european-union.html›.

23   Leonidas Stergiou, "What a Brexit Could Mean for Greece," *Kathimerini English Edition*, June 24, 2016; online at ‹www.ekathimerini.com/209868/article/ekathimerini/comment/what-a-brexit-could-mean-for-greece›.

24   Angeliki Koutantou, "Greece Revises Hellinikon Property Deal, Unlocking Bailout Funds," *Reuters*, June 7, 2016; online at ‹www.reuters.com/article/us-eurozone-greece-privatisation-idUSKCN0YT1AW›. Nektaria Stamouli, "Greece Stymies Its Own Plan to Sell Assets," *Wall Street Journal*, October 3, 2016, A1, A14; online as "What's Derailing Greece's Plan to Sell State Assets? Its Own Government"; online at ‹www.wsj.com/articles/the-greek-government-is-both-for-and-against-its-own-privatization-plan-1475428917›.

25   "Beach Volley, Courts and Julia Alexandratou," *Protagon.gr*, May 9, 2016; online (in Greek) at ‹www.protagon.gr/epikairotita/44341130858-44341130858›.

26   Bloomberg Editorial Board, "Don't Let Greek Pensions Threaten the Euro," *Bloomberg View*, February 2, 2016; online at ‹www.bloomberg.com/view/articles/2016-02-02/don-t-let-greek-pensions-threaten-the-euro›. Kerin Hope, "Tsipras Calls on Businesses to Invest in Greece," *Financial Times*, September 11, 2016; online at ‹www.ft.com/content/92e7ee34-779e-11e6-97ae-647294649b28›.

27 Catherine I. Risen, "The Background for John Trohopoulos' Departure from Niarchos Foundation," *Protagon*, April 17, 2016; online at ‹http://www.protagon.gr/epikairotita/allagi-igesias-ektos-kentrou-politismou-idryma-stavros-niarxos-o-giannis-troxopoulos-44341111372›.

28 "Work Starts on New Pipeline Bringing Azeri Gas to Italy," Associated Press, May 17, 2016; online at ‹www.yahoo.com/news/starts-pipeline-bringing-azeri-gas-143952643.html›.

29 Nasos Koukakis, "Tsipras Inaugurates TAP Gas Pipeline in Greece," *CNBC News*, May 16, 2016; online at ‹www.cnbc.com/2016/05/16/tsipras-inaugurates-tap-gas-pipeline-in-greece.html›.

30 Niki Kitsantonis, "Greek Officials Approve Austerity Legislation," *New York Times*, May 23, 2016, B3; online at ‹www.nytimes.com/2016/05/23/business/greek-lawmakers-narrowly-approve-austerity-legislation.html›.

31 International Monetary Fund, "Report for Selected Countries and Subjects," *World Economic Outlook Database*, October 2016 (Washington, D.C.: International Monetary Fund, October 4, 2016); online at ‹www.imf.org/external/pubs/ft/weo/2016/02/weodata/weorept.aspx?pr.x=70&pr.y=20&sy=2014&ey=2016&scsm=1&ssd=1&sort=country&ds=.&br=1&c=174&s=NGDPD%2CNGDPDPC%2CPPPGDP%2CPPPPC&grp=0&a=›.

32 International Monetary Fund, "Greece Preliminary Debt Sustainability Analysis—Updated Estimates and Further Considerations," Country Report No. 16/130, May 2016; online at ‹http://www.imf.org/external/pubs/ft/scr/2016/cr16130.pdf›.

33 "Vague Promises of Debt Relief for Greece," *New York Times*, May 30, 2016, A18; online at ‹www.nytimes.com/2016/05/30/opinion/vague-promises-of-debt-relief-for-greece.html›. International Monetary Fund, "Greece Preliminary Debt Sustainability Analysis," May 2016.

34 Jörg Rocholl and Axel Stahmer, "Where Did the Greek Bailout Money Go?" ESMT White Paper No. WP-16–02, 2016; online at ‹https://www.esmt.org/where-did-greek-bailout-money-go›.

35 Ana Swanson, "The Forgotten Origins of Greece's Crisis Will Make You Think Twice About Who's to Blame," *Washington Post*, July 1, 2015; online at ‹www.washingtonpost.com/news/wonk/wp/2015/07/01/the-forgotten-origins-of-greeces-terrible-crisis-will-make-you-think-twice-about-whos-to-blame/›.

36 Lesley Wroughton, Howard Schneider, and Dina Kyriakidou, "How the IMF's Misadventure in Greece is Changing the Fund," *Reuters*, August 28, 2015; ‹www.reuters.com/investigates/special-report/imf-greece/›.

37 Gillian Tett and Barney Jopson, "Turkish Turmoil Strengthens Case for Greek Debt Relief, Says US," *Financial Times*, July 20, 2016; online at ‹https://www.ft.com/content/97f8a4be-4e26-11e6-8172-e39ecd3b86fc›. Wroughton, Schneider, and Kyriakidou, "How the IMF's Misadventure in Greece."

38 "03 October 2016/66th Regular Assembly of the Special Advisory Committee of the Greek State with the SNF for the SNFCC," Stavros Niarchos Foundation website, accessed October 12, 2016; online at ‹http://www.snf.org/en/newsroom/news/2016/10/66th-regular-assembly-of-the-special-advisory-committee-of-the-greek-state-with-the-snf-for-the-snfcc/›.

39 "Tsipras: We Will Manage the SNFCC Responsibly," *Kathimerini Newspaper*, August 31, 2016; online (in Greek) at ‹www.kathimerini.gr/872903/article/epikairothta/ellada/tsipras-8a-diaxeiristoyme-ypey8yna-to-kentro-politismoy-toy-idrymatos-st-niarxos›. "Tsipras Thanks Dracopoulos for the Stavros Niarchos Foundation Cultural Centre," *National Herald*, August 31, 2016; online at ‹http://www.thenationalherald.com/135040/›.

40 "The Stavros Niarchos Foundation Invites the Greek State to Accept Delivery of the Stavros Niarchos Foundation Cultural Center," Stavros Niarchos Foundation website, December 28, 2016, online at ‹http://www.snfcc.org/news-room/news/2016/12/the-stavros-niarchos-foundation-invites-the-greek-state-to-accept-delivery-of-the-stavros-niarchos-foundation-cultural-center/›.

41 Hope, "Tsipras Calls on Businesses." *Financial Times,* September 11, 2016.

42 President Barack Obama's speech in Athens, Greece. See Gardiner Harris, "'American Democracy Is Bigger Than Any One Person,' Obama Says," *New York Times,* November 16, 2016; online at ‹http://www.nytimes.com/2016/11/17/world/europe/barack-obama-greece-donald-trump.html?_r=0›.

43 See "Agora," note 1.

Afterword

1 Neil Clemson, in conversation with the author, June 25, 2014, and e-mail to the author, May 31, 2016.

2 Bernard Tschumi and Joel Rutten, Acropolis Museum project architect, in conversation with the author, June 20, 2016.

3 Martin Hirko, in conversation with the author, November 23, 2015.

4 Andreas Dracopoulos, in conversation with the author, November 5, 2015.

5 Joanna Woronkowicz, D. Carroll Joynes, and Norman M.

Bradburn, *Building Better Arts Facilities: Lessons from a U.S. National Study* (London and New York: Routledge, 2015): 2–3.

6 Essential maintenance items for the building that require a regular schedule: cleaning of the solar panels; general visual inspection, cleaning, and repainting of the exposed ferro-cement surface of the canopy, as well as the exposed structural steel elements; monitoring, inspection, and maintenance for potential cracking and water damage to the ferro-cement surfaces (for which a specially designed electronic monitoring system will be installed) and for the column heads on which the canopy rests.

7 Hirko, in conversation with the author, June 24, 2016.

8 "Workers in Peril at Athens Sites," *BBC News,* July 23, 2004; online at ‹http://news.bbc.co.uk/1/hi/world/europe/3920919.stm ›.

9 See, for example, the report that the SNF allocated 20 million euros, or more than $22 million, toward the municipal governments of Athens and Thessaloniki "to cover the immediate needs of citizens in the large urban centers, who are experiencing the consequences of the deepening crisis more severely," *New York Times*, July 11, 2015; online at ‹http://www.nytimes.com/2015/07/12/world/europe/greece-debt-crisis-athens-poverty-inequality.html›.

10 Maria Katsounaki, "Domino Changes in Culture," *Kathimerini Newspaper,* January 12, 2016; online (in Greek) at ‹www.kathimerini.gr/845367/article/epikairothta/ellada/ntomino-allagwn-ston-politismo›.

11 Alexis Papachelas, "A Symbol of the Country We'd Like," *Kathimerini English Edition*, August 1, 2016; online at ‹http://www.ekathimerini.com/210875/opinion/ekathimerini/comment/a-symbol-of-the-country-wed-like›.=

12 Vasili Tsamis and Stelios Vasilakis of the SNF, in conversation with the author, August 3, 2016.

13 Cour des comptes, Chambres regionals et territoriales des comptes, "Construction de la "Philharmonie de Paris," accessed on September 26, 2016; online at ‹https://www.ccomptes.fr/Publications/Publications/Construction-de-la-Philharmonie-de-Paris›.

14 "Qui change tout?" "Philharmonie de Paris, Conférence de presse de Jean Nouvel," June 18, 2015; online at ‹http://www.jeannouvel.com/mobile/projets/DP_PHILA_18JUIN2015_PRINT.pdf›.

15 For information on the brief opening and subsequent completion of National Taichung Theater, I am indebted to Joanna Lee and Ken Smith (music critic for the *Financial Times*), who toured the building in October 2015, and Nick Frisch (a freelance music journalist and doctoral student in East Asian studies at Yale University), who toured it on January 12, 2016.

16 Corinna de Fonseca-Wollheim, "Finally, A Debut for Hamburg's Hall," *New York Times,* January 11, 2017, c1.

17 Christopher Ingenhoven, Meinhard von Gerkan, and Pierre de Meuron, "The Men Behind Germany's Building Debacles," *Spiegel Online*, June 14, 2013; online at ‹http://www.spiegel.de/international/germany/de-meuron-von-gerkan-and-ingenhoven-on-german-construction-headaches-a-905472.html›.

18 "Greek Artists Unhappy at Being Left Out by Festival's Belgian 'Curator' Jan Fabre," *Kathimerini English Edition,* March 31, 2016; online at ‹www.ekathimerini.com/207517/article/ekathimerini/life/greek-artists-unhappy-at-being-left-out-by-festivals-belgian-curator-jan-fabre›. "Greek Director Vangelis Theodoropoulos to Head Festival after Fabre Resignation," *Kathimerini English Edition,* April 4, 2016; online at ‹www.ekathimerini.com/207595/article/ekathimerini/news/greek-director-vangelis-theodoropoulos-to-head-festival-after-fabre-resignation›.

19 Rachel Donadio, "Suffering for Art in Greece and Matching the National Mood," *New York Times,* April 8, 2016; online at ‹www.nytimes.com/2016/04/09/arts/design/suffering-for-art-in-greece-and-matching-the-national-mood.html›.

20 James Glanz and Rami Nazzal, "Palestinian Museum Prepares to Open, Minus Exhibits," *New York Times*, May 16, 2016; online at ‹www.nytimes.com/2016/05/17/world/middleeast/palestinian-museum-birzeit-west-bank.html›.

21 Tony Perrottet, "Mining Magnate Bernardo Paz's Dedication to Inhotim," *Wall Street Journal*, August 20, 2013; online at ‹www.wsj.com/articles/SB10001424127887324354704578638281663481150?mg=id-wsj›.

22 Doreen Carvajal, "Plans Take Shape for Pinault Museum in Paris," *New York Times*, August 4, 2016, C1, 4; online at ‹www.nytimes.com/2016/08/04/arts/design/plans-take-shape-for-francois-pinault-museum-in-paris.html›.

Index

Page numbers in italic type
refer to illustrations.

Illustration Credits

Every effort has been made to contact copyright holders. Please contact the publisher if there are any additions or corrections.

AKG-Images: 74 bottom right
Amsterdam City Archives: 199 right
AntyDiluvian: 126 left
Artists Rights Society (ARS), New York/ADAGP, Paris: 77 top right, 93 left (Fondation Le Corbusier); 121 bottom left; 126 right (The Museum of Modern Art/Licensed by SCALA/Art Resource, NY/VG Bild-Kunst, Bonn); 127 left (John J. Heartfield)
Arup: 142, 144 top, 144 center left, 144 center right, 145, 146, 147, 151 right
A-Savin, Creative Commons: 159 bottom
Austrian National Library/Hajduk: 160 left
Irini-Kallistheni Avdelidi: 77 left
Iwan Baan: 2, 99 right, 195 bottom right, 213, 228 left
Manolis Baboussis: 77 bottom right
Alejo Bagué © Carlos Ferrater, Office of Architecture in Barcelona: 193
La Bibliothèque de l'École du Breuil: 69 right
Bill Barekas: 202–3
Matt Barrett: 79 top right
William Beaucardet: 246 right
Yannis Behrakis © Reuters Pictures: 136
Nathan Benn/Ottochrome/Corbis: 162 top left
Bernard Tschumi Architects: 200 top
BETAPLAN: 119 left, 123, 151 left, 152, 153, 162 right, 169 right, 230, 231 top left, 235 left
Haris Bilios: 144 bottom
Bill and Melinda Gates Foundation, Courtesy Veria Library: 169 center
Hélène Binet: 183
Nicolas Borel © Jakob + MacFarlane Architects: 169 left
Canadian Centre for Architecture/Centre Canadien d'Architecture, Cedric Price fonds: 127 right
Cooper Robertson: 50 left
Deborah Nevins & Associates: 180, 184, 186, 187 left, 192 left, 194 left, 234

Dowland/Matthew Chrislip: 85
John Drysdale: 199 left
Andrew Duthie: 200 bottom
European Pressphoto Agency: 237
Expedition Engineering: 88 (annotations by Dowland/Matthew Chrislip), 89 left, 99 left, 195 left, 195 top right
Flickr: 125 bottom right (Mark Palmer), 181 left (GiChristof), 192 right (Francesc_2000)
Fondazione Renzo Piano: 128 top right (Paul Vincent), 130 (Fregoso & Basalto)
Foster + Partners: 98 right (Nigel Young), 121 bottom right (Peter Blundell Jones)
Fu Jing, China Daily: 172
Gravetye Manor: 185
Farrell Grehan/Esto: 143
Clement Guillaume: 52 top left
Christopher Hagelund/Birdseyepix.com: 51 top right
Hellenic Literary and Historical Archive–Cultural Foundation of the National Bank of Greece: 74 top right, 75 right
Herman Miller, Inc.: 198 top
Mary Hollinshead: 194 right
May Iosotulano: 50 right
Kharbine-Tapabor/The Art Archive at Art Resource, NY: 191
Panos Kokkinias: 132
John Kolesidis/Reuters Pictures: 188
Dionysis Kouris: 79 bottom right
Danica O. Kus: 246 left
Gregory E. Larson AIA: 189
Antonis Lemonakis, Courtesy Cyclades Festival: 141 bottom
David Leventi, Courtesy Rick Wester Fine Art: 51 bottom right
Library of Congress, G. Eric and Edith Matson Photograph Collection: 22
LoveGreece.com: 235 right
Charalambos Luizidis © Yannis Aesopos: 79 left
Alex S. Maclean: 201 right
MAXXI Architecture Collection, Pier Luigi Nervi Archive: 93 bottom right
Norman McGrath: 98 left
Mecanoo Architecten: 167, 168 top left, 168 bottom left
Myron Michailidis: 140 right
Adam Mørk © Schmidt Hammer Lassen Architects: 171
MPFP: 198 bottom
Eric Nathan/LOOP IMAGES/Corbis: 67 bottom

National Library of Greece: 174
Neues Museum, Berlin: 62 right
New York Public Library: 231 bottom right
Oleve Family Estate and Products: 197 bottom
Sam Omans: 232, 241 left
Onassis Foundation Archive: 24 bottom right
Princeton University Library, Manuscripts Division, Department of Rare Books and Special Collections, Xochimilco Photographs: 95 left
Frode Ramone: 182
Renzo Piano Building Workshop: 55, 56, 58, 59, 61, 64, 65, 67 top, 72, 74 left, 86, 91, 116, 118 right, 119 right, 120, 125 top right, 131 right, 134, 138, 156, 158, 159 top, 168 top right, 168 bottom right, 176, 181 right; 48 (Courtesy Andreas Dracopoulos, Photographed by Erika Barker); 52 bottom right, 128 bottom (Paul Hester); 53 left (Aldo Ippoliti); 53 top right, 57 (Moreno Maggi); 53 bottom right (Christian Richters); 62 bottom left, 114, 141 top, 178, 218, 231 top right (Michel Denancé); 66, 129 top (Enrico Cano); 93 top right, 125 left, 129 bottom right, 187 right (Nic Lehoux); 95 right (Stephano Goldberg/Publifoto); 129 bottom left (John Gollings); 131 left (Gianni Berengo Gardin); 137 (Vincent Mosch); 179 top (Nicolas Robin photographe); 179 bottom (Tom Fox, SWA Group)
Renzo Piano Building Workshop and Faliro 2014, Courtesy Helli Pangalou & Associates: 84
RMN–Grand Palais/Art Resource, NY: 69 left
Gillian Roe: 162 bottom left
Rogers Stirk Harbour + Partners and Renzo Piano Building Workshop: 52 top right, 128 top left (Gianni Berengo Gardin)
Philippe Ruault: 52 bottom left (© Ateliers Jean Nouvel), 70 left (OMA)
Joint Venture Salini Impregilo-Terna: 34, 36–37, 38, 39, 40, 41, 102, 105, 113
Shawna Coronado © Gustafson Guthrie Nichols: 70 right
Stavros Niarchos Foundation: 10, 24 left, 24 top right, 154

Jochten Tack © Foundation Zollverein: 201 left
Theatre Project Consultants: 140 left
Thies Rätzke: 248 left
Toyo Ito & Associates: 247
twa © Wolfgang Tschapeller ZT GMBH: 163
US Embassy in Athens, Courtesy Stavros Niarchos Foundation: 241 right
Van den Berk Nurseries: 190
Manuel Gonzalez Vicente © The Foundation for the City of Culture of Galicia: 249
Eirini Vourloumis: 164
James Willis: 51 left
Yiorgis Yerolymbos, Courtesy Stavros Niarchols Foundation: 6–7, 21, 32–33, 35, 42, 43, 44–45, 46–47, 62 top left, 63, 68, 81, 83, 89 right, 94, 97, 100, 101, 104, 106–7, 108–9, 110, 111, 112, 115, 118 left, 121 top, 122, 149, 150 (annotations by Dowland/Matthew Chrislip), 161, 196, 197 top, 204, 205, 206–7, 208, 209, 210, 211, 212, 214–15, 216–17, 219, 220, 221, 222–23, 224, 227, 231 bottom left, 233, 238
Michael Zapf: 248 right